FOND DU LAC PUBLIC LIBRARY

P9-CME-457

WITHDRAWN

HOME CHEESE MAKING

HOME CHEESE MAKING

RECIPES FOR 75 HOMEMADE CHEESES

RICKI CARROLL

Storey Publishing

The mission of Storey Publishing is to serve our customers by
publishing practical information that encourages
personal independence in harmony with the environment.

Edited by Dianne M. Cutillo and Karen Levy
Cheese-maker profiles and additional text by Susan Mahnke Peery
Cover photo by Sabine Vollmer von Falken
Illustrations by Elayne Sears
Cover design by Wendy Palitz
Text design by Karin Stack and Cindy McFarland
Text layout and production by Susan Bernier and Jennifer Jepson Smith
Indexed by Susan Olason / Indexes & Knowledge Maps

© 2002 by Ricki Carroll
Previous editions © 1996, 1982 by Storey Publishing, LLC
Recipes on pages 218, 234, and 250 appear courtesy of Paula Lambert, *The Cheese Lover's Cookbook and Guide,* © 2000, all rights reserved.
Home Cheese Making was first published in 1982 as *Cheesemaking Made Easy* and revised in 1996. All of the information in the previous edition was reviewed and updated, and 115 new recipes were added.

All rights reserved. No part of this book may be reproduced without written permission from the publisher, except by a reviewer, who may quote brief passages or reproduce illustrations in a review with appropriate credits; nor may any part of this book be reproduced, stored in a retrieval system, or transmitted in any form or by any means — electronic, mechanical, photocopying, recording, or other — without written permission from the publisher.

The information in this book is accurate and complete to the best of our knowledge. All recommendations are made without guarantee on the part of the author or Storey Publishing. The author and the publisher disclaim any liability in connection with the use of this information. For additional information, please contact Storey Publishing, 210 MASS MoCA Way, North Adams, MA 01247.

Storey books are available for special premium and promotional uses and for customized editions. For further information, please call 1-800-793-9396.

Printed in the United States by Edwards Brothers Malloy
30 29 28 27 26

Library of Congress Cataloging-in-Publication Data

Carroll, Ricki.
    Home cheese making : recipes for 75 homemade cheeses / Ricki Carroll.
      p. cm.
    New edition of: Cheesemaking made easy.
    Includes index.
    ISBN 978-1-58017-464-0
    1. Cheesemaking.   2. Cookery (Cheese)   I. Carroll, Ricki. Cheesemaking made easy. II. Title.
SF271 .C37 2002
637'.3 — dc21   2002007749

CONTENTS

FOREWORD

Many people have asked me, "How did you get into cheese?" I have a simple answer: "It got into me." My love affair with cheese began at an age that surely preceded my ability to express that predilection. But while my fondness for cheese grew as I did, my knowledge about cheese did not. All I knew was that cheese was made from milk, and after that, it magically appeared as a flat orange square neatly wrapped in cellophane. It came in convenient packages of eight.

My universe of cheese expanded once I began to shop for myself. Brie quickly became my cheese of choice, as no party was complete without it. But Brie was also an inadvertent educational tool. It was the first cheese I ever tasted that had a rind. Although most party guests assiduously avoided the snowy white rind, I liked the contrast it offered in texture and flavor. And more, it looked like cheese. What a marvelous discovery!

By now irrevocably hooked on cheese, I began to explore it with determination and intensity. It didn't take long to see that there was a virtual explosion of cheese makers who were making wonderful cheese right here in the United States. It was a revelation that would lead to my book, *The New American Cheese,* in which I chronicled the lives of the cheese makers who bring real cheese (with rinds) to our table and who work so hard in doing so. As I researched my book, I also discovered one individual who was playing a quiet but integral role in helping many of the cheese makers I'd come to know. That person was Ricki Carroll.

These days, cheese has become perhaps the hottest culinary trend to take hold since artisanal bread. But far ahead of any trend, Ricki Carroll has steadily been leading the charge in home and commercial cheese making for decades. Her company, New England Cheesemaking Supply, has been answering the ongoing needs of cheese makers, and her book, *Cheesemaking Made Easy,* was the necessary bible for aspiring and experienced cheese makers. Precious few readable resources for cheese making existed before she wrote that book.

Ricki has long been the cheese making "answer woman" at the other end of the line when cheese makers call in a state of panic wondering what went wrong with their batch of cheese or wanting to know how to elevate their cheese from good to great. Ricki's home, in which she offers ongoing cheesemaking seminars, has been a refuge for cheese makers wishing to improve their craft, and her ability to source hard-to-find equipment has been crucial to the careers of many cheese makers.

It is fitting that in this time of cheesemania, Ricki is once again answering the call of wanna-be cheese makers — hobbyists and professionals alike — by revising and updating this book. She is providing an essential tool to anyone with a modicum of interest in cheese and, at the same time, servicing the needs of experienced cheese makers. Her easy-to-understand manner and, most important, years of hands-on experience qualify her as one of the nation's preeminent cheese-making mentors.

To guide milk into cheese is a heady experience. Yet that is the very opportunity Ricki is giving all of us with this book. I have no doubt that after you start reading *Home Cheese Making,* you won't be able to stop yourself from imagining which cheese you're going to make first, which milk you're going to make it from, and even how to fashion a place to age it.

Cheese has now captured the fancy of culinarians and aficionados across the United States, and that is largely because so many fantastic cheeses now grace our shops and markets. But long before cheese was a trend, Ricki was helping cheese makers develop cheeses that were worthy of the shops and marketplaces. Ricki Carroll has always made cheese making a little easier, and with this book, she helps us see that, in fact, there's a cheese maker in each of us.

— LAURA WERLIN
Author of *The New American Cheese*

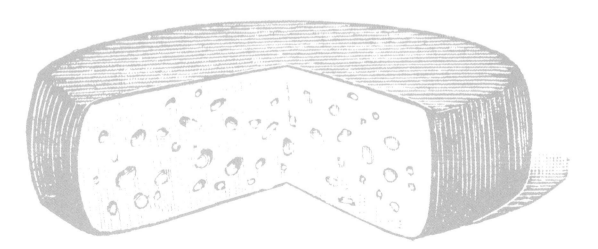

PREFACE TO THE NEW EDITION

I take great pleasure in having participated in the renaissance of artisanal cheese making in the United States over the past two decades. It has been thrilling to watch people take their cheeses from the kitchen to the Winners' Circle at the American Cheese Society and other prestigious competitions. Although only a small percentage of cheese makers aspire to that level of commercial cheese making, this book will enable *everyone* to have fun making delicious cheeses. You will surely become a winner within your own circle of family and friends.

This book is written with the beginner in mind, to show that it's possible — even easy — to make cheese at home. It's a wonderful family activity and makes a great science lesson. The recipes here are a "grate whey" to learn this traditional art and perhaps begin traditions of your own. For those who approach cheese making as a hobby or an occasional activity, you'll find plenty of recipes and enough technical explanation to ensure success.

I hope to increase awareness and appreciation of cheese and cheese making. Even if you make cheese only once, you'll have a greater respect for this ancient art. The next time you purchase artisanal cheese, you'll realize how much passion went into that log of fresh chèvre, wheel of Brie, or wedge of Cheddar. It will also remind you of how important it is to support farmhouse cheese makers (those who make cheese with milk from their own farms) and other small-scale farmers, who steward some of our most valuable land.

Cheese making involves some fascinating science, but it is the myriad variables in milk that lend uniqueness to the final product. Climate, humidity, pasture type, breed of animal, time of year, and subtle differences in how a cheese maker handles the milk all contribute to produce a range of distinctive cheeses. Although you may not have access to a wide variety of milk, your art will develop from experimenting with time, temperature, and milk brands that you purchase from the grocery store.

This new edition includes many more recipes, tips and recipes from cheese lovers, stories about cheese makers, and little cheesy tales — all in keeping with my belief that cheese making is fun. Once you understand the basic process, try some of the recipes that have trickled in from my customers over the past 25 years. They have been passed down through generations and appear as I received them in the recipe boxes throughout this book. Above all, don't be afraid to experiment. I have demystified the process for you, leaving in the fun and excitement of making this culinary delight at home.

I have been inspired by home cheese makers who have written over the years, thrilled with the success of their first cheese, and I would love to hear about your experiences as well. Welcome to the world of cheese making. I hope "ewe" have a very "Gouda" time!

— Ricki Carroll

ACKNOWLEDGMENTS

I would like to thank the following wonderful people for their support:

Denise Pavao, for her patience and beautiful calming energy while sitting
with me at the computer and holding my hand while I wrote the manuscript.

Kathy Martel, for her smile and loving support and for keeping
New England Cheesemaking Supply Company running smoothly.

Viki and Glenda, for their friendship and laughter.

Jamie Eckley, for his love, inspiration, and caring.

Dianne Cutillo, for letting me go a few weeks over the deadline
— and then telling me to stop!

Susan Peery, for her stories on cheese makers, which enrich this book.

Jim Wallace, for his fantastic experiments that have taken him
to great new heights in just one year.

Karen Levy, for helping me sort it all out and much, much more!

Dave Potter and Bill Wendorff, for always being there
to answer my technical questions.

Judy Schad, for her endless energy and loving support.

My customers at New England Cheesemaking Supply Company,
for their support, ideas, and many questions,
which have brought me great joy over the past two and a half decades.

And most of all, the artisanal cheese makers,
whose love of their craft brings me to tears.

"*I made my first batch of cheese, and it turned out great. It was simple, quick, and awesome to the taste buds. It was very interesting to watch all the chemical changes and the metamorphosis from liquid to lumps of curds and then finally to pressed and molded cheese.*"

— Marjorie, Seattle, Washington

THE ART OF CHEESE MAKING

Those of us who remember our first attempts at bread making look back with an indulgent smile upon the bowl of sticky, disobedient dough that clung to everything it touched and defied our inexperienced hands at every turn. The indulgent smile is possible because we also remember that

we finally beat it into submission and that it did everything the cookbook promised it would. We kneaded it into a wonderful elastic mass that rose up gloriously under its dampened cloth cover and filled the entire house, just an hour later, with one of the most heavenly smells.

No one seems to know why the art of bread making fled the factories and settled with delicious comfort in our

homes so far ahead of the art of cheese making. Bread, wine, and cheese, besides being (collectively and individually) among life's greatest pleasures, share another bond: They are all produced by a process of fermentation. Bread rises in the pan, and wine matures its heady excellence from the action of yeast and sugar. Cheese, as if by magic, emerges from a pot of milk because of the action of bacteria upon milk sugar.

CHEESE, THE ORIGINAL SLOW FOOD

In our fast-paced world, any organization whose official symbol is the snail must have its heart in the right place. Slow Food is an international movement that started in Italy in 1986 as a protest against McDonald's bringing its golden arches into historic Rome.

But Slow Food isn't just against change: It is a growing voice in favor of family farms, sustainable agriculture, biodiversity, eating seasonally and regionally, and many other laudable goals. Most of all, Slow Food's message is this: Food should taste good. That means fresh ingredients, careful preparation, and respect for recipes and traditions that have lasted for generations. "Slow food" often is simple food. It tastes best eaten at a table with friends and family.

Cheese may be the original slow food. Slow is the only way to go if you make cheese, wine, bread, or even pickles, which all require age-old processes that cannot be rushed. Slow Food appreciates the care that home and farmstead cheese makers take in recalling the old alchemy of transforming milk into cheese every time they slowly warm milk, slowly stir the curds, and patiently wait for their cheese to age to perfection.

There's a Trick to It

Just as there's a knack to handling bread dough, there are tricks to turning milk into cheese. You may have learned to make bread by watching your mother. Today, however, there are few mothers indeed who can be counted on to hand down the techniques of cheese making to the next generation.

This book is designed to keep alive the art and pleasures of cheese making. If you follow directions carefully (especially the ones about cleanliness), I can almost promise you smooth sailing and the undeniable thrill of watching a guest smack her lips over a slice of your very own Gouda, and you saying to her, "I made it myself!" But if the going gets rough, or the curds won't set, or your cheese turns out less than perfect, there is an excellent troubleshooting section that will answer all your questions.

It All Began . . .

Cheese is one of the earliest foods made that is still consumed by people. It dates back to the initial domestication of animals, estimated to at least 9000 B.C.E. Archaeologists have established that cheese was well known to the Sumerians (4000 B.C.E.), whose cuneiform tablets contain references to cheese, as do many Egyptian and Chaldean artifacts. It was a staple in biblical times, along with honey, almonds, and wine, and is associated with stories of great daring: David was delivering cheese to Saul's camp when he encountered Goliath.

It's fun to speculate about how cheese may have been discovered. I like the oft-told tale about the nomad who poured his noon ration of milk into a bottle made from a sheep's stomach and plodded across the desert all morning, only to find, at noon, that his liquid lunch had solidified! It must have been a shock for the poor wanderer. He may not have been as brave as the person who ate the first raw oyster, but I imagine our hero eating a rather late lunch that day.

Once he finally tasted it, however, he probably became the first traveling salesman, singing the praises of that new food at all his overnight oasis stops. I suppose it didn't take long for his customers to recognize a good thing when they tasted it and for a cheese-making mystique to take hold and spread around the world.

Cheese making was important to the ancient Greeks, whose deity Aristaios, a son of Apollo, was considered the giver of cheese. Homer sang of cheese in the *Odyssey*. And Greek Olympic athletes trained on a diet consisting mostly of cheese. A Greek historian named Xenophon, born c. 431 B.C.E., wrote about a goat cheese that had been known for centuries in Peloponnesus.

The art of cheese making was carried westward to Rome. The Romans refined techniques, added herbs and spices, and discovered how to make smoked cheese. Many varieties were made during those times, and the Romans feasted on curd cheeses, Limburger-type cheeses, soft cheeses, and smoked and salted cheeses. They exported their hard cheeses and experimented with a cheese made from a mixture of sheep's and goat's milks.

In addition, they learned to use different curdling agents besides the rennet they extracted from the stomach of a weanling goat or sheep. Thistle flowers, safflower seeds, and fig bark were soaked in water to make extracts that would set a curd. Baskets and nets and molds were devised to shape their cheeses. When Julius Caesar sent his soldiers to conquer Gaul, they packed rations of cheese for the long marches. Wherever they went, northern tribesmen quickly learned to copy their captors' delicious food.

Factories, Finally

In the 15th century, far up in the Alps, Swiss farmers milked their cows in the fields and brought the milk back to their farms to make cheese. It wasn't until about 1800 that they realized they could make cheese down in the valleys as well as high in the hills. In 1815, the first cheese factory was opened in the valley at Bern. It was such a successful venture that 120 cheese factories sprouted in the next 25 years, with the number growing to 750 by the end of the 19th century.

The early Swiss factories had a fire pit in the corner, with a copper kettle hanging over it on a crane so they could swing the kettle above or away from the fire. They tested the temperature on their forearms. Their rennet solution, made from the stomach lining of a calf, was so strong that they claimed it could set milk in the time it took to recite The Lord's Prayer. (This is a lovely idea, but when I tried it, reverently and slowly, I was able to drag it out only to 30 seconds, a trifle short for the setting time in most of my recipes.)

The first American cheese factory was established in 1851 in Rome, New York, by an ingenious entrepreneur named Jesse Williams. Earlier companies, as far west as Ohio, had been set up to buy homemade curds from local farmers and process the curds into cheeses weighing from 10 to 25 pounds. Williams realized that cheese made from several different batches of curd lacked uniformity in taste and texture. He also knew that it takes exactly the same length of time to make a curd from 1,000 pounds of milk as it does from 1 pint, so he set up his factory to make cheese from scratch.

He bought milk from local farmers to add to the output of his own herd of cows, and in its first years of operation, his factory produced four cheeses per day, each weighing at least 150 pounds. Springwater was circulated around the vats to cool them, and steam, produced by a wood-fired boiler, heated them. It is recorded that his costs averaged about 5½ cents a pound for an aged cheese and that he sold this entire stock on contract for a minimum of 7½ cents a pound. The financial success of the operation was enhanced by the sale of pork from his large herd of hogs, which were fed the factory's whey output.

Modern scientific methods, developed throughout the latter half of the 19th century by entrepreneurs like Jesse Williams, have taken the guesswork out of commercial cheese making. Models of cleanliness and efficiency, cheese factories are equipped with steam-jacketed stainless-steel vats, thermostatic controls, mechanical agitators, and curd cutters. Sterile conditions largely eliminate the possibility of unwanted bacterial invasion at any stage of a cheese's development. Today, about one-third of the world's annual milk production is processed into approximately 400 varieties of cheese bearing more than 800 names.

When I started making cheese in the early 1970s, I was part of a do-it-yourself culture. In our concern for the environment, as well as for our poor, overburdened budgets, more and more of us were trying to reclaim some of the techniques of self-sufficiency that made our ancestors the independent folks they were. We learned how to heat with wood, bake our own bread, brew our own beer, and make our own cheese. Since then, an entire artisanal cheese movement has grown up in the United States.

Before You Begin

The cheese recipes in this book are divided into six categories: soft cheese, hard cheese, Italian cheese, whey cheese, goat cheese, bacteria- and mold-ripened cheese, and there are recipes for other dairy products as well. Each chapter includes a variety of cheeses that are all made in a similar fashion and involve the same basic steps and techniques. Just as we must all walk before we can run, it is smart to start cheese making with the simpler varieties. Begin with the soft cheese recipes and make a few of these cheeses before you graduate to the complexities of the hard cheeses. The soft cheeses I recommend for beginners are Queso Blanco, Fromage Blanc, and Whole-Milk Ricotta (all in chapter 4), and 30-Minute Mozzarella (in chapter 6). For your first hard cheeses, try Farmhouse Cheddar and Gouda. Keep accurate records so you can benefit from your successes and learn from your mistakes.

> "*If I had a son who was ready to marry, I would tell him, 'Beware of girls who don't like wine, truffles, cheese, or music.'*"
>
> — Colette

Family Cheese Making Apparatus.

GETTING

STARTED

CHAPTER 1

INGREDIENTS

In the beginning, God created goats, they produced milk, and that was good. Then he was so excited that there came sheep, cows, and other milk-producing mammals. Then came human beings, who used wondrous, wholesome milk to feed their families. When they realized that milk in stomach pouches coagulated, it was their first miracle. They had discovered cheese! And that was VERY good! Stomach linings became their source for rennet, soured milk and whey became their source for cultures, and fingers were turned into instant thermometers (but that we'll save for the equipment chapter). The miracle of cheese solved an age-old question of how to save milk. After a while, naturally occurring molds added vim and vigor to cheeses and introduced variety to the palate.

Today, we use the same ingredients but obtain them in more sophisticated ways. Cultures and rennets are now made and standardized in factories and can be obtained from cheese-making supply houses. Milk comes in bottles and is bought at the grocery store. But hark! I hear the artists calling, because in the right hands, these ingredients can be turned into gastronomic delights. Read on, and happy cheese making.

Milk

Milk means different things to different people. For the shopper in a grocery store, milk is the white liquid found in plastic jugs in the dairy case. For the owner of a dairy animal, milk is obtained in the course of a day's chores. Milk is a complicated substance. About seven-eighths of it is water. The rest is made up of proteins, minerals, milk sugar (lactose), milk fat (butterfat), vitamins, and trace elements. Those substances are called milk solids.

When we make cheese, we cause the protein part of the milk solids, called *casein,* to coagulate (curdle) and produce curd. At first the curd is a soft, solid gel, because it still contains all the water along with the solids. But as it is heated, and as time passes, the curd releases liquid (whey), condensing more and more until it becomes cheese. Most of the butterfat remains in the curd and very little passes into the whey. Time, temperature, and a variety of friendly bacteria determine the flavor and texture of each type of cheese.

Throughout history, people have used milk from many animals. The familiar cow, goat, and sheep have fed people for centuries, along with less common animals such as the yak, camel, water buffalo, llama, ass, elk, mare, caribou, zebu, and reindeer. When making the cheeses in this book, you may use whatever milk you have available in your area. Cow's and goat's milks are the most readily available in the United States; you may find some sheep's and water buffalo's milks, if you are very lucky. You may make the cheeses in this book with store-bought milk, as long as it is not Ultrapasteurized (UP), and you can use dried milk powder for all the recipes in chapter 4, "Soft Cheese," and in chapter 10, "Other Dairy Products."

No matter what type of milk you use for cheese making, it must be of the highest quality. Always use the freshest milk possible. If it comes from the supermarket, do not open the container until you are ready to start. This will prevent possible contamination from bacteria in the air. Above all, if the milk tastes sour or "off," throw it away — the cheese-making process will not make your milk taste better! When purchasing milk, remember that 1 gallon yields 1 pound for hard cheeses or 2 pounds for soft cheeses. This varies from milk to milk. Yields from goat's milk and nonfat milk are lower, and the yield from sheep's milk is higher. The following list includes the many types of milk used in the cheese-making process.

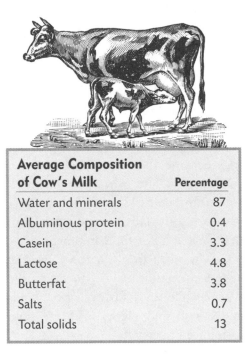

Average Composition of Cow's Milk	Percentage
Water and minerals	87
Albuminous protein	0.4
Casein	3.3
Lactose	4.8
Butterfat	3.8
Salts	0.7
Total solids	13

Cow's Milk

In the United States today, cow's milk is the most popular for use in cheese making. This is not the case in the rest of the world, however, as goats and sheep feed the majority of the globe's population. Cows are more difficult to raise; they eat more and therefore take up much more grazing land and natural resources. Yet cow's milk is abundant, the curd is firm and easy to work with, and it produces many wonderful cheeses. If you are considering buying your own cow, start with a Jersey — its rich milk will produce a high cheese yield because it has a high butterfat content, and Jerseys are very sweet animals.

Goat's Milk

Goat's (doe's) milk has smaller butterfat globules than cow's milk, making it more easily digested. It is more acidic than cow's milk, so it ripens faster, and it has no carotene, so it produces a whiter cheese. Because of its natural homogenization, goat's milk makes a slightly softer cheese than that from cow's milk, though the butterfat content is about the same. Cheese made from raw goat's milk has a distinct peppery hot pungency caused by naturally occurring lipase enzymes and fatty acids. During the renneting process, you may lower the temperature five degrees, because goat's-milk curd tends to be more delicate. Remember to treat these softer curds very gently.

If you are looking for your own goats, Nubians and Alpines are good producers and tend to have the sweetest milk. Saanens often produce more milk, but it has a stronger flavor. Toggenburgs pro-

Average Composition of Goat's Milk	Percentage
Water and minerals	87.5
Albuminous protein	0.7
Casein	3.0
Lactose	4.0
Butterfat	4.2
Salts	0.6
Total solids	12.5

duce a slightly lower yield, but also a strong flavor. Nigerian Dwarf goats have the highest butter fat of all breeds and very sweet milk.

Sheep's Milk

Sheep's (ewe's) milk is one of the most nutritionally valuable foods available. It is high in protein and vitamins, which so often have to be artificially added to our diet. Sheep's milk contains almost 10 percent less water than cow's or goat's milk and is almost twice as high in solids as cow's milk; therefore, it produces a very high cheese yield — almost 2½ times what you would expect from cow's or goat's milk.

Milking sheep are now making an appearance in the United States, and

Average Composition of Sheep's Milk	Percentage
Water and minerals	79.6
Albuminous protein	1.1
Casein	4.6
Lactose	4.7
Butterfat	9.0
Chloride salts	1.0
Total solids	20.4

not a possibility in the United States at this time.

Raw Milk

Several terms need to be defined, so that you know what I am talking about when I use the word *milk*. Raw milk comes directly from a farm animal and is filtered and cooled before use. It is not pasteurized, so it has a higher vitamin content than heat-treated milk. Raw milk brings out the fullness and richness of flavors, and it has the added advantage of bringing the subtleties of pasturing and the diet of the animal into your final cheese.

Raw milk contains natural flora, many of which are very useful in cheese

there are some differences to note if you use sheep's milk for cheese making. When adding rennet, use three to five times less than that used for cow's milk, and top-stir carefully. When cutting the curd, make larger cubes; when ladling, take thicker slices, or you will lose too much butterfat and the cheese will be too dry. Use half the amount of salt called for and exert only light pressure when pressing.

Water Buffalo's Milk

This milk has twice as much butterfat as cow's milk and is traditionally used to make mozzarella. Unless you have your own herd, using water buffalo's milk is

Average Composition of Buffalo's Milk	Percentage
Water and minerals	85.0
Albuminous protein	0.7
Casein	3.8
Lactose	4.5
Butterfat	6.0
Total solids	15.0

making. It may also contain harmful bacteria, known as pathogens, that can produce disease in humans. Pathogens that may be found in milk include *Mycobacterium*, which causes tuberculosis; *Brucella*, which cause brucellosis; and *Salmonella*, which causes salmonellosis.

A few salmonella outbreaks in recent decades, however, all have occurred in pasteurized milk. Typically, salmonella outbreaks are caused by a lack of cleanliness in factories, where the thinking is that "pasteurization will take care of it." Taking precautions to avoid food-borne illness is important for everyone, but especially for those most vulnerable to disease — children, the elderly, and people with weakened immune systems.

If you consume raw milk or use raw milk to produce cheese that is aged fewer than 60 days (this includes almost all fresh cheeses), *you must be absolutely certain that there are no pathogens in the milk*. To ensure that your raw milk is pathogen-free, consult a local veterinarian for advice. A good rule to follow is: *If in doubt, pasteurize.*

When using raw milk, never use milk from an animal that is suffering from mastitis (inflammation of the udder) or receiving antibiotics, which will destroy the helpful bacteria that are essential in making cheese. (If you make raw-milk cheese for sale, U.S. federal law dictates that it must be aged longer than 60 days to prevent the development of pathogenic bacteria.) That said, raw-milk cheeses are some of the best in the world.

FREEZING MILK

Many people wonder whether freezing milk has an effect on cheese making. I have found that goat's milk keeps well for 30 days frozen and can then be used in cheese making, at least for the soft and semisoft varieties. Cow's milk does not freeze well, because the cream separates after freezing.

Homogenized Milk

This milk has been heat-treated and pressurized to break up the butterfat globules into very small particles so that they are distributed evenly throughout the milk and do not rise to the top. Homogenized milk produces a curd that is smoother and less firm than that of raw milk, so I recommend adding calcium chloride during cheese making.

Cream-Line Milk

This milk has not been homogenized and has a "line" that separates the cream on the top from the milk on the bottom. (This is delicious! If you're my age, you remember the glass bottles on the porch — that was cream-line milk.)

Pasteurized Milk

This type of milk has been heat-treated to destroy pathogens. In effect, it kills all bacteria, which is why you need to add bacterial starter to most cheese recipes. Pasteurization makes proteins, vitamins, and milk sugars less available, and it also destroys the enzymes that help the body assimilate them.

How to Pasteurize Milk. If you acquire milk directly from a cow or a goat and need to pasteurize it, follow this simple procedure:

1. Pour the raw milk into a stainless-steel or glass pot (do not use aluminum) and place the pot into another, larger pot containing hot water. Put the double boiler on the stovetop.

2. Heat the milk to 145°F, stirring occasionally to ensure even heating. Hold the temperature at 145°F for exactly 30 minutes. The temperature and time are important. Too little heat or too short a holding time may not destroy all the pathogens. Too much heat or too long a holding time can destroy the milk protein and result in a curd that is too soft for cheese making.

3. Remove the pot of milk from the pot of hot water and put it into a sink filled with ice water that is at the same level as the milk. Stir constantly until the temperature drops to 40°F. Rapid cooling is important to eliminate conditions that support the growth of unwanted bacteria.

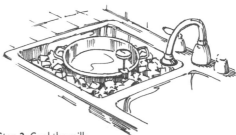

Step 3: Cool the milk as rapidly as possible in ice water.

4. Store pasteurized milk in the refrigerator until you're ready to use it.

Ultrapasteurized Milk

Scientists working for large corporations have figured out that if you heat-treat milk to ultrahigh temperatures, you can keep it for a very long time prior to opening. This allows large milk companies to buy out the smaller ones and transport your milk all across the country and still get it to your table in all its dead glory. The protein is completely denatured and you may as well drink water. Please ask your local storekeepers to get the real thing for you. You *cannot* use this type of milk for the wonderful 30-Minute Mozzarella (see page 134); it will only make a mushy ricotta.

Step 2: To pasteurize milk, hold it at 145°F for 30 minutes.

ULTRAPASTEURIZATION: BAD NEWS FOR HOME CHEESE MAKERS

First there was raw milk. This is milk as it comes out of the cow, sheep, or goat. Most cheese makers believe it is the very best choice for making cheese. United States law mandates that raw-milk cheeses be aged for at least 60 days to ensure that any pathogens are destroyed.

Then there was pasteurization. This heating process (145°F for 30 minutes or 161°F for 15 seconds) destroys pathogenic bacteria, including *Mycobacterium tuberculosis*. As a public health measure for the sale of fluid milk, pasteurization has saved countless lives. As far as cheese making goes, it changes the flavor of the milk slightly and denatures 4 to 7 percent of the whey proteins, which in turn generates a slightly weaker curd. For home cheese making, cream-line milk (which has minimum pasteurization and no homogenization) is ideal, but it is hard to find.

Now there is ultrapasteurization. To the dismay of home cheese makers (and consumers who simply like to drink milk), more and more of the milk and cream in grocery dairy cases is ultrapasteurized (UP). This means it is heated to 191°F for at least 1 second, which destroys all organisms in the milk.

It also gives milk a slightly cooked taste, like that of evaporated milk. The purpose of UP treatment is to give the product greater shelf life. UP milk and cream will last at least 28 days, as long as they are refrigerated and not opened. (Once opened, they keep only as long as conventionally pasteurized milk and cream.)

UP milk is less than ideal for home cheese making; the protein structure is damaged and the enzymes are destroyed. It has no real advantage as fluid milk for the consumer but is convenient for the processor, who can buy less milk, transport it farther, and keep it on the shelf longer. It doesn't even taste good. UP cream is nasty stuff that leaves a greasy film on coffee and is difficult to whip. Large processors market UP milk by pandering to people's fears about food safety, though conventionally pasteurized milk and cream are perfectly safe.

Talk to your grocer. Demand an alternative to UP milk. Drive out of your way to buy non-UP dairy products. Support local milk suppliers who are willing to provide a fresh, healthful product. If all else fails, buy a cow, a few sheep, some goats. Drink good milk, and learn to make cheese.

Ultra-Heat-Treated (UHT) Milk

UHT milk, or "long-life" milk, sold in foil-lined containers, is flash-heated at a temperature between 275 and 300°F. It has a shelf life of several months. If this is the only milk available to you, you can use it to make soft cheese, but this product comes in a box — need I say more?

Whole Milk

Milk that still has all of its original ingredients and a butterfat content of 3.5 to 4 percent is called *whole milk*. Whole milk contains cream.

Nonfat (Skim) Milk

Milk that has most of the cream removed and a butterfat content of 1 to 2 percent is called *nonfat* or *skim milk*. Nonfat milk is used for making prepared starter and hard, grating cheeses, such as Romano and Parmesan. It may also be used as a low-fat alternative to make soft cheeses (see chapter 4) and for a number of other dairy products (see chapter 10).

Dry Milk Powder

This product is simply dehydrated milk solids; 1⅓ cups of dry milk powder dissolved in 3¾ cups of water makes 1 quart of milk. Dry milk powder does not need to be pasteurized, as the drying process destroys unwanted bacteria. You may use either skim or whole milk powder to make soft cheeses and other dairy products.

I have used dry milk powder in the tropics to make fromage blanc with great success. Simply add a packet of starter to the powder, mix it with water, shake, set, and drain, and voilà — cheese for the island!

Soy Milk

Made from the milk of soybeans, soy milk can sometimes be used to make soft cheeses and other dairy products. You will have to experiment with your local brands.

Buttermilk

Originally, buttermilk was the liquid drained from the churn after butter was made. Little of that is available today. Instead, the buttermilk we buy is made from pasteurized skim milk to which bacterial starter has been added. Today, it is quite simple to use direct-set buttermilk starter to make your own buttermilk (see page 195).

Cream

There are many types of cream, depending on the butterfat content. If you are buying cream at a store, light cream and half-and-half are ideal for making soft cheeses. Whipping cream and heavy cream are frequently too high in butterfat to set properly. Avoid ultrapasteurized cream.

Rennet

Rennet is a substance used to coagulate milk. It contains enzymes that act on the milk protein casein, separating the milk into curds (solids) and whey (liquid). If raw milk is left for a few days, it will curdle on its own due to the action of naturally occurring bacteria that convert milk sugar (lactose) to lactic acid. The longer it is left, the more acidic it becomes, until it finally curdles. In cheese making, however, it is not desirable to have coagulation take place at a high acidity level, because the milk will coagulate too quickly. Therefore, rennet is used to bring about coagulation while the milk is still sweet.

Rennet comes in liquid, tablet, and powdered forms and is available from cheese-making supply houses. Keep liquid rennet in the refrigerator; store rennet tablets and powdered rennet in the freezer. If refrigeration is unavailable, store rennet in a cool place away from light. Exposure to light can cause rennet to break down. At temperatures below 50°F and above 130°F, the activity of rennet practically ceases.

Animal Rennet

Animal-derived rennet is extracted from the fourth stomach of a calf and contains the enzymes rennin (chymosin) and pepsin. In the days before modern laboratory technology produced standardized rennet, most cheese makers made their own rennet on the farm. When they slaughtered a calf or kid, they cleaned and salted the stomach and hung it up to dry in a cool place until it was needed. At cheese-making time, they broke off a small piece of the dried stomach and

OLD-TIME RENNET

An old method of making rennet involved the stomach of a calf or kid slaughtered at not more than 2 days old. The stomach contains milk with a high percentage of colostrum. Cheese makers drained the milk, cleaned the stomach, returned the milk to the stomach, tied off the tip, and hung it up to age. Cheese makers also added a tiny amount of finely grated, dried cheese to the milk as it was replaced in the stomach, producing a rennet that was both a culture and a coagulant.

Antique rennet-testing equipment

soaked it in cool, fresh water for several hours, then added a bit of the solution to ripened milk to produce a curd.

Vegetable Rennet

A number of plants have coagulating properties. In ancient Rome, cheese makers used an extract of bark from the fig tree *(Ficus carica)*. An infusion made of our lady's bedstraw *(Galium verum)* or stinging nettle *(Urtica dioica)* may also be used. The flower of the thistle plant *(Cynara)* is used in Portugal to make Sera de Estrella cheese. Legend has it that at one time in northern Europe, the butterwort plant (cheese flower) was fed to cows just before milking time, causing the milk to coagulate 3 hours later. Today, vegetable rennet contains an enzyme derived from the mold *Mucur miehei*. Liquid vegetable rennet is usually kosher.

Note: Cheese made with vegetable rennet and aged for a long time tends to develop a slightly bitter flavor.

Chymosin

This high-quality rennet is suitable for many vegetarians and is frequently used by commercial cheese makers. The genes responsible for producing chymosin (the enzyme found in rennet) are transferred from calf cells to bacterial cells. When the altered bacterial cells reproduce, the daughter cells produce chymosin that is identical to calf chymosin. This rennet is available under a number of trade names, including Chymostar Classic, Chy-Max, and Chymogen.

Junket Rennet

Junket is a weak form of rennet. Although it is possible to curdle milk with junket rennet and to use it in some soft-cheese making, it should not be used in hard-cheese making. Cheese rennet tablets are four or five times stronger than junket rennet tablets.

Unchlorinated Water

Since chlorine can destroy the action of rennet, you must use nonchlorinated water to dilute rennet. If your source of water is municipal, check with your local water department to find out whether it chlorinates your water supply. Many

---

PLANTS USED AS COAGULANTS

Over the years, I have had numerous inquiries about what types of plants may be used as coagulants. In addition to the plants mentioned under vegetable rennet, the following plants can be used as coagulants. To use the plant extracts (sap), crush the plant matter and strain it before adding the liquid to the milk.

- Nettles *(Arctium minus)*
- Butterwort leaves *(Pinguicula vulgaris)*
- Knapweed *(Centaurea species)*
- Mallow *(Malva sylvestris)*
- Teasel *(Dipsacus sylvestris)*
- Yarrow *(Achillea millefolium)*

Liz McAlister, Cato Corner Farm
Colchester, Connecticut

Liz McAlister loves her cows. To keep them and her family farm afloat in a rapidly urbanizing region, she makes cheese from spring to fall, producing classic aged Italian-, English-, and Dutch-style cheeses with rich, distinctive flavors. In the winter, when the cows are eating hay and silage, she sells fluid milk.

The 70 Jerseys (about 40 of them are milkers) on Liz's farm are named and loved. "We also keep four Guernseys," Liz says with an easy laugh. "They're big and friendly, and tourists love them." Liz and her son Mark work full time on the farm, and interns from around the world join them to learn about dairying and cheese making.

Liz started making cheese many years ago from the first edition of this book (her original copy is falling apart), but she didn't start selling cheese until 1996. "I started with dairy goats," Liz explains, "but I just enjoy cows more, and I like the range of cheeses made from cow's milk. Our cheese called Vivace is based on the recipe for montasio, with a few alterations."

Liz and Mark are in the process of building a cheese cave, with the aid of matching funds from the state of Connecticut's Farm Enhancement Grant program. Built into the side of a hill near the barn, the cave will provide a cool, humid environment perfect for aging, allowing Liz to expand the range of cheeses she can offer.

Anyone who visits Cato Corner Farm is likely to find Liz out in the barn with her cows or in the cheese-making room. It's hard to catch her indoors, except on the coldest winter day. Her son is just as enthusiastic about cheese making and as committed to keeping the farm in the black — and in the family — as she is.

> *If you love cows and you love cheese, you might think Liz McAlister has the perfect life. She would agree*

cities and towns add chlorine to kill harmful microorganisms in water. If your tap water is chlorinated, you may use bottled water or distilled water, which can be purchased at grocery and other stores.

Starter

A starter is a culture of bacteria that is added to milk to assist in the process of cheese making. Starter converts milk sugar (lactose) into lactic acid, bringing about conditions that allow a number of changes to take place. For instance, starter helps develop the proper level of acidity in milk. The acid helps the rennet coagulate the milk, aids in expelling the whey from the curds, checks the growth of pathogens, and helps preserve the final cheese. Starter also contributes to the body, flavor, and aroma of a cheese. The process of using a starter to increase the acidity of milk is referred to as *ripening*. When milk has reached the proper level of acidity, it is referred to as *ripened*.

Direct-Set Starter vs. Prepared Starter (Mother Culture)

Traditionally, starters were made from the whey from the previous day's cheese making. Over the years, starters were prepared and then propagated from one batch to the next — these were known as *mother cultures* (reculturable starters).

In the late 1980s, a new technology of home starter cultures, known as direct-set starters, was introduced for home cheese making. They are added directly to the milk, which eliminates the lengthy process of making the prepared starter. They save time, are very easy to use, and dramatically reduce the possible contaminants that can enter the milk during the cheese-making process.

There are direct-set cultures for all types of cheeses as well as for other dairy products. They are available to home cheese makers in freeze-dried powdered form and can be stored in the freezer unopened for up to 2 years. They may be purchased from cheese-making supply houses.

Mesophilic Starter vs. Thermophilic Starter

Another important distinction between starter cultures is that of mesophilic and thermophilic starters (although a variety of starter cultures are used in cheese making, those are the two basic categories). *Mesophilic starters* are used to make low-temperature cheeses; *thermophilic starters* are used to make high-temperature cheeses.

Making Prepared Mesophilic Starter. You may prefer to prepare your own mother culture, which then may be propagated for 1 to 6 months, depending on your attention to cleanliness. To make your first batch of prepared mesophilic starter, add a freeze-dried packet of starter to sterilized, then cooled, skim milk. As time passes, the bacteria reproduce rapidly; after 15 to 24 hours, there are an astronomical number of starter bacteria living in the milk, enough to turn milk protein into a solid white gel. (If you make a mother culture with goat's milk, it will have the consistency of runny buttermilk rather than of gel.)

1. Sterilize a clean 1-quart canning jar and its lid by placing them in boiling water for 5 minutes.

2. Cool them and fill the jar with fresh skim milk, leaving ½ inch of headspace. Tightly cover the jar with the sterilized lid.

3. Place the jar in a canner (or a big deep pot) with the water level at least ¼ inch above the top of the lid.

4. Place the pot on the burner and bring the water to a boil. Note when the water begins to boil, then let it continue at a slow boil for 30 minutes.

Step 4: Sterilize the jars in slowly boiling water for 30 minutes.

5. Remove the jar from the water and let it cool to 72°F, away from drafts. (Monitor the room's temperature with a thermometer to avoid contaminating the milk.)

Step 6: Pour the culture into the cooled, sterilized milk.

6. Inoculate the milk (still at 72°F) by adding the contents of the freeze-dried mesophilic starter culture packet. Quickly add the powder to minimize the milk's exposure to air. Cover the jar with the lid and swirl the jar to mix and dissolve the powdered culture. (If you are making a second batch, add to the sterilized milk 2 ounces of fresh or frozen mother culture rather than the packet of powder.)

7. Place the jar where the milk's temperature can be kept at 72°F for 15 to 24 hours during the ripening period. Sixteen hours usually does the trick, but if the milk hasn't coagulated by then, leave it for another 8 hours or so. (If the kitchen seems too cool, place the jar on a top shelf, where the temperature of the room is usually 10 degrees warmer.)

8. The culture will have the consistency of good yogurt. It will separate cleanly from the sides of the jar and its surface will be shiny. Taste it — it should be slightly acidic and also a bit sweet.

9. Once it has thickened, chill it immediately. You may keep the starter refrigerated for up to 3 days before using it. Unless you plan to make a large amount of cheese right away, however, the best thing to do is to freeze it for future use.

10. To freeze the prepared starter culture, sterilize two plastic ice cube trays. Fill the trays with starter culture, cover with plastic wrap, and freeze them solid in the coldest part of your freezer. Transfer the cubes to airtight plastic bags and put them back in the freezer. They will keep their strength for up to 1 month. Each cube of starter culture is a convenient 1-ounce block, which may be thawed at any time and used to make cheese or another batch of starter culture. Always label your bags with the name of the starter you made and the date.

Step 10: To store the culture, freeze it in sterilized ice cube trays.

Making Prepared Thermophilic Starter. The directions for preparing thermophilic starter culture are similar to those for mesophilic starter, with some differences in steps 5, 6, and 7.

1. Follow steps 1 through 4 for Making Prepared Mesophilic Starter on page 20.

2. Remove the jar from the water and let it cool to 110°F, away from drafts.

3. Inoculate the milk with thermophilic culture when the temperature is still 110°F. Quickly add the powder to minimize the milk's exposure to air. Cover the jar with the lid and swirl the jar to mix and dissolve the powdered culture. (If you are making a second batch, add to the sterilized milk 2 ounces of fresh or frozen mother culture rather than the packet of powder.)

4. In step 7, allow the milk to incubate at 110°F for 6 to 8 hours, until a yogurtlike curd is produced. (If the kitchen seems too cool, place the jar on a top shelf, where the temperature of the room is usually 10 degrees warmer.)

Cheese Coloring

The characteristic color of a finished cheese is as much a part of its identity as its flavor. For example, goat's milk, which does not contain carotene, produces a white cheese. Cow's milk, which has a very high carotene content, makes a perfect yellow Cheddar. At the far end of the color spectrum is the deep orange of longhorn and colby cheeses.

In times past, yellow cheese was thought to be a higher-quality cheese,

PROBLEMS WITH STARTER PREPARATION

If you are careful to sterilize everything and monitor the timing and the temperature, probably nothing will go wrong with your starter culture. But . . .

1. If your starter tastes sharply acidic, or even slightly metallic, it may mean that it has overripened. Next time, use a little less starter, or incubate the milk at 70°F instead of 72°F for mesophilic culture or at 108°F instead of 110°F for thermophilic culture.

2. If your starter won't coagulate, it may be because of any (or all) of the following:
  a. The temperature dropped below 72° (110°F for thermophilic culture) during the ripening period.
  b. The inoculating culture didn't contain live bacteria.
  c. The milk contained antibiotics. This happens occasionally when a dairy must give antibiotics to a cow. The medicine is absorbed into the animal's system and is expressed in the milk.
  d. While cleaning your utensils, you used bleach or a strong detergent and didn't rinse thoroughly. Residual amounts of either can halt bacterial action.

  e. You didn't add enough starter culture. This is unlikely in your first batch, because the packets of freeze-dried culture are carefully premeasured. In your second and succeeding batches, be sure to add 2 ounces of fresh starter or two cubes (1 ounce per cube) of frozen starter culture from your freezer supply.
  f. Also unlikely, but still possible, is that organisms hostile to lactic acid–producing bacteria were present in the culture.

3. If you find bubbles in your finished starter culture, discard it. Bubbles may mean:
  a. The milk was not properly sterilized in the canning-jar step. Gas-producing organisms, such as yeasts and coliform bacteria, manufacture bubbles. They are present in a starter because of faulty preparation techniques.
  b. Your equipment was not clean enough.

If you have *any* reason to believe that your starter culture is not quite right, *throw it out and begin again with a fresh culture.* It would be heartbreaking to wait 6 long months for your cheese to age, only to find that the wrong bacteria have been at work spoiling it.

because it was made from milk rich in butterfat. Cheese makers soon discovered they could artificially color their cheeses and command a premium price for cheeses made with inferior milk. At one time, marigold petals, hawthorn buds, saffron, and turmeric were used to color cheese.

In reality, coloring depends not on the butterfat content but on the concentration of carotenes (natural pigments) in the butterfat. Animals absorb carotenes through their feed and convert some of it, including beta-carotene, into vitamin A. Some of the excess beta-carotene is stored in the butterfat in their milk. Carotene concentration also varies with the breed of animal. Added cheese coloring has no effect on the flavor of a cheese, except for Roquefort and blue cheeses, because their identifying blue flecks are caused by the same mold or fungus that imparts its delectable flavor.

Cheese coloring is a safe, nontoxic vegetable dye that attaches to milk protein (casein) during the cheese-making process. The ingredient responsible for the color is annatto, an extract from the seeds of *Bixa orellana,* a South American shrub. Cheese coloring comes in liquid form and may be purchased from cheese-making supply houses. Store it in a cupboard; it has an indefinite shelf life.

Cheese Salt

Salt enhances the flavor of cheese. Cheese salt is a coarse, noniodized flake salt that is similar to pickling salt. It is usually added to the curds just before they are pressed and, in some cases, rubbed gently on the outside of a cheese after the rind has formed. Cheese salt is also used to make a saturated brine solution in which cheeses are soaked.

Cheese salt performs many important functions. It draws moisture from the curd, helps drain the whey by causing the curd to shrink, inhibits the growth of lactic bacteria toward the end of the cheese-making process, and acts as a preservative by suppressing the growth of undesirable bacteria. Cheese salt is available from cheese-making supply houses. As an alternative, Diamond Crystal salt company sells a crystal kosher salt that is very good. Do not use iodized salt; iodine inhibits the growth of starter bacteria and slows the aging process.

Herbs

Herbs and spices add a variety of flavors and a touch of color to cheeses. It is best to use fresh herbs; if you can, pick them fresh and use them as soon as possible. The amount to use depends on your own taste buds, but if you use dried

"*Only peril can bring the French together. One can't impose unity out of the blue on a country that has 265 different kinds of cheese.***"**
—Charles de Gaulle

herbs, you need far less. Use about 1 teaspoon of dried herbs for every tablespoon of fresh herbs. Popular herbs for hard-cheese making are cumin and caraway seeds. For soft-cheese making, some herbs that I enjoy using from my garden include chives, parsley, thyme, garlic, dill, oregano, basil, and sage. I also like to roll soft cheeses in peppercorns and herbes de Provence. Soft cheeses made with fresh herbs should be allowed to set in the refrigerator for a day or two so the flavors can permeate the cheese. Allow soft cheeses made with dried herbs to set in the refrigerator for several days, because dried herbs are not as aromatic as fresh ones.

Calcium Chloride

Calcium chloride is a salt solution used to restore balance to the calcium content of milk that has been heat-treated. This is especially important when vegetable or microbial rennet will be used. The heat used in pasteurization decreases the amount of calcium in milk and has an adverse effect on its clotting properties. This means that the renneting action in pasteurized milk is significantly slowed. Adding calcium chloride helps bring this process back into balance and produces a firmer curd. Calcium chloride has an indefinite shelf life.

Note: We do not recommend using calcium chloride when making mozzarella because it may prevent the cheese from stretching properly in the final step.

> ### RIND DEVELOPMENT
> Proper rind development is important to the success of white mold–ripened cheeses. *Penicillium candidum* is better suited to cow's-milk cheese, where it breaks down proteins and fats and enhances flavor. However, it may grow too quickly on goat's-milk cheese, creating a layer of liquid under the skin and causing the rind to slip off the cheese. The slower-growing mold of *Geotrichum candidum* helps eliminate "slipskin" in goat's- and sheep's-milk cheeses. Although it may be used on its own, it is often combined with *Pencillium candidum* to produce a more full-flavored cheese.

Acids

Although rennet is used to aid coagulation of most cheeses, various acids may also be used for this purpose when making soft bag cheeses. Chapter 4, "Soft Cheese," contains recipes that use the following acidifying agents: vinegar; citric acid; tartaric acid; and lemon, lime, and orange juices. Citric and tartaric acids can be obtained from cheese-making supply houses.

Lipase Powder

Lipase is an enzyme that is added to milk to create a stronger-flavored cheese. It is added to many Italian cheeses and occasionally to blue cheese. Lipase powder is stored in the freezer and keeps for 4 to 6 months.

Bacteria and Molds

Bacteria and molds are added to bacterial and mold-ripened cheeses to enhance their flavor and aroma. They are available from cheese-making supply houses.

Penicillium candidum
(White Mold)

This mold is generally used as a surface mold on soft cheeses, such as Brie. It gives the cheese its characteristic appearance, and its rapid spread over the surface inhibits the growth of undesirable molds. Its capacity to break down lactic acids allows it to neutralize the acidity of cheese, thereby influencing taste and structure. It also contributes to the ripening process, especially in regard to flavor. This powder is stored in the freezer and will keep for 3 to 6 months.

Geotrichum candidum
(White Mold)

This mold produces white to cream-colored, flat, sometimes almost transparent colonies that may also appear powdery. It is used together with *P. candidum* for the production of soft cheeses, such as Camembert and Brie. This mold plays a significant role in the ripening process and greatly influences the appearance, structure, and flavor of those cheeses. In red-smear cheeses (see below), *G. candidum* helps neutralize the surface of the cheese and stimulates the development of *Brevibacterium linens*. This powder is stored in the freezer and will keep for 3 to 6 months.

Penicillium roqueforti
(Blue Mold)

This mold produces the typical bluish green mottling. It restricts undesirable mold growth, and its enzymes influence the development of a cheese's piquant taste and creamy consistency. This liquid is stored in the refrigerator and will keep for 3 to 6 months, but it can't be frozen.

Brevibacterium linens
(Red Bacteria)

This bacterium is an important component of red-smear cheeses, such as brick cheeses. It provides the desired color, protects against unwanted mold growth, and is important in flavor formation. This powder is stored in the freezer and will keep for 3 to 6 months.

Ash

Sometimes called activated charcoal, ash is a food-grade charcoal used on some soft cheeses to neutralize the surface and create a friendly environment for mold growth. Ash is found at drugstores or through cheese-making supply houses.

CHAPTER 2

EQUIPMENT

For centuries, cheese has been made using indigenous materials, such as clay, wood, and tree bark for molds; straw for cheese baskets and mats; tea towels for draining; and animal stomachs for renneting. Many of these

items are still being used today in places where the art of cheese making has been handed down from generation to generation, and it is fascinating to watch delicious cheeses still being produced in time-tested fashion. And though improvising is fun and possibly less expensive, be aware that using untested materials means sanitation becomes a lot more difficult. Therefore, for the purpose of home cheese making, the following is a list of more modern-day equipment and utensils.

You must take precautions to scrupulously care for and clean all equipment regularly. Stainless steel, enamel, glass, and food-grade polypropylene are used in the kitchen today. They are easy to keep clean and are the most nonreactive

with regard to acidity produced during the cheese-making process. Note that aluminum and cast-iron pots are *not* used in cheese making because of the reaction of acids with metallic salts, which, when absorbed by the curds, cause unpleasant metallic flavors. Acids also corrode the pots, making sanitation very difficult. Do not use PVC pipe, which is not a food-grade material, or coffee cans, which may be soldered with lead.

Equipment Essentials

Most of these items can be found in your own kitchen. What you don't have on hand you can easily purchase at a department store or from a cheese-making supply house.

Atomizer

An atomizer is a bottle with a fine spray nozzle. For mold-ripened cheeses, it delivers a fine mist of mold solution on the surface of your cheese. Too much moisture may result in the growth of undesirable mold.

Bowl

An alternative to heating the pot of milk in a sink full of hot water is to use a 13-quart bowl. Set the pot in the bowl, then add hot water to heat the milk. In essence, you are making a hot-water-jacketed cheese vat on the table.

Butter Muslin

This has a slightly closer weave than cheesecloth and is used for draining all soft cheeses. Butter muslin is a must; after the time you spend with the cheese-making process, you don't want to lose the curds down the drain before you get to eat your cheese. Clean butter muslin in the same way you wash cheesecloth (see page 29). Cheese-making supply houses are the best places to purchase this. Have at least one packet on hand at all times.

Cheese Boards

These are useful as draining platforms for cheeses such as Brie, Camembert, and Coulommiers. A 6-inch, well-seasoned hardwood, such as birch or maple, works well. Do not use oak or cherry; the tannins in the wood could be harmful to you and/or your cheese. Cheese boards also may be used for air-drying and aging. Keep at least two boards handy.

Cheese Mats

These reed or food-grade-plastic mats may be purchased from a cheese-making supply house. Alternatively, you may use sushi mats or the squares found in the needlework section of a craft store. Cheese mats are essential for draining Brie, Camembert, and Coulommiers. They may also be used for the air-drying period that follows the pressing of a cheese. Have at least one pair of mats on hand.

Butter muslin

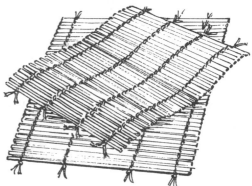
Cheese mats

Cheese Trier (optional)

This stainless-steel implement is used to take samples as the cheese ages to determine whether it is properly matured and ready for eating. It is available only through a cheese-making supply house.

Cheese trier

Cheese Wax

This pliable wax creates a protective coating to inhibit bacteria and prevent cheese from drying out during the aging process. Cheese wax comes in three colors: natural (yellow), red, and black. It may be purchased from a cheese supply house. Proper cheese wax, which is reusable, is stronger and more pliable than brittle paraffin.

Cheese Wrap

This breathable cellophane is used to wrap soft and mold-ripened cheeses to keep them in peak condition during storage. It is available through cheese-making supply houses.

Cheesecloth

This cotton cloth is used to drain curds and line molds for hard cheeses. After using cheesecloth, rinse it in cold water (some people recommend using a bit of whey, which helps loosen the curds stuck in the fibers), then wash it right away, occasionally adding a little bleach to the water. Boiling the cheesecloth in water to which washing soda has been added

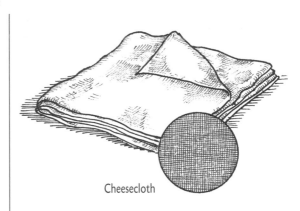

Cheesecloth

NYLON TRICOT
I find that nylon tricot makes terrific milk strainers and cheesecloths. It is strong and easy to clean, has no frayed edges, and lets the liquid through very quickly but catches every speck of solids. (It is the best material for straining and reusing wax, too.)

— Winnie, Pont Hill, Indiana

helps maintain freshness. Please obtain this from a cheese-making supply house: Professional-quality cheesecloth remains strong enough to wash, boil, and use over and over again. (The cheesecloth you may find in a grocery store is not woven tightly enough, and it would be a sad story to make your cheese and lose it through those wide holes.) Have at least one packet on hand at all times.

Colander

Use this for draining the curds and whey. Any type will work fine because you'll line it with cheesecloth.

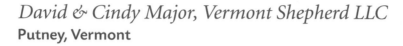

David & Cindy Major, Vermont Shepherd LLC
Putney, Vermont

Prizewinning Vermont Shepherd cheese (sheep), Putney Tomme (cow), Timson (cow), and other sheep's-milk cheeses come from Major Farm and members of the Vermont Shepherd Cheese Guild, which David and Cindy Major organized. The cheeses aging in the Putney cave distill the rocky soil, sunny pastures, blazing maples, and fresh water of Vermont into nutty, mellow, distinctive cheese.

Cindy's dad, who ran a dairy and cheese plant in New York state, suggested that David and Cindy milk their sheep. "We started selling the milk fresh," David remembers, "and he said, 'Why not try making cheese?' So we did. It was in the late 1980s."

"The first cheese we made was terrible," Cindy says. "We entered it in a competition and it came in last."

In 1993, the couple went to the French Pyrenees and studied with small-scale cheese makers. They found out that what they had been doing was mostly wrong. They had been freezing the milk so they could make cheese in large batches, and they had not been careful. When they returned home, they started using small batches of fresh milk that they heated and cooled slowly, stirred slowly, and treated gently. That year their cheese won first place in the American Cheese Society competition.

David advises novice cheese makers to start small, then plan on experimenting for a couple of years "to figure out what you like to make best and what you're good at." Rather than their many prizes, "making our small Vermont farm a success and helping others do the same is what I'm happiest about," David says. "There's such a trick to it! But we've shown there is hope for small farms."

Cindy continues, "In France, the philosophy of farming is to capture the essence of the land in your food. When we feel we have done that, it makes us happy. We've learned to work with the process, not try to speed it along." (David and Cindy's favorite ways to eat their Vermont Shepherd cheese are featured on pages 230 and 234.)

Curd Knife

A curd knife has a blade long enough to reach the bottom of the pot without immersing the handle and has a flat end rather than a pointed one.

Curd knife

Dairy Thermometer

The temperature range of a dairy thermometer is 0 to 220°F. Any thermometer with this range that can be inserted in milk is acceptable. If you need to check its accuracy, dip it in boiling water. If it doesn't read exactly 212°F, you'll need to make adjustments when using it. A variety of glass and stainless-steel thermometers are available from cheese-making supply houses. The stainless-steel dial-head thermometers are faster in their response to temperature changes and most have a bracket to hold them on the side of a pot. A floating glass thermometer is another option. (The temperature range of a candy thermometer is too high for cheese making.)

Dairy thermometer

Drip Tray

Put a tray under your press or mold to catch the whey, so it doesn't drain all over the counter. You may use a baking sheet or purchase a drip tray from a cheese-making supply house. The tray also protects the wood surface of the cheese press from moisture while the cheese is being pressed.

Hygrometer (optional)

This instrument is used to measure proper humidity readings in your aging area. It is easily obtainable at hardware stores and is especially useful for bacteria- and mold-ripened cheeses.

Kitchen Scale (optional)

This may be used to weigh ingredients.

Measuring Cup

Glass is best for this, because you will be using it for rennet and need to keep it sterile. Plastic may be used, but it could cause contamination if scratched, making it impossible to clean properly.

Measuring Spoons

Stainless steel is advised.

Molds and Followers

Molds, which come in a variety of shapes and sizes, are used to contain the curds

Molds and followers

during the final draining period. The mold determines the shape of the final cheese. The ones obtained from cheese-making supply houses come in stainless steel and food-grade plastic and have drainage holes. To create a homemade mold, select a food-grade-plastic container and punch holes from the inside into the sides and bottom.

Followers are thin, flat disks that fit inside the mold and sit on top of the curds. They press the curds evenly by distributing the weight from the press across the surface of the cheese. Followers are made of stainless steel, food-grade plastic, or wood. If you make your own wooden followers, cut them smaller than the diameter of your mold, as wood expands and contracts with moisture. Use ash or fir; maple tends to mold quickly, and cherry gives off tannins. Don't use pressure-treated wood or wood that has been treated with chemicals.

Notebook

Record keeping is an essential part of cheese making. When things go wrong — and when they go right — you will want to know exactly what you did or did not do. When you keep notes, the reasons for variations in your final cheeses will be more understandable. You may want to repeat a "mistake" or set of conditions that resulted in a particularly delicious cheese! Copy the Cheese Record Form on page 34 when making your cheeses.

Perforated Ladle

You will use a perforated ladle, also called a skimmer, to transfer the curds of some soft and mold-ripened cheeses into molds. You may also pour the rennet through the ladle to distribute it evenly over the surface of the milk. As with all utensils, stainless steel is best. You will find this in a local super-market if not already in your kitchen drawer.

Perforated ladle

Pots

Use stainless-steel, glass, or unchipped enamel pots that are large enough to hold 1 to 3 gallons of milk, depending on the recipe. You may also choose to heat the ingredients indirectly in a stainless-steel double boiler.

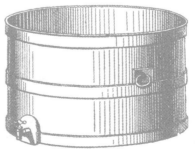

CHEESE-TUB.

THE CHEESE PRESS — HOW TO MAKE IT*

I added this historical design here because it is still a viable way to press cheese, and the design is similar to that of the Off-the-Wall cheese press plans used today. If you make your own press, those plans give you the exact directions for calculating the pressure.

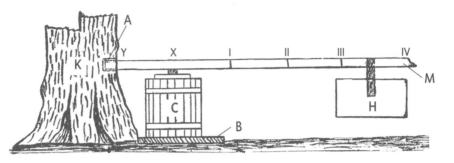

"There was a large stump (K) left just outside my house – indeed the veranda projected over it – and this I used, as shown in the illustration above. I first levelled the ground and laid a 2-inch plank (B) as close to the stump as possible, then placed the hoop (C), allowing space for the follower and a cross-piece. I mortised a hole (A) in the stump, 3 inches square and 4 or 5 inches deep. When used, a long pole (M) was placed with one end in the hole (A), and, the hoop being in position, a bucket or box (H), filled with stones, was attached at the other end.

"To calculate the pressure, the distance from Y to X is measured, and in this case it was 12 inches. If the weight of the bucket is 100 lbs., and it is hung at I, which is 12 inches from X, the pressure is 100 lbs.; if at II, or 24 inches from X, it is 200 lbs.; and if between III and IV, it is 350 lbs.

*from *A.B.C. in Cheese-Making*, J. H. Monrad, 1908

"Such a press can be fixed on any solid wall, by simply spiking a piece of scantling (h) to the wall, as shown in the illustration at right and putting the end of the lever-pole under it. More convenient still is to have one end of the pole fixed by a very strong hinge to the wall, while the other is hung up by a cord to the ceiling, so that the pole can be hoisted up out of the way when not in use, but this will not do for heavy pressure.

"There is only one drawback to these cheap and yet efficient presses, and that is the fact that unless you watch them very carefully, the pole is apt to slant a little one way or the other, and the result is a lopsided cheese (as shown here)."

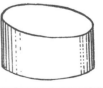

HOMEMADE CHEESE RECORD FORM

Type of
Cheese _____   Date
                          Made _____   Type
                                          of Milk _____   Amount
                                                                     of Milk _____

1. RIPENING

Type of starter_____

Amount of starter_____

Time at adding starter_____

Milk temperature at
time of adding starter_____

2. RENNETING

Type of rennet _____

Amount of rennet _____

Time at adding rennet _____

Milk temperature at
time of adding rennet _____

3. CUTTING THE CURD

Size of curds _____

Time at cutting curds _____

4. COOKING THE CURD

Time of cooking curd_____

Temperature at start of cooking _____

Temperature at finish of cooking _____

5. DRAINING THE CURD

Time of draining _____

6. MILLING THE CURD

Time of milling_____

7. SALTING THE CURD

Amount of salt added _____

Type of herbs added _____

Amount of herbs added _____

8. PRESSING THE CURD

Time at start of pressing _____

Amount of pressure at start _____

Amount of pressure at end _____

Date at end of pressing _____

9. AIR-DRYING

Date started _____

Date finished _____

10. WAXING

Date waxed _____

11. AGING

Temperature during aging _____

12. EATING

Date of first bite _____

COMMENTS AND OBSERVATIONS

_____

_____

_____

Press

Essential for making hard cheese, a press needs to be easy to assemble and clean, and it must provide a way to measure the amount of pressure that is applied to your cheese. Several types of presses and press plans are available from cheese-making supply houses, or you can build one yourself following the diagram on page 33. You may even be able to wheedle one out of your next-door neighbor's workshop — maybe in exchange for some homemade cheese.

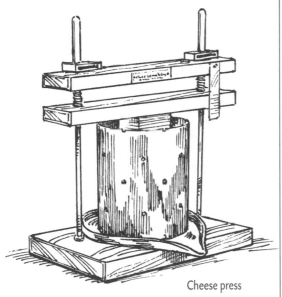

Cheese press

"*A cheese may disappoint. It may be dull, it may be naïve, it may be over-sophisticated. Yet it remains cheese, milk's leap toward immortality.***"**

– Clifton Fadiman

Wax Brush

This is used for brushing wax on your finished cheese. Any natural-bristle brush will work. Do not try to use nylon, which will melt right into the wax, leaving you with a nub when you remove it. Do not use the brush for anything else because you'll never get it completely clean and it will come in contact with food.

Wax Pot

For melting wax, any type of pot will do. If you want to dip your cheese into the wax, the pot must be large enough to hold a 5-pound block; a 1-gallon pot is just the right size for that. If you want to apply wax with a brush, you'll have to melt only a 1-pound block, which will fit into a 1-quart saucepan. Don't plan to use this pot for anything else — cleaning it will be nearly impossible.

Cleaning and Caring for Your Equipment

All utensils must be cleaned scrupulously before and after cheese making. Most home cheese making failures are caused by unclean or unsterile equipment and/or mishandling of the milk. Remember that the entire process of making cheese is based on the action of friendly bacteria. Unclean and unsterile conditions add the undesirable factor of "war between the good guys and the bad guys."

Before getting started, thoroughly rinse your equipment and utensils in hot water; sterilizing them is best. While you are making cheese, make sure all utensils that come in contact with milk are first rinsed in cold water, then wash again in hot water. Rinsing them first in cold water prevents the buildup of milkstone, which creates unwanted bacterial accumulation and may contaminate your final cheese.

Sterilizing Your Equipment

Sterilizing your equipment before and after use is always a good idea, but don't let that scare you. Use common sense to keep things clean while making cheese. People have been doing this for years under all types of conditions. However, the more you sterilize your equipment, the more likely you will have a great cheese-making experience. Sterilizing is done in the following ways.

1. Immerse equipment in a pot of boiling water for 5 minutes.

2. Steam utensils for 5 minutes in a large kettle with about 2 inches of water in the bottom and a tight lid on top.

(Wooden items, such as cheese boards, may be scrubbed and air-dried. Between uses, mats must be boiled or steamed for at least 20 minutes.)

3. Sterilize plastic food-grade equipment by dipping it in a solution of 2 tablespoons of household bleach (sodium hypochlorite) per 1 gallon of water. Dampen a clean cloth in the bleach solution and wipe all work areas.

4. You may also use bleach with stainless-steel utensils, but make sure that you rinse them thoroughly afterward, because a residue of sodium hypochlorite will interfere with the growth of cheese-making bacteria and may kill rennet.

5. Air-dry all rinsed equipment and store in a clean place. Just before using them again, resterilize the equipment.

cheese mold.

CHAPTER 3

TECHNIQUES

" *A small garden, figs,*
a little cheese, and,
along with this,
three or four good friends
— such was luxury to Epicurus. "

— Friedrich Nietzsche

The techniques presented here are all used at one time or another in cheese making. Each type of cheese (e.g., soft, hard, mold-ripened) involves techniques common to all or most of the cheeses within that group. I recommend that you read through this chapter to familiarize yourself with the various techniques before jumping in and making cheese. Then, while you follow a recipe, refer to the appropriate sections for a quick review as needed.

The next four pages provide a quick, at-a-glance summary of the cheese-making process. Remember that the steps will vary according to what type of cheese you are making, so not all the steps will be used for all cheeses.

The remainder of the chapter provides a detailed overview of the techniques specific to each step. The directions are easy to follow, and as you progress, you will get the hang of it relatively quickly.

CHEESE MAKING AT A GLANCE

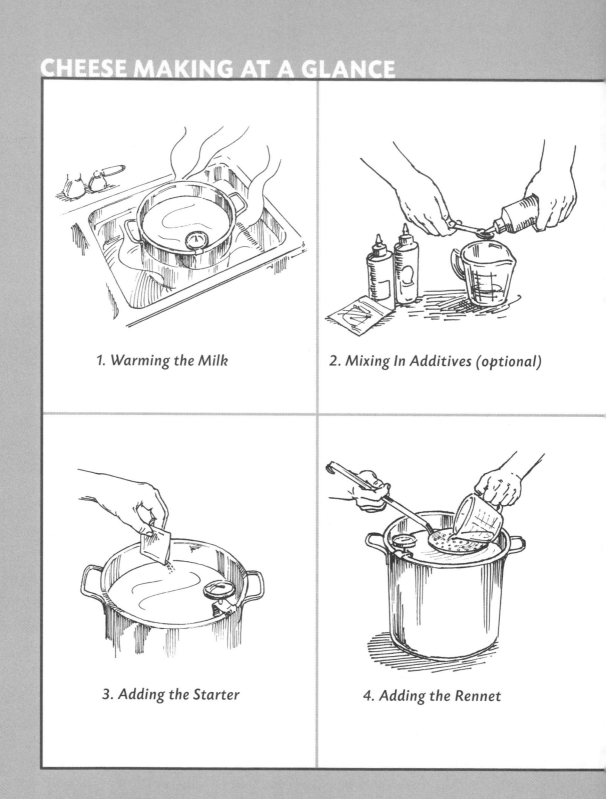

1. Warming the Milk

2. Mixing In Additives (optional)

3. Adding the Starter

4. Adding the Rennet

5. Letting Set until the Curd Gives a Clean Break

6. Cutting the Curds

7. Cooking the Curds

8. Draining the Curds

(continued on next page)

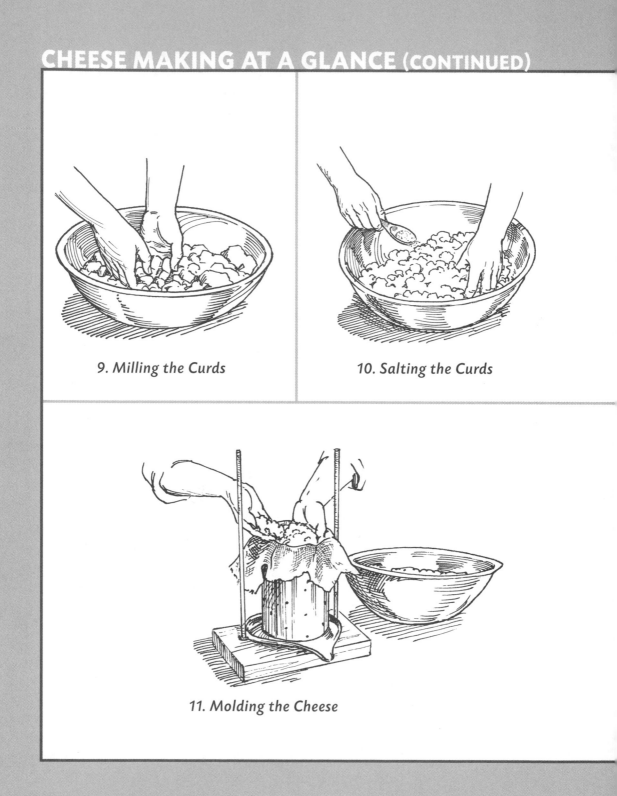

9. Milling the Curds

10. Salting the Curds

11. Molding the Cheese

12. Pressing the Cheese
(hard cheese only)

13. Misting Mold-Ripened
Cheese

14. Air-Drying the Cheese
(hard cheese only)

15. Waxing the Cheese
(hard cheese only)

Final Step: Aging the Cheese

Ripening

The first step in making cheese is to ripen the milk. In the ripening process, milk sugar is converted into lactic acid. The increase in acid in the milk aids in the expulsion of whey from the curd, helps the rennet coagulate the milk, helps preserve the final cheese, and assists in flavor development.

To ripen milk, heat it to the temperature and in the manner specified in the recipe. When the milk reaches the required temperature, add cheese starter culture (starter). The starter contains active lactic acid–producing bacteria, which ripen (acidify) the milk, usually over a period of 30 to 60 minutes. The increase in acidity must proceed at the proper rate. We control the acidity by planning the ripening time so that the level of lactic acid will be just right. If too much acid is produced, the cheese will sour and could leak whey during the aging process. If too little acid is produced, the cheese may have little flavor and could have numerous gas holes caused by contaminating yeast or coliform bacteria.

Remember that cheese is alive. The starter must be healthy and active during cheese making. Pay particular attention to preparing and storing your starter (see page 20). Also, make sure that the milk is heated to the correct temperature, at the correct rate, and in the correct manner. During the ripening process, milk is heated in one of two ways: directly or indirectly.

Direct Heating – Stovetop

In this method, milk is heated directly on your stovetop. Direct heating can heat your milk unevenly, and it is never used in hard-cheese making. Use this method when you see the stovetop icon (⬛) in the recipe.

Indirect Heating – Water Bath

This is done by placing a pot of milk into a bowl or sink full of hot water. (The water is typically 10 degrees warmer than the target temperature of the milk.) If the temperature of the milk starts to climb too high, remove the pot from the water. If the temperature falls too low, place the pot back into the water. Add hot or cold water to the outer bowl or sink as needed to maintain the temperature of the milk. Use this method when you see the water-bath icon (🍲) in the recipe.

Adding Starter

A healthy starter is the key to good-quality cheese. Starter converts the lactose in milk to lactic acid to produce controlled ripening (see page 20). The categories of starter and how to use them are described below.

Mesophilic

A moderate temperature–loving starter, mesophilic starter grows best when the temperature is between 80 and 86°F. Temperatures lower than 70°F inhibit bacterial growth during the initial ripening period; those higher than 86°F do not encourage optimal growth. A temperature above 104°F destroys the bacteria.

Thermophilic

This heat-loving starter is used for cheeses in which the curd is cooked at temperatures of up to 132°F. The optimum temperature for the addition of thermophilic starter is between 86 and

Adding prepared starter:
Thermophilic

107°F. These bacteria thrive at high temperatures. At lower temperatures, thermophilic starter remains inactive.

Direct Set

To use direct-set starter, open the packet and add the contents directly to the milk. Stir to distribute evenly. Once mixed, do not stir for the remainder of the ripening period; excessive aeration reduces the rate of acid production, which may extend the ripening time.

Adding starter:
Direct set

Prepared

To use prepared starter, make your own mother culture, store it, and then propagate it as needed (see pages 20–22). Add the required amount of prepared starter to the milk and stir to distribute evenly. Once mixed, do not stir for the remainder of the ripening period; excessive aeration reduces the rate of acid production, which may extend the ripening time.

Additives

You may find it necessary or desirable to add various ingredients to enhance flavor, provide color, or aid coagulation. It is a good idea for beginning cheese makers to sterilize the water that will be used to dilute various additives. This eliminates one variable and enables you to rule out contamination at this step if you have a problem with your final cheese.

To sterilize water, bring the required amount to a boil, cool it, and store it in a sterilized bottle in the refrigerator. Below are the various types of additives and how to use them.

Calcium Chloride

If you are using pasteurized/homogenized milk, we recommend adding calcium chloride. This restores the calcium that was lost during heat treatment. Use ¼ teaspoon calcium chloride per gallon of milk. Dilute the calcium chloride in ¼ cup of nonchlorinated water and add the mixture when you begin heating your milk. Then, after adding your rennet, allow the milk to set three to five minutes longer than usual before cutting your curds.

Using additives:
Calcium chloride

Coloring

Cheese coloring can destroy the coagulating ability of rennet, so add it to ripened milk before the rennet. Remember: When you add coloring to milk, there is still a lot of water in it, so the color will not be apparent until you drain the curds.

Dilute coloring in 20 times its own volume of cool water (¼ cup of water is usually sufficient for the amount of coloring you'll use) and thoroughly mix it into the milk. If it is not mixed adequately prior to adding the rennet, it may cause streaking in the finished cheese. If you plan to use the same bowl or cup to dilute the rennet, make sure you wash it carefully. The annatto in the coloring, if concentrated, will weaken the action of the rennet.

Lipase

Lipase enzyme produces additional acid in milk, so it may be necessary to adjust the amount of rennet used, depending on the firmness of your curds.

Dissolve lipase in ¼ cup of cool water. Let sit for 20 minutes before adding the mixture to the milk.

Bacteria and Molds

These are added to certain types of cheese to produce a characteristic flavor and texture.

Brevibacterium linens (Bacteria linens). This bacteria is added to the milk at the same time that you add your culture. After brining, it is smeared by hand on the surface of the cheese. To do this, gently wash the cheese each day with salted water (½ pound salt per gallon of water). Wearing sterilized gloves, wet the palm of one hand with the salted water and dampen all surfaces of the cheese.

Geotrichum candidum. This mold powder is added to the milk in conjunction with *Penicillium candidum* in a ratio of one part *Geotrichum* to five parts *Penicillium*.

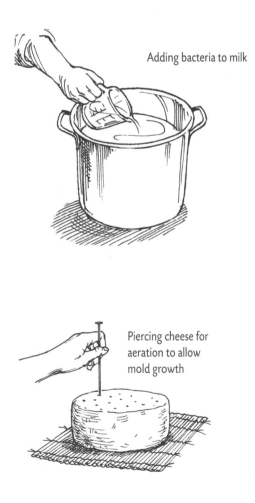

Adding bacteria to milk

Piercing cheese for aeration to allow mold growth

Penicillium candidum. This white mold powder is added to the milk at the same time that you add your culture. It works best when combined with a tiny bit of *Geotrichum candidum*.

Penicillium roqueforti. This mold is rehydrated and added to the milk at the same time that you add your culture or sprinkled on the curds when molding.

Renneting

In this step, rennet is added to the ripened milk. The milk is left to set until it has coagulated. The enzyme rennin (or, in the case of vegetable rennet, a microbial enzyme) causes the protein portion of the milk to precipitate out of solution, becoming a solid white custardlike mass called curd. Trapped within this mass of curd are the butterfat and whey. The whey contains water, milk sugar, albuminous protein, and minerals, and it may be saved to make other recipes (see chapter 7).

Rennet works most efficiently at 105°F, but that temperature is usually not used in cheese making because the resulting curd would be too firm. If the milk is warmer or cooler than that, the action slows. Rennet works faster in milk with a high acid content.

Measure rennet carefully. Too little will not set the milk properly; too much will result in a rubbery and possibly bitter-tasting cheese. The perfect curd is one that produces the highest yield of cheese from any given amount of milk.

DETERMINING COAGULATION AND SETTING TIME

If you notice how long the rennet takes to start coagulating the milk, you can estimate the setting time to be 2½ times that long. Here are two ways to determine when the milk has begun to coagulate:

1. Float a clean, sterile toothpick on the surface of the milk; the toothpick will stop moving the instant the milk begins to coagulate.

2. Put a drop of water on the surface of the milk. When it lies on the surface or makes a slight indentation in the surface, coagulation has begun.

Diluting Rennet

If rennet is not diluted, it will be unevenly distributed in the milk, which could produce a faulty curd. Always dilute rennet (liquid, powder, or tablet) in 20 to 50 times its own volume of cool, unchlorinated potable (drinking) water (¼ cup is sufficient for a 1 or 2 gallon recipe) before adding it to the ripened milk. If using powdered rennet, let sit for 30 minutes, stirring occasionally, to completely dissolve it before use. If using a rennet tablet, crush it with the back of a spoon and let sit for 10 to 30 minutes to completely dissolve before use.

Adding Rennet

Pour the diluted rennet through a perforated spoon and into the milk to help disperse it evenly. Mix gently for several minutes with an up-and-down motion, making sure you reach the bottom of the pot. Cover the pot and let the milk set for the amount of time specified in the recipe. Do not stir the milk once it has started to coagulate; it will cause severe loss of butterfat. It is also very important not to disturb the pot during setting, because it may break the bonds forming between protein molecules and they will not rejoin, thus producing a weak curd.

Adding rennet

Top-Stirring

If your milk is not homogenized, top-stir it for several minutes longer when adding rennet to mix any butterfat that has risen to the surface back into the body of the milk. To top-stir, simply stir the top ¼ inch of the milk with the bottom of a slotted spoon or skimmer.

Top-stirring

Cutting Curds

The curd is carefully cut into small, uniform cubes to increase the surface area, which allows the whey to continue draining. Uneven or crushed curds have much more surface area, resulting in more rapid and uneven drainage and increased loss of butterfat and solids. It's important to cut the curd at the right moment. If you cut it too soon, it will be soft and unworkable; if you wait too long, it will become too firm. If it is too firm, the knife will crush the curd rather than cut it cleanly.

The curd is ready for cutting when it gives a clean break. This can be determined by placing a thermometer or a clean finger into the curd at a 45-degree angle. If the curd separates cleanly and clearly around the inserted thermometer, you have a clean break and the curds are ready for cutting. If the curd does not show a clean break, wait 5 minutes longer and test it again. Immediately after cutting, the whey will be whitish because of the small amount of butterfat that escapes during cutting. Shortly after, the butterfat will seem to disappear and the whey will take on a greenish hue and turn clear.

Note: A good rule for cutting the curd is to time how long it takes for the curd to set and multiply by 3. For example, if the curd first sets in 12 minutes, the cutting time is after 36 minutes.

Ladling and Slicing Soft and Mold-Ripened Cheese

These curds are soft and must be treated very gently. The less you break up the curds at this point, the creamier your final cheese will be.

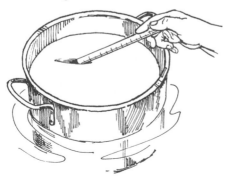

Checking for a clean break

Ladeling soft curds

Gently dip into your curd with a ladle to remove thin slices of curd and place them into a mold or a butter muslin–lined colander.

Cubing Hard Cheese

The curd is cut according to the directions in the recipe, and the range is from ¼-inch to ½-inch cubes.

CUTTING HARD-CHEESE CURDS

If you are cutting the curd into ½-inch cubes, place your curd knife ½ inch from the left side of the pot; gently draw the knife through the curd in a straight line, making sure you reach the bottom of the pot. Make a second slice ½ inch to the right of the first one. Continue making ½-inch slices across the pot. Now you have a pot of curd cut into ½-inch slices.

Turn the pot 90 degrees and repeat the cutting. When you are done, you will have a checkerboard pattern of ½-inch-square curds.

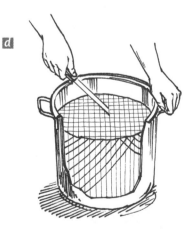

Then, with the knife at a slant and using the previously cut lines, cut the curd at a 45-degree angle.

Turn the pot 90 degrees and repeat the cutting.

Your aim is to cut the entire curd into ½-inch cubes. When all the curd has been cut at a 45-degree angle in both directions, gently stir the cubes, turning them over from bottom to top, and cut any pieces that are still too big.

Don't be alarmed if you do not cut each curd to the correct size. You simply want to have all of the curds as close as possible to the same size. Let the curds set for 5 minutes to firm up, then stir them very gently with a ladle, cutting any oversized pieces with the curd knife. If the recipe calls for cutting the curd into ¼-inch cubes, use a stainless-steel whisk. Be careful not to stir too much — butterfat is trapped in the curds, and stirring too vigorously will result in a loss of butterfat and produce a cheese of poor consistency.

Cooking Curds

After the curds have been cut into uniform cubes, you will notice the cubes floating in more liquid. Each cube is slowly losing whey and shrinking in size. At this point, the cubes are soft and jelly-like, and they must be handled very gently to avoid damaging the curd and losing butterfat. The cubes are then heated indirectly to expel more whey, to firm and dry the curds, and to increase acidity. Too much acid may result in a cheese that is sour and/or bitter, with a moist, soft texture. Too little acid can produce a cheese with little flavor.

As with ripening, the temperature of the curds is controlled by the temperature of the water surrounding the pot. The curds are gently stirred to keep them from matting. For many cheeses, it is important to increase the temperature of the curds by no more than two degrees every 5 minutes. If the curds are warmed too quickly, they will develop a skin that traps the whey inside and prevents adequate drainage, which may leave the final cheese with excess moisture. As the

Cooking hard-cheese curds

Hard-cheese curds cooked to the proper consistency

Carol Lively, Home Cheese Maker
Rowe, Massachusetts

As her name would suggest, Carol Lively enthusiastically makes cheese as a hobby, using the excess goat milk that her family doesn't drink. Her milk, butter, and cheese recently won first place at the Shelburne Grange Fair near Carol's home.

Thinking back on what inspired her to start making cheese, Carol muses, "I'm a city kid who grew up in Framingham, Massachusetts, but in November of 2000 I got three goats so I could start milking them for my daughter. A friend of mine who also had goats made lemon cheese, and I thought, 'I could do that.'" She took a one-day course and started making cheese with her extra milk. She uses the whey in pizza and bread dough. "We've never wasted a drop of the milk, and I'm so amazed at how much I've done," she says. "Even when my cheese isn't great, it's still good!"

Reflecting on some of the main lessons she has learned, Carol says, "I'm good at following instructions, so that probably helps. You need an accurate thermometer, and you really have to pay attention to the details. How much you handle the cheese (especially with mozzarella), how you press it, how you store it — all of those things make a big difference."

Currently, Carol makes Camembert, Cheddar, chèvre, feta, goat ricotta, Gouda, lemon cheese, mozzarella, and Ziegerkase. "I can't legally sell it," she says, "but I give it away as gifts, and my friends say, 'You're a hero!' I think my soft cheese is just as good as some commercial brands, but I'm still working on the hard cheeses." (Carol's delicious recipe using goat ricotta is on page 246.)

> *This hobbyist is a hero to her lucky friends*

temperature slowly increases, the cubes shrink in size as they expel more whey. The amount of whey in the pot will noticeably increase.

Draining

After the curds are cooked, they are drained to remove more whey. The draining process varies depending on the type of cheese being made.

Soft Cheese

Soft-cheese curds are placed in butter muslin and hung to drain.

Line a colander with butter muslin and gently ladle in the curds. Tie the corners of the muslin into a knot and hang the bag over the sink. A bungee cord hung from a hook over the sink makes a great draining tool.

Hard Cheese

Hard-cheese curds are usually drained between 5 and 60 minutes. The whey may be saved for further cheese making, but it must be used within 3 hours of collecting it.

Line a colander with cheesecloth and carefully pour the curds and whey into the colander. You can also carefully pour off or ladle out the whey, leaving the curds in the pot.

Bacteria- and Mold-Ripened Cheese

For these types of cheeses, the curds drain under their own weight, rather than by

Draining soft cheese in butter muslin

Draining hard cheese in colander lined with cheesecloth

Draining bacteria- and mold-ripened cheese through holes in mold being pressed (see page 54). Drainage takes place either through the holes in the mold or through the mat on which the cheese sits inside a mold sandwich.

Mold Sandwich. This method is used to drain certain types of bacteria- and mold-ripened cheeses. The cheese mold is placed on a cheese mat that rests on a cheese board and is situated in a sink or a pan. The mold is filled to the top with curd and drainage begins immediately. A second cheese mat is placed on top of the mold and a second wooden board is placed on top of the mat. After a period of draining, the entire assemblage is flipped over. The cheese mat that is now on the top is gently peeled away, which

Making a mold sandwich

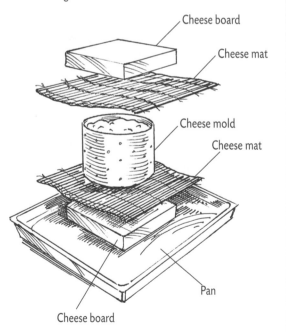

Cheese board

Cheese mat

Cheese mold

Cheese mat

Pan

Cheese board

allows the cheese to fall gently to the bottom of the mold. The cheese mat is then replaced and the process is repeated at regular intervals.

Milling

After draining, most hard-cheese curds are broken into small pieces without squeezing out any moisture. This requires great care; otherwise, a serious loss of butterfat will occur.

With your hands, break the curds into small pieces ranging in size from a thumbnail to a walnut, depending on the recipe's directions.

Salting

Salt enhances the flavor of the cheese and acts as a preservative by suppressing the growth of undesirable bacteria. It also helps inhibit the growth of lactic bacteria toward the end of the cheese-making process. Cheese salt also draws moisture from the curds, causing them to shrink and drain more whey.

However, in making aged cheeses, you may be surprised to learn that the more salt you add to your cheese, the less salty it may taste once it is aged.

This is because salt slows down the aging process, which naturally produces its own salts. There are different ways to salt cheese, depending on the type being made.

Directly

In this case, salt is added directly to the curd. For soft cheese, remove the curds from the muslin bag, add salt to taste, and mix well. For hard cheese, sprinkle cheese salt over the milled curds according to the recipe's directions, and gently but thoroughly mix it into the curds. For mold-ripened cheese, rub salt on the outside of the cheese prior to drying and aging.

Brining

Brining is used mainly on cheeses that have a short aging time. Some cheeses, such as feta and Gouda, are not salted before pressing; rather, they are put into a brine bath after pressing. A brine bath may range from lightly salted water to a saturated salt solution (in which the water is so saturated with salt that some salt precipitates out of the solution). The amount of salt needed for a brine solution depends on the type of cheese being made.

To make a saturated salt solution, stir 2 pounds of cheese salt into 1 gallon of nearly boiling water. Allow the water to chill before using. When chilled, some salt will precipitate out, demonstrating saturation. An olive will float on the top of a saturated salt solution.

Salting soft cheese

Salting hard cheese

Salting bacteria- and mold-ripened cheese

Brine can be stored in the refrigerator for future batches of cheese. Because it loses some of its salt to the cheese and may become contaminated with unwanted bacteria over time, it's important to use and store a brine bath properly. After using a brine bath, boil it, add additional salt until the salt no longer dissolves in the water, cool the brine, and keep it in the refrigerator.

Note: The first time you use a brine, add 1 tablespoon calcium chloride per gallon of water. This prevents the brine from leaching calcium out of the cheese. If you reuse this brine, you will not have to add calcium chloride again.

Molding

Once the curds have been milled and salted, they are ready to be molded and pressed. Select the mold in which the curds will be pressed and line it with cheesecloth. (Remember that the mold determines the shape of the cheese.)

Place the curds into the mold. For cheese that will be pressed lightly or not at all, pack the mold lightly, so the curds will not lose butterfat. For cheese that will be pressed at high pressure (most hard cheeses), pack the curds firmly. In most cases, the curds must not be pressed before their temperature has fallen to 70°F or lower or much of the butterfat will be lost, ruining the flavor and texture of the cheese.

Pressing

The cheese is then pressed for varying lengths of time to compress the curd and expel additional whey. The amount of pressure determines the final texture of your cheese. It is important to apply pressure to cheese gradually. Heavy pressure at the beginning will cause a lot of

Molding
hard cheese

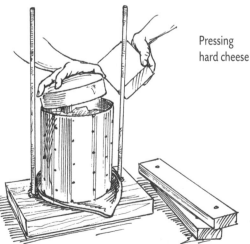

Pressing
hard cheese

butterfat to be expelled, forming a hard coat and preventing the cheese from draining properly.

Line a mold with cheesecloth. Place the mold on a drip tray, which will allow the whey to drain into a sink or small container. Ladle the curds into the mold. Lay a piece of cheesecloth on top of the curds and cover it with a follower that fits the mold. Once the follower is in place, pull the cheesecloth snug to eliminate any bunching of the cloth.

Generally, you will apply light pressure to the cheese for the first 10 to 15 minutes. After that, take the mold out of the press and remove the cheese from the mold. Gently peel the cheesecloth from the cheese and turn over the cheese. Wrap the cheese in the same cheesecloth or use a new one. This is called re-dressing, and this procedure prevents the cloth from sticking to the cheese. Turning the cheese also results in even pressing. Return the cheese to the mold and replace the follower. The cheese is then pressed at an increased pressure according to the recipe's directions. The cheese is usually flipped

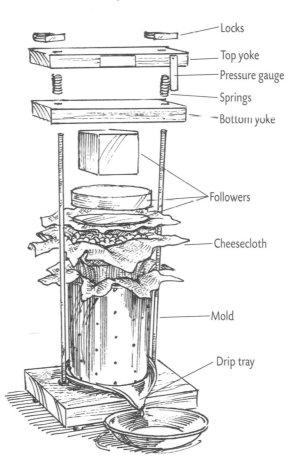

Locks
Top yoke
Pressure gauge
Springs
Bottom yoke
Followers
Cheesecloth
Mold
Drip tray

several more times and pressed at increasing amounts of pressure, until it is finally left in the press at full pressure for at least 12 hours.

Air-Drying

During this process, the cheese is prepared for aging.

Remove the pressed cheese from the mold and gently peel away the cheesecloth. Place the cheese on a cheese board or cheese mat and air-dry at room temperature for several days, or until it is dry to the touch. Turn over the cheese

Air-drying hard cheese on a cheese board

several times a day to allow even drying of all surfaces. *Note:* Some cheeses are placed in a brine solution (see page 53) immediately after coming out of the press and are air-dried after brining.

PRESSING IDEA ROLLS 300

I had trouble with lopsided cheese due to my follower slipping, so I came up with a solution that works great. I found a can that is exactly the same size as my mold, and filled it with melted wax to within 2 inches of the top. I let the wax harden in the refrigerator to make it easier to remove from the can. It also leaves an indentation in the top of the wax, which my press, a bowling ball, fits perfectly. After the wax hardens, I remove it and

melt or pare down the sides so it effortlessly slides up and down in the mold.

Another good thing about a wax follower is the cleanliness. It can be melted down (either partially or completely) after each use. I have an assortment of bowling balls, weighing from 10 to 16 pounds. A person can obtain these very inexpensively from Goodwill or the Salvation Army.

MILDRED,
GIG HARBOR, WASHINGTON

CONTINUOUS PRESSURE GANG PRESS.

CONTINUOUS PRESSURE

Removing unwanted mold

If any unwanted mold develops on the surface of the cheese, dip a piece of cheesecloth into a bowl of vinegar or lightly salted water. Wring it out so it is merely damp. Rub the surface of the cheese to remove the mold.

Bandaging

Instead of air-drying, try bandaging Cheddar cheese for a deliciously pronounced flavor. It is perfectly normal for mold to develop on bandaged cheeses; the mold will protect the inside of your cheese from drying out while allowing it to breathe and develop optimal flavor.

Cut a piece of butter muslin as wide as the depth of the cheese and 1½ times its circumference in length. Cut four circular pieces to act as caps for the top and bottom, but make them larger than the cheese so they will fold over the sides. Rub a thin coat of lard or solid vegetable shortening on the cheese and place two caps at each end. Wrap the bandage around the cheese, sticking it down as you go.

This larding technique is a traditional English method that produces a drier, flakier Cheddar than the buttery-textured Cheddars more commonly produced in the United States. Store the cheese at the temperature indicated in the recipe and keep it bandaged until it is ready to be cut and served. The lard and mold will be on the outside of the bandage and will come off when you remove the bandage.

Waxing

Once the cheese is dry, it may be waxed to keep it from drying out and to retard the growth of mold during the aging process. Some cheeses, such as Swiss and Parmesan, have a thick natural rind and are not waxed. However, if you make those types of cheese and they are 2 pounds or less, you may want to wax them to prevent excess drying and a very hard texture.

Cool the cheese in the refrigerator for several hours prior to waxing, so that the wax will adhere better. Melt the cheese wax in a double boiler on a stovetop that is vented with a hood fan. Wax vapors are highly flammable, so use caution when melting it. For precaution against

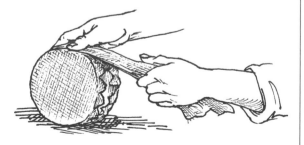

Bandaging hard cheese

Applying wax
with a brush

mold, wipe cheese with a cloth dampened lightly with vinegar and let dry on a clean surface. Apply the wax with a natural-bristle brush, working on one surface of the cheese at a time. Allow it to cool for several minutes before turning it over and waxing the other surfaces. Cheese wax dries very quickly. It takes at least two thin coats of wax to protect the cheese. Subsequent coats of wax may be applied as soon as the first coat dries.

Alternatively, dip your cheese into the wax pot one side at a time with a quick in-and-out motion so that you do not melt the previous layer. Use extreme caution in the dipping process — the wax is very slippery. Allow the wax to dry between coats.

For accurate labeling, write the name of the cheese and the date it was made on a piece of paper, and wax it onto the cheese when you apply the last coat. If mold growth appears on the surface of the cheese, cut it off before eating. It will not hurt the cheese. (*Note:* If you plan to smoke the cheese, smoke it first, then wax it.)

Reusing Cheese Wax

Cheese wax is so pliable that when your cheese is ready to eat, you can peel it off and use it over and over again.

To reuse it, simply melt the wax and strain it through a piece of butter muslin.

Dipping cheese into wax

Straining used cheese
wax for reuse

Aging

During this stage, cheese begins to develop its flavor and character. Aging can take anywhere from just a few days to 6 years. Store cheese in a temperature- and humidity-controlled environment to promote proper maturation. The temperature at which you age your cheese is important in allowing the good bacteria introduced by the starter to grow and produce enough acidity to preserve your final cheese. Most cheeses prefer an aging temperature between 46 and 60°F and a relative humidity of 75 to 95 percent. The constant exchange of ripening gases from the cheese (including carbon dioxide and ammonia) and oxygen in the air is critical for flavor development.

If you do not have a suitable location for aging, a spot where the room temperature will not exceed 68°F is preferable to the household refrigerator. If the aging temperature is too cold, the starter culture won't produce the proper acid development for safe and flavorful cheese. If the aging temperature is too warm, the cheese may develop a sharper, more pungent flavor than is pleasing and the texture may begin to deteriorate. Also, the cheese may develop undesirable mold growth and will require more frequent checks.

Mold may also develop if the aging room is too damp. If the aging room is not damp enough, however, the cheese may shrink and possibly crack. If small cracks appear, simply smear over them with a little bit of butter. The precise details for aging vary according to the type of cheese being made.

Soft Cheese

Soft cheeses are typically not aged, but you may want to do some experimenting once in a while and lightly press and age one or two for a short time. Some recipes, such as those for Gervais and Bondon (see pages 81 and 83), include more detailed information for pressing and aging soft cheeses.

Hard Cheese

Store hard cheese on a clean cheese board in a spot where the temperature will remain at a constant 55°F and have a relative humidity of 65 to 85 percent. Many home basements will satisfy this requirement.

You might consider purchasing a secondhand refrigerator or a small dorm-size fridge. Place a bowl of water in the bottom of the refrigerator and keep the setting at 55°F, and you will have an ideal cheese storage chamber.

Turn over the cheese each day for the first few weeks, and several times a week thereafter. This prevents moisture from accumulating on the bottom of the cheese, causing rot.

The longer a hard cheese ages, the stronger its flavor becomes. A minimum of 60 days is required for most hard cheeses. Some of the hard grating cheeses (such as Parmesan) may be aged for years to develop a very sharp flavor. If you are beginning this art, you might be tempted to taste your cheese sooner, but you will have a real treat if you can be patient.

Using a Cheese Trier. After a month or more of aging, a trier is sometimes used to sample a hard cheese to determine whether it has aged sufficiently. Judges in cheese competitions use triers to ascertain information on flavor, aroma, acidity, butterfat and moisture content, texture, and body.

Push the trier into the side of the cheese (as you do this, note the resistance of the curd). Turn the trier one or two complete turns and carefully withdraw the plug of cheese. Remove a small piece of the plug and roll it between your

---

SMOKING

Smoking your cheese is another way to add flavor. The smoke evaporates moisture, bringing butterfat to the surface of the cheese; when combined with the smoke, which contains antimicrobial substances, the butterfat has a preservative effect, provided the cheese is kept dry. In addition to a wonderful smoky flavor, this procedure also imparts an attractive light brown color to the surface of the cheese. (Note: Do not wax the cheese until after it is smoked.)

The key to smoking is low heat. Smoking should not heat the cheese, which could cause it to lose butterfat. Hang the cheese in a cold, smoke-filled room at a temperature no higher than 40°F. Oak and apple wood shavings are two appropriate woods for this purpose. Smoke the cheese from 4 to 6 hours, an hour or two longer for milder cheeses. (Although I do not recommend it because it is chemically derived, liquid smoke is an alternative that may be added either at milling or along with the salt, or the cheese may be dipped in a solution of liquid smoke. Follow the directions on the bottle.)

If you do not have a smoker, use this simple smoking method. Put some dampened hardwood sawdust into a metal pan and place it on a few warm coals that have been allowed to burn down on the bottom of your outdoor grill. Set the cheese on a rack well above the smoking material. Cover the grill and allow the smoke to escape through the vent in the grill's cover. Keep a close eye on your cheese to make sure it doesn't get too warm (above 90°F). Smoke the cheese until the exterior is golden brown.

cheese

dampened hardwood sawdust

outdoor grill

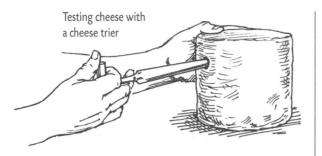

Testing cheese with a cheese trier

TEMPERATURE CONVERSION

Centigrade to Fahrenheit: Multiply by 9, divide by 5, and add 32.

Fahrenheit to Centigrade: Subtract 32, multiply by 5, and divide by 9.

fingers to warm it. Smell and taste the warmed piece of cheese for aroma and flavor (an "off" flavor is easily detected at this stage). Replace the plug carefully and seal the gap around the plug by smearing a piece of the warmed cheese from the plug with your finger. Now continue aging, if necessary.

Bacteria- and Mold-Ripened Cheese

These cheeses are aged in cool, moist temperatures to allow the prolific growth of mold on both the surface and the interior of the cheese. A temperature of 45°F and a relative humidity of 85 to 95 percent is typical. For a detailed description of the aging technique for bacteria- and mold-ripened cheeses, see page 156.

Temperature

As is probably clear by now, temperature plays an important role in the cheese-making process. Although the temperature indicated at each step in a particular recipe is meant to provide the conditions necessary for the successful production of that cheese, experience will teach you that there is room for experimentation.

A recipe presents general guidelines to follow when learning to make cheese. Once you master the techniques, you may experiment with varying the temperatures up or down by as much as five degrees to produce subtle changes in the final cheese, turning your hobby into an art form.

DOUBLING RECIPES

When you make 1 pound of cheese, you use the same techniques and ingredients that you would if you were making 1,000 pounds of cheese. Once you become comfortable with a recipe and know how long ripening and coagulation take, you may double or triple the recipe (or more). The preparation time is the same; all you need are larger pots and molds.

The proportion of ingredients to add to the milk depends, in part, on the quality of the milk. A good rule is to increase the ingredients proportionately; however, you will have to check the speed of coagulation and adjust the rennet in future trials so that you use the amount that results in coagulation at the normal time for that recipe. This often means that you will need less rennet.

Temperature Troubleshooting

Procedure	If Temperature Is Too High	If Temperature Is Too Low
Starter preparation	Kills active bacteria or makes for very slow acid development	Inhibits bacterial growth
Ripening	Produces a milk that is overly acidic; may kill bacteria	May not be warm enough to allow starter to grow
Renneting	Interferes with starter growth; may decrease rennet activity; at temperatures higher than 130°F, rennet activity virtually ceases	May result in a curd that takes too long to set and is too soft to cut
Cooking	Scalds the curds, creating a skin that prevents proper drainage	Interferes with milk's ability to produce the proper amount of acidity
Aging	Encourages undesirable mold growth and perhaps too rapid an acid development	Prevents the proper amount of acidity from building up. As proper acid development is important to the safe preservation of your cheese, this is an important consideration.

Acidity Testing

The times and temperatures indicated in the recipes throughout this book are designed to provide the proper levels of acidity required for successful home cheese making. I have been following these recipes since 1982, much to the delight of my family and friends.

However, there may come a time when you find yourself intrigued by the fascinating science behind cheese making and feel the need to delve into the

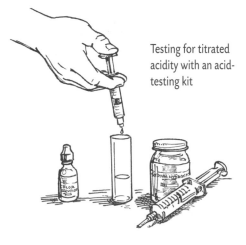

Testing for titrated acidity with an acid-testing kit

specifics of acidity. Or you may decide to begin selling some of your cheese and find that customers expect uniformity in your products. In either case, you will want to test for acidity at various stages during cheese making. Determining acidity ensures that the optimum conditions are met to obtain uniform results.

Acidity is determined by measuring either pH value (true acidity) or titrated acidity. The pH of milk is determined by its content of hydrogen ions and is measured by simply comparing pH strips to a known color chart. A value of 7.0 indicates neutral pH. Values above 7.0 indicate an alkaline condition; values below 7.0 indicate an acid condition.

Testing for titrated acidity is a bit more involved. Basically, a few drops of a color indicator, called phenolpthalein,

which is colorless in acid, are added to the milk. As long as the milk is in an acid state, the indicator will remain colorless. The moment the liquid becomes alkaline, the color changes to pink, indicating the instant when the acid was neutralized. Titrated acidity is therefore the amount of an alkaline solution that will neutralize an acidic liquid. Fresh milk has a titrated acidity of 16 to 18. Acid-testing kits are available from cheese-making supply houses.

Storing and Re-storing Cheese

Because cheese is a living, breathing organism, it continues to ripen from the day it is made to the moment you eat it. Temperature and humidity during storage are important because they affect taste and texture. In addition, remember that the firmer the cheese, the longer it will stay fresh, if treated properly. Although hard cheeses, such as aged Cheddar and Parmesan, can be kept (wrapped) in your refrigerator for many months, most soft cheeses, especially after they are cut, will last only for about 2 weeks.

In an earlier time, before insulation and central heating, many homes had a buttery, or cool pantry, on the north side of the house, where cheese, butter, milk, and even meat were stored during much of the year. Today, lacking that, we have to turn to our refrigerator. Most sources advise refrigerating cheese at temperatures of 38 to 42°F. If your refrigerator has a little cubby in the door that is

---

TESTING ACIDITY THE TRADITIONAL WAY

Here is a traditional method for testing acidity at the curd stage. Squeeze a piece of curd between your fingers until it is dry. Rub it on a hot iron frying pan. In a continuous motion, slowly draw the curd away from the pan. The length of the thread indicates the amount of acidity according to the following chart.

¼ inch	= 0.17–0.19% acidity
½ inch	= 0.24% acidity
¾ inch	= 0.45% acidity
1 inch	= 0.65% acidity
1½ inches	= 0.85% acidity
2 inches	= 0.95% acidity

Bruce & Ellen Clement
Westmoreland, New Hampshire

After just two seasons of cheese making, the Clements entered a wheel of creamy sheep's-milk cheese at the American Cheese Society show in 2000. The cheese, aged in the Vermont Shepherd cave in Putney, and marketed by David and Cindy Major (see page 30), was named Best of Show.

The Clements have farmed sheep for meat and wool since 1973, but once their children were grown, they began to consider sheep dairying as a possible source of retirement income and a pleasurable activity to do together. Bruce, who has worked as a County Extension educator for more than 25 years, had long known the Majors, and he and Ellen made a careful business plan.

They figured they would spend about four hours per day milking their 60 Dorset ewes; another two hours every second or third day making cheese; and another one to two hours a day brining and turning the cheese.

A smart business plan pays off with prizewinning cheese

They knew they could age their cheese in the Majors' cave and take advantage of Vermont Shepherd's marketing expertise. They bought secondhand equipment and built a 16- by 16-foot cheese-making room. They also started breeding their Dorset ewes to East Friesian and Lacaune rams to get a longer lactation period (up to 180 days) and a higher average milk yield.

All of the careful planning paid off, and they produced about 1,500 pounds of cheese — including the prize wheel — in their second year. Then "life" intervened in the form of an employment offer that Bruce couldn't refuse, and their cheese making is currently on hold until they both can devote the time they know is required to make good cheese. Meanwhile, their flock is thriving and the Clements are looking forward to resuming their cheese-making business as soon as it is practical.

labeled CHEESE, don't use it. Instead, store cheese in one of the vegetable bins in the bottom of the fridge, where it will be out of the airflow. Check the temperature in the bin to be sure it isn't too cold.

Keep cheese in its original wrapping until you are ready to use it. Wrap cut pieces in aluminum foil, wax paper, or plastic wrap. Check the cheese frequently to see how it is doing; if it gets moldy, trim off the mold and rewrap the cheese in a clean piece of foil or plastic. Some cheese makers advise perforating the foil or plastic wrap so the cheese can breathe. If you do that, check to make sure the cheese isn't drying out too much.

Cheese needs the moisture it has, not more or less, so monitor the cheeses you are storing. If a semihard or a hard cheese becomes dry or cracked on the surface, wrap it for 1 to 2 hours in a damp towel. You can also cover hard cheeses with a cloth dipped in wine or salt water and wrung out.

HOW TO MARKET YOUR CHEESE

Okay, so you are ready to take the next big step. You love making cheese, you have experimented at home and come up with a recipe that you like and all your friends and neighbors exclaim over, and you want to sell your cheese, perhaps at the local farmers' market or to restaurants in town. What do you do?

I asked Vicki Dunaway, whose Hometown Creamery Revival project is dedicated to helping small farms and small-scale processors find customers. She claims that the biggest logistical hurdle for cheese makers going commercial is meeting the plethora of state and federal regulations. Get in touch immediately with your state's dairy inspector. He or she will be well informed about federal regulations that may apply to your operation.

Vicki publishes two newsletters, *Home Dairy News* and *Creamline,* and has also published *The Small Dairy Resource Book* (see Resources, pages 266–67). Other helpful Web sites are listed on page 265.

Once you have met the criteria that permit you to sell your cheese, you still need to convince someone to buy it. This is much more subjective. Most of the groups listed above offer tips, anecdotes, and strategies for succeeding at the business end of cheese making. But sometimes you have to convince just one key person – the buyer.

For advice about this, I consulted Steve Jenkins, a.k.a. The Big Cheese, cheesemonger for The Fairway in New York City and easily one of the most knowledgeable and influential people in the country on the subject of cheese. Steve claims he has only one criterion: memorability. "If it pleases me," he says, "I'll buy it. If it's forgettable, I won't. I'm either enthused or not. I don't care about quantity, either. If it's memorable, I'll take whatever they have." What does "memorable" mean to Steve? "Rusticity is very important to me. That, and the honesty of the cheese. It's about the food – nothing else."

RECIPES
FOR ALL
TYPES OF
CHEESE

Camembert Mould.

CHAPTER 4

SOFT CHEESE

These cheeses require little equipment and are excellent choices for beginning cheese makers. Usually high-moisture cheeses that are eaten fresh, soft cheeses are quick, delicious, and easy to make. They are perfect for experimentation because you can vary them simply by adding herbs, spices, honey, or other flavorings (see the box on page 75 for suggestions).

Most of these cheeses have a creamy, spreadable consistency. Many are called "bag cheeses," because the curds are drained in a bag of butter muslin. They are made by coagulating milk or cream with cheese starter or with an acid, such as vinegar or lemon juice. Some recipes call for a little rennet to help firm the curds.

It's important to drain these cheeses in a place where the temperature stays close to 72°F (usually the kitchen). If the temperature and humidity are too high, you will have problems with yeast, which may produce a gassy, off-flavored cheese. If the temperature is too low, the cheese will not drain properly. The yield from 1 gallon of milk is usually 1½ to 2 pounds of soft cheese, depending on the type of milk you use and the desired consistency of the cheese. The greater the butterfat content, the higher the cheese yield.

Soft cheeses will keep for 1 to 2 weeks in the refrigerator. Although it is not my first choice, they may also be frozen. If you want to salt your cheese, it's best to wait until after thawing to add the salt; salt will increase the freezing temperature of the cheese and therefore it will not keep as well. The techniques used in this section are very straightforward; see chapter 3 to review them, as needed.

Note: When a recipe calls for warming the milk, do not use direct heat (on the stove), unless specified. Heat the milk indirectly, with the cheese pot resting in a bowl or sink full of hot water.

lactic cheese

This is a delicious, soft, spreadable cheese that is easy to make and ready to eat in 24 hours. You may add herbs in a variety of combinations for truly tantalizing taste treats. I find that a combination of freshly ground black pepper, 1 clove of chopped garlic, chopped fresh chives, and a dash of paprika makes a savory cheese. Try rolling plain or sweetened cheese in crêpes and topping with fruit sauce for a gourmet dessert. I like to make this cheese at night and drain it in the morning.

1 gallon pasteurized whole or skim milk

1 packet direct-set mesophilic starter or 4 ounces prepared mesophilic or prepared fresh starter

3 drops liquid rennet diluted in ⅓ cup cool, unchlorinated water

Cheese salt (optional)

Herbs (optional)

1. Heat the milk to 86°F. Add the starter and mix thoroughly.

2. Add 1 teaspoon of the diluted rennet and stir gently with an up-and-down motion. Cover and let set, undisturbed, at a room temperature of at least 72°F for 12 hours, or until a solid curd forms. The curd will look like yogurt.

3. Slowly pour the curd into a colander lined with butter muslin. Tie the corners of the muslin into a knot and hang the bag to drain for 6–12 hours, or until the cheese reaches the desired consistency. A room temperature of at least 72°F will encourage proper drainage. If you want the curds to drain more quickly, change the muslin periodically.

4. Place the curds in a bowl and add the salt to taste, if desired. Add the herbs, if desired.

5. Store in a covered bowl in the refrigerator for up to 2 weeks. (If the cheese has a hard, rubbery texture, add less rennet next time. If the cheese is too moist, add a little more rennet.)

YIELD: About 2 pounds

fromage blanc

French in origin, fromage blanc simply means "white cheese." The word fromage is derived from the Greek word formos, *the name for the wicker baskets used by the Greeks to drain whey from cheese. Fromage blanc is fresh and easy to prepare and makes an excellent spread — it has the consistency of cream cheese but a fraction of the calories and cholesterol. Add herbs and spices to it, or use it plain as a substitute for cream cheese or ricotta in cooking. Fromage blanc can be made with either whole or skim milk. If you use nonfat milk, the yield will be lower and the cheese will be drier. I like to make this cheese at night so I can drain it when I get up in the morning.*

1 gallon pasteurized whole or skim milk

1 packet direct-set fromage blanc starter

1. Heat the milk to 86°F. Add the starter and mix thoroughly.

2. Cover and let set at 72°F for 12 hours.

3. Line a colander with butter muslin. Ladle the curd into the colander. Tie the corners of the muslin into a knot and hang the bag to drain.

4. Let the curd drain at 72°F for 6–12 hours, or until it reaches the desired consistency. A shorter draining time produces a thinner, more spreadable cheese. A longer draining time produces a cream cheese–type consistency.

5. Store in a covered container and refrigerate for up to 2 weeks.

YIELD: About 2 pounds

mascarpone with culture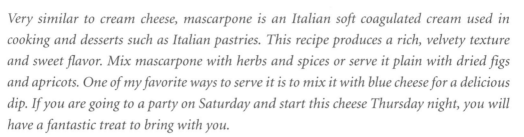

Very similar to cream cheese, mascarpone is an Italian soft coagulated cream used in cooking and desserts such as Italian pastries. This recipe produces a rich, velvety texture and sweet flavor. Mix mascarpone with herbs and spices or serve it plain with dried figs and apricots. One of my favorite ways to serve it is to mix it with blue cheese for a delicious dip. If you are going to a party on Saturday and start this cheese Thursday night, you will have a fantastic treat to bring with you.

1 quart pasteurized light cream or half-and-half

1 packet direct-set crème fraîche starter

1. Heat the cream to 86°F. Add the starter and mix thoroughly.

2. Cover and let set, undisturbed, at room temperature for 12 hours, or until coagulated.

3. If a thicker curd is desired, ladle the curd into a colander lined with butter muslin and drain in the refrigerator for 1–4 hours or longer, depending on the desired consistency.

4. Cover and store in the refrigerator for up to 4 weeks.

YIELD: About 1 pound

RECIPE FROM A HOME CHEESE MAKER

potato cheese

This cheese is made in Germany and has been adapted in the United States by many in the Amish community. Make a curd from farm-fresh sour milk. Peel, boil, and mash potatoes and combine in various proportions with the curd (3 parts potato to 2 parts curd, or 1 part potato to 2–3 parts curd). Add salt and caraway seeds, if desired. Age the cheese for 2–4 days, mix again, and put into a mold for 1 day. Remove the cheese from the mold and air-dry it. Cover with beer or cream, if desired, and age in a tub for 1 to 2 weeks.

mascarpone with tartaric acid

Delicious in cannolis! This may also be served on slices of sweet bread. The consistency is similar to that of butter, depending on the amount of time drained. Tartaric acid is a natural vegetable acid derived from the seed of the tamarind tree, which is found throughout the Caribbean.

> 1 quart light cream or half-and-half
>
> ⅛–¼ teaspoon tartaric acid

1. In a double boiler, heat the cream to 185°F.

2. Add ⅛ teaspoon of the tartaric acid and stir for several minutes. The mixture will slowly thicken into a cream-of-wheat consistency, with tiny flecks of curd. If the cream does not coagulate, add a speck more of the remaining tartaric acid and stir 5 minutes longer. Be careful not to add too much tartaric acid, or a grainy texture will result.

3. Line a stainless-steel colander with a double layer of butter muslin. Ladle the curd into the colander and drain for 1 hour.

4. Place the finished cheese in a covered container and refrigerate for up to 2 weeks.

YIELD: About 1 pound

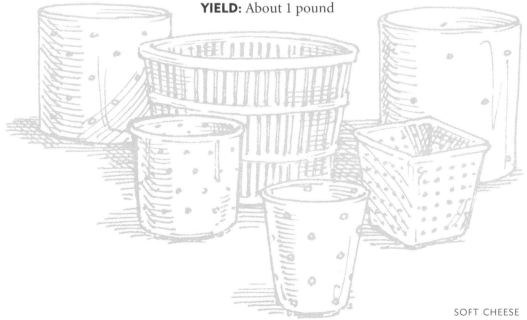

moist buttermilk cheese

This cheese is made from cultured buttermilk. It is best to use fresh, homemade, cultured buttermilk made from a packet of buttermilk starter, as it will have a thick, clabbered consistency (to make buttermilk, see page 195). Let set for several hours at 72°F. This cheese is fairly moist, because the curds are not heated before draining.

1 quart freshly made cultured buttermilk

1 drop liquid rennet diluted in 6 teaspoons cool, unchlorinated water (if using goat's-milk buttermilk)

Cheese salt (optional)

Herbs (optional)

1. Let the buttermilk come to room temperature (72°F). If you are using buttermilk made with goat's milk, add 1 teaspoon of the diluted rennet to the buttermilk.

2. Pour the buttermilk into a colander lined with butter muslin. Tie the corners of the muslin into a knot and hang the bag to drain for 12–24 hours, or until the cheese reaches the desired consistency.

3. Place the cheese in a bowl. Add a pinch of the salt and/or the herbs to taste, if desired. Store in a covered bowl in the refrigerator for 1–2 weeks.

YIELD: 6–8 ounces

RECIPE FROM A HOME CHEESE MAKER

appetitost (appetite cheese)

This is a Danish buttermilk cheese. Some people make it by heating farm-fresh sour buttermilk to boiling, but others prefer to heat the buttermilk to 120°F. Stir well and allow to settle. Drain as much whey as possible. Cover the semiliquid mass and set in a warm place. Fermentation will make the curd sticky. Knead the curd and allow it to ferment again. Repeat the process until the mass is yellowish and soft but tough and viscous. When it has thoroughly fermented, heat the mass to 120°F and add salt and spices to taste. Work them into the cheese and form the cheese into fancy shapes.

dry buttermilk cheese

Made from fresh, homemade cultured buttermilk, this cheese is heated, so its texture is fairly dry. It has a grainy, spreadable consistency and a slightly acidic flavor.

1 quart fresh cultured buttermilk

Cheese salt (optional)

Herbs (optional)

1. In a medium-sized pot, directly heat the buttermilk to 160°F, stirring now and then. The curds will separate from the whey. (If not, increase the temperature to 180°F.)

2. Pour the curds into a colander lined with butter muslin. Tie the corners of the muslin into a knot and hang the bag to drain for 6–12 hours, or until the curds have stopped dripping and reached desired consistency.

3. Place the cheese in a bowl. Add the salt and herbs to taste, if desired.

4. Store in a covered bowl in the refrigerator for 1–2 weeks.

YIELD: 6–8 ounces

TASTY ADDITIONS TO SOFT CHEESE

You can make any soft cheese into a tasty dessert cheese by adding the following to 6–8 ounces of cheese and mixing well:

- 2 tablespoons honey
- 1 teaspoon cinnamon
- ¼ teaspoon allspice
- ¼ teaspoon nutmeg
- ¼ teaspoon vanilla extract

For a flavorful herb cheese, add the following and mix well:

- 2 tablespoons chopped fresh chives
- 1 teaspoon chopped fresh dill
- 1 small clove garlic, chopped
- ¼ teaspoon freshly ground black pepper
- Pinch of salt

real buttermilk cheese  and

This cheese is made from "real" buttermilk, the liquid that remains after cream is churned and butter is produced. Buttermilk can be used in cooking (such as buttermilk pancakes) or to make cheese. This cheese has a spreadable consistency and a light, sour flavor. It cannot be purchased in any cheese store.

> 1 gallon fresh buttermilk
>
> Cheese salt (optional)

1. Allow the buttermilk to set at 72°F for 24 hours. This will lightly sour it. (If you prefer a less sour cheese, omit this step.)

2. In a large pot, directly heat the buttermilk to 160°F. At that temperature, the buttermilk should separate into curds and whey. (If not, increase the temperature to 180°F.)

3. Line a colander with butter muslin; pour the coagulated buttermilk into it. Tie the corners of the muslin into a knot and hang the bag to drain for 3–4 hours, or until the cheese reaches the desired consistency.

4. Place the cheese in a bowl. Add the salt to taste, if desired.

5. Store in a covered bowl in the refrigerator for up to 2 weeks.

YIELD: 1½ pounds

yogurt cheese

With the tart flavor characteristic of fresh yogurt, this cheese is a tasty treat on crackers or bagels and may be enhanced with herbs. It is best made from fresh yogurt; however, store-bought yogurt also works well.

1 quart fresh plain yogurt

Cheese salt (optional)

Herbs (optional)

1. Let the yogurt come to room temperature (72°F).

2. Pour the yogurt into a colander lined with butter muslin. Tie the corners of the muslin into a knot and hang the bag to drain for 12–24 hours, or until the yogurt has stopped dripping and has reached the desired consistency.

3. Remove the cheese from the bag. Add the salt and/or herbs to taste, if desired.

4. Store in a covered container in the refrigerator for up to 2 weeks.

YIELD: About 8 ounces

SERVING IDEAS FOR YOGURT CHEESE

To serve yogurt cheese as an appetizer, try this Syrian dish known as *Laban Dahareej.* Roll the cheese into balls, make a depression with the back of a knife, put in a drop of olive oil, and sprinkle with chopped mint. Or place on a tray or serving dish and allow to set overnight in the refrigerator until firm. Place in a glass jar, cover with olive oil, and secure with a tight-fitting lid. To serve, place in a small dish and spoon a small amount of oil over the yogurt balls to keep them soft enough to spread on Syrian bread.

kefir cheese

Kefir is a cultured milk drink that has been used for thousands of years in Caucasia, a region of Russia. It is made by adding kefir culture to fresh whole milk, which is coagulated by the culture and fermented slightly with yeast. It has a light, bubbly sparkle and is often referred to as the "champagne of milk." The delicious summertime drink can also be made into a very tasty cheese. Using homemade kefir is preferable, as it produces a much thicker curd than does commercial kefir. (To make kefir, see pages 196–98.)

1 quart fresh kefir
Cheese salt (optional)
Herbs (optional)

1. Let the kefir come to room temperature (72°F).

2. Pour the kefir into a colander lined with butter muslin. Tie the corners of the muslin into a knot and hang the bag to drain for 12–24 hours, or until the cheese has stopped draining and has reached the desired consistency.

3. Place the drained cheese in a bowl. Add the salt and herbs to taste, if desired.

4. Store the cheese in a covered container and keep in the refrigerator for 1–2 weeks.

YIELD: About 8 ounces

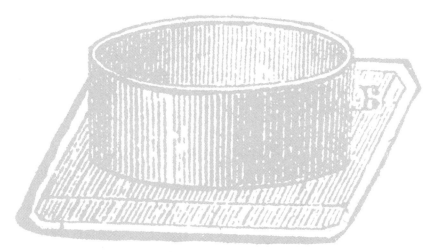

lemon cheese

This moist cheese has a spreadable consistency and a mild, lemony flavor.

½ gallon whole milk

Juice of 2–3 large lemons or approximately ¼ cup

Cheese salt (optional)

Herbs (optional)

1. In a large pot, directly heat the milk to 185–200°F. Add the juice from two of the lemons and stir well.

2. Cover and let the milk set for 15 minutes. (You are looking for a clear separation of the curds and whey, not milky whey.) If the milk has not yet set, add more of the remaining lemon juice until it does set.

3. Pour the curds into a colander lined with butter muslin. Tie the corners of the muslin into a knot and hang the bag to drain for 1–2 hours, or until the curds have stopped draining. (If you drain the curds for only 20 minutes, you can then chill the mixture and add mint leaves for a refreshing summertime drink.)

4. Remove the cheese from the bag. Add salt and herbs to taste, if desired.

5. Store in a covered container in the refrigerator for 1–2 weeks.

YIELD: About 1 pound

RECIPE FROM A HOME CHEESE MAKER

lemon and orange curd cheese

This cheese makes a lovely spread. Heat 1 gallon of milk to 205°F, stirring to prevent scorching. Remove from the heat; stir in the juice from 6 lemons and 6 oranges and let set for 15 minutes. Line a colander with butter muslin and ladle in the curd. Tie the corners of the muslin into a knot and hang the bag to drain for 1 hour. You may have to scrape the outside of the bag a few times to unclog the pores in the cloth and encourage drainage. Add salt to taste. Cover and refrigerate. Will keep for up to 1 week.

neufchâtel

Originally from the town of Neufchâtel in Normandy, France, this cheese is made from whole milk enriched with cream. Americans tend to eat it fresh; the French prefer it ripened with a white surface mold. Once you perfect this recipe, spice it up with chives, garlic, onions, scallions, olives, or pickles. For a sweet flavor, try chopped pineapple.

1 gallon pasteurized whole milk

1 pint pasteurized heavy cream

1 packet direct-set mesophilic starter or 4 ounces prepared mesophilic starter

3 drops liquid rennet diluted in ⅓ cup cool, unchlorinated water

Cheese salt (optional)

Herbs or condiments (optional)

1. Combine the milk and cream. Heat to 80°F.

2. Add the starter and mix thoroughly.

3. Add 1 teaspoon of the diluted rennet. (The exact amount of rennet is important. Too little, and the cheese will drain through the muslin; too much, and the cheese will be hard and rubbery. You will have to adjust the amount of rennet after experimenting with your milk.) Stir gently with an up-and-down motion.

4. Cover and let the mixture set at a room temperature of at least 72°F for 12–18 hours, or until a thick curd has formed. (It will look like yogurt.)

5. Pour the curd into a colander lined with butter muslin. Tie the corners into a knot and hang the bag to drain for 6–12 hours, or until the bag has stopped dripping and the cheese has reached the desired consistency.

6. Put the bag into a colander lined with butter muslin; place the colander in a pot. Put a plate on the bag and place a weight on the plate (the weight of two bricks is sufficient). Cover the pot; refrigerate for 13 hours.

7. Remove the cheese from the bag and put it in a bowl. Add the salt and herbs to taste, if desired, and mix thoroughly. Knead the cheese briefly by hand until it holds together, then divide into four rounds.

8. Shape into patties and wrap each one separately in cheese wrap. Store in the refrigerator for 1–2 weeks.

YIELD: About 2 pounds

gervais

Gervais is a French cheese made from a mixture of milk and cream. It is similar to Neufchâtel but richer and creamier. This is a fresh cheese that is best consumed within several days; for that reason, it is rarely found in cheese stores. It is traditionally made with cow's milk but you may use goat's milk.

2⅔ cups pasteurized whole milk

1⅓ cups pasteurized heavy cream

1 packet direct-set mesophilic starter or 2 ounces prepared mesophilic starter

1 drop liquid rennet diluted in 2 tablespoons cool, unchlorinated water

Cheese salt

Herbs (optional)

1. Combine the milk and cream. Warm to 80°F.

2. Add the starter and mix thoroughly.

3. Gently stir in the diluted rennet and mix with an up-and-down motion for 5 minutes. If the milk starts to coagulate, stop stirring. Cover and let the milk set for 24 hours.

4. Ladle the curds into a colander lined with butter muslin. Tie the corners of the muslin into a knot and hang the bag to drain for 4–6 hours, or until the curds stop dripping. You may need to take down the bag periodically and scrape the sides with a spoon to open the pores of the muslin for better drainage.

5. Put the curds in a fresh piece of butter muslin, place in a cheese mold, and press at 15 pounds of pressure for 6–8 hours.

6. Remove the cheese from the mold and transfer it to a bowl. Add a small amount of salt to taste and mix thoroughly. The cheese will be creamy and smooth. If it's a bit lumpy, force it through a strainer.

7. Add the herbs, if desired.

8. Place the cheese in small molds lined with wax paper. Traditionally, these molds are 2¼ inches wide by 1¾ inches deep. This size will make four cheeses. Store in a covered bowl in the refrigerator for 1–2 weeks.

YIELD: 8–10 ounces

Constantine "Dean" Zoulamis
Home Cheese Maker
Bowdoinham, Maine

With years of restaurant cooking under his belt, Dean Zoulamis and his wife, Clay Theberge, moved to their 18-acre property near the Maine coast to set up a self-sufficient life for themselves and their son, Elias.

Their small goat herd of Alpine-Nubian crosses provides several gallons of milk a day, which Dean heat-treats two gallons at a time and turns into cheese and yogurt. As an alternative to rennet, he uses an infusion of bull thistle flower as a curdling agent.

Dean's dream is to build a certified kitchen and make enough cheese to sell. He also is working on improving his pasture and hay fields to ensure a steady supply of forage for the goats. "People assume that goats will eat anything," he says, "but they seem to do best on pasture and hay, with no grain to change their pH."

An experienced cook turns to cheese making to follow his dream

Dean loves to experiment, and he remembers making a batch of feta cheese simply by using a little bit of real feta as a starter. "I tried to do it again, without ever reading directions, and ended up with a metallic-tasting batch," he said. "My advice, based on this, is to follow directions closely until you feel confident, and *then* start experimenting."

The family spreads its soft goat cheese on bread, uses it in quesadillas, and rolls it in chives that have been roasted in the oven to intensify their flavor. When Dean has too much cheese, he freezes it unsalted, adding herbs, salt, and other amendments after it is thawed. The cheese freezes beautifully.

bondon

Bondon is another fresh French cheese made from whole milk and is similar in taste and texture to Neufchâtel. Traditionally, this cheese is made from cow's milk, but you can use goat's milk with this recipe.

1 quart pasteurized whole milk

1 packet direct-set mesophilic starter or 2 ounces prepared mesophilic starter

1 drop liquid rennet diluted in 2 tablespoons cool, unchlorinated water

Cheese salt (optional)

Herbs (optional)

1. Warm the milk to 65°F. Add the starter and mix thoroughly.

2. Add the diluted rennet, stirring gently in an up-and-down motion for several minutes. Cover and let the milk set at 65°F for 24 hours.

3. When the curd has coagulated, ladle it into a colander lined with butter muslin. Tie the corners of the muslin into a knot and hang the bag to drain for 6–8 hours, or until the bag has stopped dripping and the cheese has reached the desired consistency. You may need to scrape the muslin with a spoon occasionally to hasten draining.

4. Remove the cheese from the muslin and place it in a mold lined with butter muslin. Press the cheese for 4–8 hours at 15 pounds of pressure.

5. Remove the cheese from the mold and put it in a bowl. Add the salt and herbs to taste, if desired. The cheese should be smooth in texture. If it is grainy, force it through a strainer.

6. Place the cheese into one or two small molds lined with wax paper. Traditionally, these molds are 2¾ inches deep and 1¾ inches wide.

7. Store in a covered container in the refrigerator for 1–2 weeks.

YIELD: About 6 ounces

cream cheese: uncooked-curd method

Easy to make, rich, and creamy, this cheese is one even your kids can make and enjoy.

2 quarts pasteurized light cream or pasteurized half-and half

1 packet direct-set mesophilic starter or 4 ounces prepared mesophilic starter

Cheese salt (optional)

Herbs (optional)

1. Bring the cream to room temperature (72°F). Add the starter and mix thoroughly.

2. Cover and let set at 72°F for 12 hours. A solid curd will form.

3. Pour the curd into a colander lined with butter muslin. Tie the corners of the muslin into a knot and hang the bag to drain for up to 12 hours, or until the bag stops dripping and the cheese has reached the desired consistency. Changing the bag once or twice will speed the draining process.

4. Place the cheese in a bowl and add the salt and herbs to taste, if desired.

5. Place the cheese into small molds and cool in the refrigerator. Once the cheeses are firm, take them out of the molds and wrap individually in cheese wrap.

6. Store in the refrigerator for 1–2 weeks.

YIELD: About 1 pound

RECIPE FROM A HOME CHEESE MAKER

lebanese guban

Combine 1 gallon of milk with 1 teaspoon of rennet and warm over medium heat, stirring, until curds form. Push the curds to the bottom and divide them into four patties. Rub them with salt and soak in a brine bath for up to 10 days. You can change the brine if it becomes slimy. Alternatively, you may store the cheeses in olive oil. Use the cheese for making round Lebanese bread (Guban + colby + flour + oil).

cream cheese: cooked-curd method

This recipe requires a bit more work and produces a slightly drier cheese than the uncooked method.

2 quarts pasteurized light cream or half-and-half

1 packet direct-set mesophilic starter or 4 ounces prepared mesophilic starter

3 drops liquid rennet diluted in ⅓ cup cool, unchlorinated water

1–2 quarts water

Cheese salt (optional)

Herbs (optional)

1. Heat the cream to 86°F. Add the starter and mix thoroughly.

2. Add 1 teaspoon of the diluted rennet and stir gently with an up-and-down motion. Cover and let the cream set for 12 hours at a room temperature of at least 72°F. A solid curd will form.

3. Heat the water to 170°F. Add enough of the hot water to the curd to raise its temperature to 125°F.

4. Pour the curd into a colander lined with butter muslin. Tie the corners of the muslin into a knot and hang the bag to drain until it stops dripping.

5. When the bag stops draining, put the cheese in a bowl and add the salt and herbs to taste, if desired.

6. Place the cheese into small molds and chill in the refrigerator. Once the cheeses are firm, unmold them and wrap individually in cheese wrap.

7. Store in the refrigerator for 1–2 weeks.

YIELD: About 1 pound

creole cream cheese

Creole Cream Cheese is a Louisiana dish. It was sold in pint containers with one big curd, topped with heavy cream, and traditionally eaten for breakfast with sugar. The following is reportedly the best recorded recipe. It was written by Myriam Guidroz and appeared in the *Times-Picayune* newspaper. For a dessert, use heart-shaped molds and top with whipped cream and sugar. (Fromage blanc made according to the recipe in this book and molded in soft cheese molds will yield the same delicious results.)

1 gallon skim milk (may be reconstituted dry milk powder)

½ cup cultured buttermilk

½ teaspoon liquid rennet

Half-and-half or heavy cream

1. Make sure the temperature of the milk is no cooler than 70°F and no warmer than 80°F. Place the milk in a large container.

2. Add the buttermilk and stir well. Add the rennet and agitate vigorously for 1 minute. Cover and let set at room temperature (72°F) for 12–15 hours.

3. After the cheese has set, ladle it into Creole Cream Cheese molds (or other perforated containers, such as heart-shaped molds or plastic butter tubs with holes punched in them) so that the whey can drain. In a large roasting pan, elevate a rack with custard cups, then place the molds on the rack. Refrigerate until no more whey drips out. The cheese will take at least 4–6 hours to form.

4. Place the cheese in clean containers. The cream cheese will keep in the refrigerator for at least 1 month. When you are ready to eat it, spoon the amount you want into a bowl and cover with half-and-half.

YIELD: 1–2 pounds

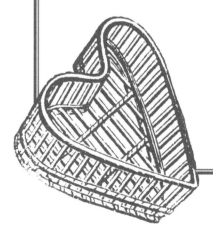

swiss-style cream cheese

This is an old recipe for a sweet cream cheese that is quite tasty.

1 quart pasteurized heavy cream

1 packet direct-set mesophilic starter or 2 ounces prepared mesophilic starter

1 drop liquid rennet diluted in 2 tablespoons cool, unchlorinated water

2 teaspoons cheese salt

Herbs (optional)

1. Warm the cream to 65°F. Add the starter and mix thoroughly.

2. Add the diluted rennet and stir gently with an up-and-down motion. Cover and let the cream set at 65°F for 24 hours.

3. Pour half of the curded cream into a colander lined with butter muslin. Sprinkle with 1 teaspoon of the salt. Pour the remaining curded cream into the colander and sprinkle with the remaining salt. (The salt will help the cream drain better.) Tie the corners of the muslin into a knot and hang the bag to drain for 12 hours.

4. Place the curd into a mold lined with cheesecloth and press for 4–6 hours at 10 pounds of pressure.

5. Remove the cheese from the mold and put into a bowl. Add the herbs, if desired.

6. Pack the cheese into small containers and refrigerate. Eat within several days.

YIELD: About 8 ounces

french-style cream cheese

This is a soft, spreadable cream cheese that is quite sweet and requires little starter culture for ripening.

2 cups pasteurized heavy cream

2 cups pasteurized whole milk

1 packet mesophilic direct-set starter or 1 ounce prepared mesophilic starter

1 drop liquid rennet diluted in ¼ cup cool, unchlorinated water

Cheese salt (optional)

Chopped fresh herbs (optional)

1–2 tablespoons heavy cream (optional)

1. Combine the cream and milk. Warm the mixture to 70°F.

2. Add the starter and rennet. Mix thoroughly. Cover and allow to set at 72°F for 24 hours.

3. Ladle the curds into a colander lined with butter muslin. Tie the corners of the muslin into a knot and hang the bag to drain for 6–12 hours, or until the curds stop dripping.

4. Transfer the curds into a bowl and mix by hand to a pastelike consistency. Add the salt and herbs to taste, if desired. For a creamier cheese, add the heavy cream.

5. Press the cheese into individual serving containers and store in the refrigerator for up to 1 week.

Note: If you find that the heavy cream will not set, use light cream next time.

YIELD: About 1 pound

RECIPE FROM A HOME CHEESE MAKER

crock cheese

Heat 1 gallon of thickened sour milk to 102°F, until you can press together curds of milk with your hand. Pour the curds into cheesecloth and thoroughly press out the whey. Melt 2 tablespoons of butter in a hot skillet, then add the curds, 1 teaspoon of baking soda, and approximately 1 teaspoon of cheese salt. Stir with a potato masher. Cook until the mixture is smooth, then add cream or milk until you have achieved the desired thickness. Pour into a bowl and serve.

whole-milk ricotta

Traditionally, ricotta is made by reheating the whey after making cheese from ewe's milk. To make ricotta from whey, see the recipe on page 152. This simple variation uses whole milk from the grocery store instead of whey; the resulting ricotta has a good flavor and a high yield.

1 gallon whole milk

1 teaspoon citric acid dissolved in ¼ cup cool water

1 teaspoon cheese salt (optional)

1–2 tablespoons heavy cream (optional)

1. Add the citric acid solution and salt (optional) into the milk and mix thoroughly.

2. In a large pot, directly heat the milk to 185 to 195°F (do not boil). Stir often to prevent scorching.

3. As soon as the curds and whey separate (make sure there is no milky whey), turn off the heat. Allow to set, undisturbed, for 10 minutes.

4. Line a colander with butter muslin. Carefully ladle the curds into the colander. Tie the corners of the muslin into a knot and hang the bag to drain for 20–30 minutes, or until the cheese has reached the desired consistency. The cheese is ready to eat immediately. For a creamier consistency, add the cream at the end and mix thoroughly.

5. Store in a covered container in the refrigerator for 1–2 weeks.

YIELD: 1½–2 pounds

ricotta salata

Ricotta salata is a dry, salted ricotta that may be eaten at a young age as a sliceable dessert cheese or when mature as a grating cheese. Traditionally, ricotta salata is made from ewe's-milk whey. Here is a variation you can enjoy at home.

1 recipe Whole-Milk Ricotta (see page 89)
1 tablespoon cheese salt

1. Follow the recipe for Whole-Milk Ricotta (see page 89) through step 4.

2. Remove the ricotta from the bag, add the remaining salt, and mix well.

3. Press the cheese into a ricotta mold and put a saucer or glass of water on top; press for 1 hour.

4. Unmold the cheese, turn it over, and put it back into the mold. Press 12 hours longer.

5. Unmold the cheese and lightly rub the surface with salt. Cover and refrigerate.

6. Turn the cheese in the mold and rub the surface with salt every day for 1 week. If any unwanted mold appears, gently rub it off with cheesecloth dampened in salt water. If the cheese becomes too soft with moisture, gently towel-dry, salt the surface again, and return it to the refrigerator.

7. Age the cheese for 2–4 weeks.

YIELD: Approximately ½ pound

panir

Panir, also spelled "paneer," is an Indian cheese similar to farmer cheese or pot cheese. Panir is one of the simplest types of unripened cheeses to make. It is rather mild and readily absorbs the flavors of the herbs and spices used with it in cooking.

---

1 gallon whole milk

8 tablespoons lemon juice or 2 teaspoons citric acid dissolved in ¾ cup hot water

1–2 cups hot water (optional)

ORIGIN OF THE WORD *CHEESE*

From the Latin *caseus* for "cheese" came the German *kaese*, the Dutch *kaas*, the Irish *cais*, the Welsh *caws*, the Portuguese *queijo*, and the Spanish *queso*. The Anglo-Saxon *cese*, or *cyse*, later became *cheese*.

---

1. In a large pot, directly heat the milk to a rolling (gentle) boil, stirring often to prevent scorching.

2. Reduce the heat to low and, before the foam subsides, drizzle in the lemon juice. Cook for 10–15 seconds.

3. Remove from the heat and continue to stir gently until large curds form. (If the whey is still milky instead of clear, return it to the heat and increase the temperature a bit or add more coagulant.)

4. Once you obtain a clear separation of curds and whey, remove from the heat and let set for 10 minutes. For a very soft cheese, add the hot water.

5. When the curds have settled below the whey, they are ready to drain. Ladle the curds into a colander lined with butter muslin. Tie the corners of the muslin into a knot and hold the bag under a gentle stream of lukewarm water for 5–10 seconds to rinse off the coagulating agent. Gently twist the top of the muslin to squeeze out extra whey.

6. At this point, either hang the bag of curds to drain for 2–3 hours or return the muslin-covered curd mass to the colander and place a bowl of water, a brick, or some other form of 5-pound weight on top and press for 2 hours.

7. Unwrap the cheese. Eat it right away or store in the refrigerator for up to 2 weeks.

YIELD: 1¾–2 pounds

chenna

Essentially the same cheese as panir, chenna is kneaded while still warm into a light, velvety smooth, whipped-cream consistency. It is an essential ingredient in many Bengali sweets.

1 recipe Panir (see page 91)

Cheese salt (optional)

Minced green chiles (optional)

Herbs (optional)

Freshly ground black pepper (optional)

Olive oil, for shallow frying (optional)

1. Follow the recipe for Panir (page 91) through step 5.

2. Return the wrapped cheese to the colander, place a 5-pound weight on top, and press for 45 minutes.

3. Unwrap the still-warm cheese and place on a smooth, clean work surface. Break it apart and press with a clean cloth to remove any remaining whey.

4. Knead the cheese by pressing out with the heel of your palm and the flat of your hand. Gather up the cheese with a spatula and continue kneading for up to 10 minutes, or until the cheese is light and velvety smooth, without any grainy texture.

5. Add the salt, chiles, herbs, and/or pepper, if desired.

6. Shape the cheese into flat patties and shallow-fry them, if desired. If you are not going to eat them right away, fry them just before serving.

7. Store in a covered container in the refrigerator. It will keep for 1 to 2 weeks.

YIELD: 1½ pounds

queso blanco

Queso blanco, which is Spanish for "white cheese," is a Latin American specialty with many variations. It is a firm cheese, with a bland, mildly sweet flavor. It is easy to make and an excellent choice if you are in a hurry or if the weather is very hot, a condition that causes problems in the production of many cheeses.

This cheese is excellent for cooking, because it has the unique property of not melting, even when deep-fried. It is often diced into ½-inch cubes and added to stir-fries, soups, or sauces (such as spaghetti) or used in Chinese cooking as a substitute for bean curd. It browns nicely and takes on the flavor of the food and spices in a recipe.

1 gallon whole milk

¼ cup vinegar (I use apple cider vinegar)

1. In a large pot, directly heat the milk to between 185° and 190°F, stirring often to prevent scorching.

2. Slowly add the vinegar, a little at a time, until the curds separate from the whey. Usually ¼ cup of vinegar will precipitate 1 gallon of milk. You may increase the temperature to 200°F in order to use less vinegar and avoid an acidic or sour taste in your cheese. (Do not boil, as boiling will impart a "cooked" flavor.)

3. Ladle the curds into a colander lined with butter muslin. Tie the corners of the muslin into a knot and hang the bag to drain for several hours, or until the cheese has reached the desired consistency.

4. Remove the cheese from the muslin. Store in a covered bowl in the refrigerator for up to 2 weeks.

YIELD: 1½–2 pounds

queso fresco

This Latin American quick farm cheese may be made using a variety of methods. The following is a simple technique you can do at home.

2 gallons pasteurized whole milk

1 packet direct-set mesophilic starter or 4 ounces prepared mesophilic starter

¼ teaspoon liquid rennet (or ¼ rennet tablet), diluted in ¼ cup cool, unchlorinated water

2 tablespoons cheese salt

1. Heat the milk to 90°F. Add the starter and mix thoroughly.

2. Add the diluted rennet and stir with an up-and-down motion for 1 minute.

3. Allow to set for 30–45 minutes, or until the curd gives a clean break.

4. Cut the curd into ¼-inch cubes.

5. Over the next 20 minutes, gradually increase the temperature to 95°F, stirring gently every few minutes to keep the curds from matting.

6. Let the curds set, undisturbed, for 5 minutes.

7. Drain off the whey.

8. Add the salt and maintain the curds at 95°F for 30 minutes longer.

9. Line a mold with cheesecloth and fill with the curds.

10. Press at 35 pounds of pressure for 6 hours. Remove the cheese from the mold and store in a covered container in the refrigerator for up to 2 weeks.

YIELD: 2 pounds

Bob and Debby Stetson, Westfield Farm
Hubbardston, Massachusetts

When Bob and Debby Stetson bought Bob and Lettie Kilmoyer's Westfield Farm in 1996, they were buying more than a 225-year-old farmhouse and 20 acres. They were buying one of America's most successful small cheese businesses, which was famous for the boost it gave to other artisanal cheese makers and known far and wide for its prizewinning Classic Blue Log.

The Kilmoyers and the Stetsons lived together for a month while the Stetsons learned to make cheese. "I always wished that I had something tangible to sell, something that I really liked," Bob Stetson says, "and my wife loved the place at first sight. We had our share of beginner's luck, and we also had plenty of batches that we threw away. Fortunately, we are able to produce the Blue Log consistently, and it's still

Falling in love with cheese making and finding excellence

a prizewinner — it's a nice fresh chèvre with a good blue 'bite' to it."

The Stetsons pick up milk from four goat farms and turn out approximately 900 pounds of cheese per week, in 15 varieties. The cheeses are stored in one of two curing rooms; the first has a steady temperature of 55°F and 75 to 80 percent humidity, and the second has variable conditions to suit the Blue Logs as they ripen over a period of two weeks.

"We strive for excellence," Bob says, "but not perfection — too often perfection can mean a lack of character. We like a few surprises. But knowing that cheese has been made long before anyone knew bacteria or microbes existed gives me confidence." (Bob and Debby's favorite ways to sample their fresh Capri and Classic Blue Log are featured on pages 233 and 239.)

small-curd cottage cheese

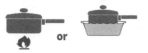

This cheese has smaller curds and is coagulated by the action of starter culture bacteria instead of by rennet. It has a pleasant, sour taste and is delicious when eaten alone or used in recipes that call for cottage cheese. If you stir the curds until they are firm and you omit the addition of heavy cream, you will have "dry curd" cottage cheese. Many people prefer the dry curd style because it has less lactose in it.

1 gallon pasteurized skim milk (whole milk may be used)

⅛ teaspoon calcium chloride diluted in ¼ cup water (if using store-bought milk)

1 packet direct-set mesophilic starter or 4 ounces prepared mesophilic starter

1–2 tablespoons heavy cream (optional)

Cheese salt (optional)

Herbs (optional)

Fresh fruit, such as chopped pineapple (optional)

1. Heat the milk to 72°F. If using calcium chloride, add it now.

2. Add the starter and mix thoroughly. Cover and let set at 72°F for 16–24 hours. The curd will be rather soft.

3. Cut the curd into ¼-inch cubes and let set for 15 minutes.

4. Increase the heat by one degree per minute until it reaches 100°F. Stir gently every few minutes to keep the curds from matting.

5. Maintain the temperature at 100°F for 10 minutes, stirring occasionally.

6. Increase the temperature to 112°F over a 15-minute period (a little less than one degree per minute).

7. Maintain the temperature at 112°F for 30 minutes, or until the curds are firm. Test for firmness by squeezing a curd particle between your thumb and forefinger. If it still has a custardlike consistency inside, it is not ready and should be cooked a little longer.

8. When the curds are sufficiently cooked, let them settle to the bottom of the pot for 5 minutes.

9. Pour off the whey. Pour the curds into a colander lined with cheesecloth. Tie the corners of the cheesecloth into a knot. If a less sour cottage cheese is desired, wash the curds by dipping the bag several times into a bowl of cool water.

10. Let the bag drain for several minutes.

11. Rinse the bag in a bowl of ice water to cool and place the bag in a colander to drain for 5 minutes.

12. Untie the bag and place the curds in a bowl. Break up any pieces that have matted. If desired, add the heavy cream to produce a creamier texture.

13. Add the salt, herbs, or fresh fruit to taste, if desired.

14. Store in a covered container in the refrigerator for up to 1 week.

YIELD: 1½ pounds

COTTAGE CHEESES

Cottage cheese originated in eastern and central Europe. It is a soft, fresh, cooked curd cheese that is usually eaten within a week after being prepared. It was quite popular in colonial America, and its name is derived from the fact that it was made in local cottages. It is also known as farmer cheese and pot cheese (because it was made at home in a pot).

In days gone by, cottage cheese was made from raw milk, which was poured into a pot and set in a spot that would stay fairly warm. In winter, that meant next to or on a cool corner of the cookstove. Within several days, because of the action of the bacteria present in unpasteurized milk, the lactic acid level would become so high that the milk protein would precipitate out into a soft, white curd. This soft curd could then be treated in a variety of ways. It was often sliced, warmed to about 100°F for several hours, then drained to produce a tasty, sour cottage cheese. Sometimes the curds were merely drained without cooking to produce a lactic acid type of cheese. Other times, the curds were pressed after cooking to produce what was called farmer cheese.

large-curd cottage cheese

Coagulated by the action of starter culture and a small amount of rennet, this cottage cheese has slightly larger curds.

1 gallon pasteurized skim or whole milk

⅛ teaspoon calcium chloride diluted in ¼ cup water (if using store-bought milk)

1 packet direct-set mesophilic starter or 4 ounces prepared mesophilic starter

¼ teaspoon liquid rennet (or ¼ rennet tablet) dissolved in ¼ cup cool, unchlorinated water

Cheese salt (optional)

Herbs (optional)

1. Warm the milk to 72°F. If using calcium chloride, add it now. Add the starter and mix thoroughly.

2. Add 1 tablespoon of the diluted rennet and mix thoroughly with a gentle up-and-down motion. Cover and let set at 72°F for 4–8 hours, or until the curd coagulates. The curd will be rather soft.

3. Cut the curd into ½-inch cubes. Allow to set, undisturbed, for 10 minutes.

4. Increase the heat by two degrees every 5 minutes, until the temperature reaches 80°F. Stir gently to prevent the curds from matting.

5. Increase the heat by three degrees every 5 minutes, until the temperature reaches 90°F, stirring gently to prevent the curds from matting.

6. Increase the heat by one degree per minute, until the temperature reaches 110°F, stirring gently to keep the curds from matting.

7. Maintain the temperature at 110°F for 20 minutes, or until the curds are sufficiently cooked and no longer have a custardlike interior. Stir gently every few minutes.

8. When the curds are sufficiently cooked, let them settle to the bottom of the pot for 5 minutes.

9. Continue the recipe as for Small-Curd Cottage Cheese, starting with step 9 (draining) on page 97.

YIELD: 1½ pounds

quark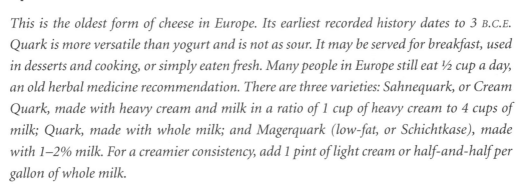

This is the oldest form of cheese in Europe. Its earliest recorded history dates to 3 B.C.E. Quark is more versatile than yogurt and is not as sour. It may be served for breakfast, used in desserts and cooking, or simply eaten fresh. Many people in Europe still eat ½ cup a day, an old herbal medicine recommendation. There are three varieties: Sahnequark, or Cream Quark, made with heavy cream and milk in a ratio of 1 cup of heavy cream to 4 cups of milk; Quark, made with whole milk; and Magerquark (low-fat, or Schichtkase), made with 1–2% milk. For a creamier consistency, add 1 pint of light cream or half-and-half per gallon of whole milk.

1 gallon pasteurized milk (see varieties above)

1 packet direct-set buttermilk starter

2–3 tablespoons heavy cream (optional)

1. Heat the milk to 88°F. Add the starter and mix thoroughly.

2. Cover and let sit at room temperature for 24 hours, or until set.

3. Ladle the curds into a colander lined with butter muslin. Tie the corners of the muslin into a knot and place the bag of curds in the refrigerator to drain overnight. You may put a container filled with water on top of the curd bag to press a bit and speed drainage.

4. If the Quark is too dry, add a few tablespoons of the cream to the finished cheese. Store in a covered container in the refrigerator for up to 2 weeks.

YIELD: 1–1½ pounds

RECIPE FROM A HOME CHEESE MAKER

quick fresh cheese

Heat ½ gallon of milk to 100°F. Add ½ teaspoon of rennet, mix well, and let set for 1 hour. Line a colander with butter muslin, ladle the curd into it, and let drain. Add herbs while draining and put into a basket mold to shape the cheese.

CHAPTER 5

HARD CHEESE

Making hard cheese is a "grate whey" to transform milk protein and butterfat into a delicious culinary delight that is both nutritious and long lasting — that is, if "ewe" can control yourself until your prize is properly "mooo-tured." The cheeses in this chapter are characteristically firm or hard in texture, due to the removal of a high percentage of moisture during the cheese-making process. They are pressed and aged for varying lengths of time for full flavor development.

You will use two different cooking methods in these recipes. Just as factories use water- or steam-jacketed vats to heat milk and curds, you too will surround your pots with warm water. This method preserves the high acidity produced in the cheese-making process, resulting in strong-flavored cheeses. In other instances, as with washed-curd cheeses, whey is replaced with hot water to heat the curds from within the pot, resulting in less acidic, mild-flavored cheeses.

Following is an overview of the steps involved in hard-cheese making. For a thorough description of each of the techniques used in these recipes, see chapter 3. I recommend starting with the recipes here and keeping detailed notes so that with time and experience you can experiment with subtle variations and produce recipes for your own unique cheeses.

Ripening

The first step in making hard cheese is ripening the milk. In the ripening process, milk sugar is converted to lactic acid by the action of a bacterial starter. Heat is applied to speed the bacterial action, because bacterial metabolism is better suited to a warm environment. The increase of acid in the milk aids in the expulsion of whey from the curd, helps rennet coagulate the milk, helps preserve the final cheese, and aids in flavor development.

Coloring

Although coloring is not necessary in cheese making, several of the cheeses in this chapter are traditionally deeper in color than a typical cow's-milk Cheddar. You may add cheese coloring to re-create those hues in your cheeses. Take care to thoroughly mix the coloring into the milk before adding rennet, or the color will be patchy or streaky.

Renneting

Having ripened the milk and regulated it to the renneting temperature, the next step is to add diluted rennet. If rennet is not diluted, it will be unevenly distributed in the milk, which can produce a faulty curd. Rennet coagulates milk protein into a solid mass of curd. Trapped within this mass are the butterfat and whey. After stirring well, keep the pot covered to help maintain a uniform temperature so the milk can coagulate evenly.

Cutting the Curd

The curd is then cut into small, uniform cubes to help remove most of the whey that is trapped inside along with the butterfat. It is important that the curd be cut when ready — either cutting it too soon or leaving it too long will result in a considerable loss of butterfat in the whey. (As soon as the curd gives a clean break, it is ready for cutting.)

Cooking the Curd

When making hard cheese, you want to remove much of the moisture from the curds so that the cheese can be safely preserved. Increasing the temperature of the curds helps expel more whey. Heating also helps firm the curd, increases acidity, and removes moisture.

Draining

Once the curds have been cooked, they are drained of any remaining whey or wash water (as in washed-curd cheeses, such as Gouda). The whey may be made into ricotta and other whey cheeses (see page 148).

Milling and Salting

Breaking the curd into smaller pieces facilitates the even distribution of salt throughout the cheese.

Molding and Pressing

The curds are placed in a mold and pressure is applied to compact the curds, expel more whey, and give the cheese its final texture and shape.

Air-Drying/Bandaging

The cheese is air-dried to form a protective rind in anticipation of the aging process. Alternatively, it may be bandaged and larded to keep its shape, preserve its coat, and prevent loss of excess moisture through evaporation.

Waxing/Oiling

Once the cheese is dry, it may be waxed to keep it from further drying out and to retard the growth of mold. Alternatively, it may be rubbed with vegetable oil to provide a protective layer that will prevent the cheese from drying out.

Aging

During this stage, the full flavor and body of the cheese are allowed to develop. This is very important and requires proper temperature and humidity. Most varieties of hard cheeses ripen best at 55 to 65°F. The longer a hard cheese ages, the stronger its flavor becomes.

An important note: U.S. law requires that raw-milk cheeses be aged for more than 60 days if they will be sold. Therefore, I must advise you to use pasteurized milk for all cheeses that will be aged for fewer than 60 days.

CHEDDAR CHEESES

Cheddar is one of the most popular cheeses in the world. Its origins go as far back as the late 1500s, and its name is taken from a small village in southern England. Legend has it that a Stone Age skeleton was found in the ancient caves overhanging Cheddar Gorge, and on the wall above its head hung a vessel containing goat's milk. Over thousands of years, the milk had hardened into a peculiar substance, pleasant to the taste – the first Cheddar cheese.

In colonial America, Cheddar was one of the most common cheeses made by farm wives. The original recipes are somewhat involved and time consuming; however, you will find the results to be well worth the effort. The cheeses included in this section all belong to the Cheddar family and involve the same basic steps. The first recipe, Farmhouse Cheddar, does not require the process of cheddaring (cutting the drained curd into strips and allowing them to set at 100°F for 2 hours), thus saving a lot of time. Farmhouse Cheddar is a good place to start when making your first Cheddar. The second recipe, Stirred-Curd Cheddar, also eliminates the cheddaring process. The third recipe, Traditional Cheddar, includes the original process of cheddaring. Other cheeses in the Cheddar family are Derby and Leicester, two English cheeses with a taste and texture very similar to those of Cheddar.

Mary Keehn, Cypress Grove Chèvre
McKinleyville, California

Cypress Grove's Humboldt Fog, perfected at the factory, is served in the finest restaurants in the United States. A soft-ripened goat cheese with a layer of ash in the center and around the outside, it looks like a layer cake when it is cut — "or maybe a foggy day along the coast," says cheese maker Mary Keehn. (The ash, which adds no flavor of its own, helps the aging process and prevents unwelcome bacterial action.) Cypress Grove also produces many other varieties, including Bermuda Triangle and Pee Wee Pyramid.

In the late 1970s, Mary and her husband bought 80 acres outside of McKinleyville. Their kids were young, and they wanted to get away from the pollution of urban areas. They raised their own goats and started making cheese at home. "I learned to make cheese the way I learned to cook — by reading and experimenting," Mary says. "When a friend opened a restaurant nearby and wanted to use our cheese, I decided to get licensed so we could sell it. At the time, I had no idea what a huge step that would be!"

A number of years ago, when the factory started to take off, they sold their Alpine goat herd intact, and Mary said she's always missed the goats. But soon they will be moving to a farm nearby and will have animals again.

Mary believes that cheese making is perfect for anyone who loves to cook and eat. "It's like magic to turn milk into something different," she says. "When people come to the factory and say, 'I want to learn to make cheese,' I tell them to get this book and then call me when they know what a curd is! If you decide to go into cheese making in a serious way, be sure you love it totally. After more than 20 years, I still love it. There are so many parts to it, including our great employees. We're a lot of women (and a few men), all making cheese."

> *Nationally renowned cheese from a small factory in northern California, where the redwoods meet the sea*

farmhouse cheddar

This recipe is a Cheddar shortcut. It's great to use when you want to have a Cheddar type of cheese but save time in the process. Farmhouse Cheddar can be dry and flaky, but is flavorful after only 4 weeks; therefore, it's a satisfying experience for your first hard cheese.

2 gallons whole milk

1 packet direct-set mesophilic starter or 4 ounces prepared mesophilic starter

½ teaspoon liquid rennet (or ½ rennet tablet) diluted in ¼ cup cool, unchlorinated water

1 tablespoon cheese salt

Cheese wax

1. Heat the milk to 90°F. (If you are using goat's milk, heat it to 85°F.) Add the starter and stir thoroughly. Cover and allow the milk to ripen for 45 minutes.

2. Add the diluted rennet and stir gently with an up-and-down motion for 1 minute. (If you are using farm-fresh cow's milk, top-stir for 1 minute with the flat underside of the ladle no more than ½ inch deep to blend the butterfat that rises to the surface.) Cover and let set at 90°F (85°F for goat's milk) for 45 minutes, or until the curd gives a clean break.

3. Cut the curd into ½-inch cubes.

4. Place the pot in a sink full of hot water and slowly heat the curds to 100°F, increasing the temperature by no more than two degrees every 5 minutes. This will take about 30 minutes. Stir gently to keep the curds from matting. The curds will shrink noticeably in size as the heating continues and you stir gently. The yellowish whey will grow in quantity as the curds shrink.

5. Cover the container and let the curds set for 5 minutes. Pour the curds into a cheesecloth-lined colander. Tie the corners of the cheesecloth into a knot and hang the bag in a convenient spot to drain for 1 hour. Do not hang in a drafty spot — the curds need to stay relatively warm.

6. Place the drained curds in a bowl and break them up gently with your fingers into walnut-size pieces. Mix in the salt.

7. Firmly pack the curds into a 2-pound mold lined with cheesecloth, then neatly fold the cheesecloth over the top. Apply 10 pounds of pressure for 10 minutes.

8. Remove the cheese from the mold and gently peel away the cheesecloth. Turn over the cheese, re-dress it, and press at 20 pounds of pressure for 10 minutes.

9. Repeat the process but press at 50 pounds of pressure for 12 hours.

10. Remove the cheese from the mold and carefully peel away the cheesecloth. Air-dry the cheese at room temperature on a wooden board until a nice rind has developed and the surface is quite dry. This can take 2–4 days, depending on the weather. Turn the cheese several times a day so moisture will not collect on the bottom.

11. Wax the cheese (see page 57).

12. Age the cheese for at least 1 month.

YIELD: 2 pounds

RECIPE FROM A HOME CHEESE MAKER

pineapple cheese

This cheese has its origins in Litchfield County, Connecticut, and is thought to have first been made in 1845. Its name comes from the surface marks, which resemble pineapple. The curd is made like Cheddar, but it is heated to a higher temperature to form a firmer curd. The curds are pressed in pineapple-shaped molds of varying sizes to produce cheeses of up to 6 pounds. After the cheeses are pressed, they are dipped in 120°F water for a few minutes and hung in a small, loose-mesh net to dry and age for several months. During aging, they are kept clean and rubbed with oil several times.

stirred-curd cheddar

When you're "pressed" for time, this Cheddar is a perfect alternative to traditional Cheddar.

2 gallons whole milk
(cow's or goat's milk)

1 packet direct-set
mesophilic starter or
4 ounces prepared
mesophilic starter

2 drops cheese coloring
per gallon of milk,
diluted in ¼ cup water
(optional)

½ teaspoon liquid rennet
(or ½ rennet tablet)
diluted in ¼ cup cool,
unchlorinated water

2 tablespoons cheese salt

Cheese wax

1. Heat the milk to 90°F. Add the starter and stir well. Cover and allow the milk to ripen for 45 minutes.

2. Add the coloring, if desired, stirring to distribute evenly.

3. Make sure the milk's temperature is 90°F. Add the diluted rennet and stir gently with an up-and-down motion for 1 minute. If using farm-fresh cow's milk, top-stir for several minutes longer. Cover and allow to set at 90°F for 45 minutes, or until the curd is firm and gives a clean break.

4. Cut the curd into ¼-inch cubes. Allow the curds to set for 15 minutes.

5. Heat the curds to 100°F, increasing the temperature no more than two degrees every 5 minutes. This should take about 30 minutes. Stir gently to keep the curds from matting.

6. Once the curds reach 100°F, maintain the temperature and continue stirring for 30 minutes. Let set for 5 minutes.

7. Drain off the whey. Pour the curds into a large colander and drain for several minutes. Do not drain too long, or the curds will mat. Pour the curds back into the pot and stir them briskly with your fingers, separating any curd particles that have matted.

8. Add the salt and blend well. Do not squeeze the curds; simply mix the salt into them.

9. Keep the curds at 100°F for 1 hour, stirring every 5 minutes to avoid matting. The curds can be kept at

100°F by resting the cheese pot in a sink or bowl full of 100°F water.

10. Line a 2-pound cheese mold with cheesecloth. Place the curds in the mold. Press the cheese at 15 pounds of pressure for 10 minutes.

11. Remove the cheese from the mold and gently peel away the cheesecloth. Turn over the cheese, re-dress it, and press at 30 pounds of pressure for 10 minutes.

12. Repeat the process but press at 40 pounds of pressure for 2 hours.

13. Repeat the process but press at 50 pounds of pressure for 24 hours.

14. Remove the cheese from the mold and peel away the cheesecloth. Air-dry at room temperature for 2–5 days, or until the cheese is dry to the touch.

15. Wax the cheese (see page 57).

16. Age it at 45 to 55°F for 2–6 months.

YIELD: 2 pounds

Curd shovel

traditional cheddar

Making Cheddar the traditional way takes longer but is well worth the effort.

2 gallons whole milk
1 packet direct-set mesophilic starter or 4 ounces prepared mesophilic starter
½ teaspoon liquid rennet (or ½ rennet tablet) diluted in ¼ cup cool, unchlorinated water
2 tablespoons cheese salt
Cheese wax

1. Heat the milk to 86°F. Add the starter and stir well. Cover and allow the milk to ripen for 45 minutes.

2. Make sure the milk's temperature is 86°F. Add the diluted rennet and stir gently with an up-and-down motion for 1 minute. If using farm-fresh cow's milk, top-stir for several minutes longer. Cover and let set, undisturbed, for 45 minutes.

3. Cut the curd into ¼-inch cubes. Allow the curds to set for 5 minutes.

4. Heat the curds to 100°F, increasing the temperature no more than two degrees every 5 minutes. This should take about 30 minutes. Stir gently to keep the curds from matting.

5. Once the curds reach 100°F, maintain the temperature and continue stirring the curds for 30 minutes longer.

6. Allow the curds to set for 20 minutes.

7. Pour the curds and whey into a colander. Place the colander of curds back into the pot and let set for 15 minutes.

8. Remove the colander from the pot and place the mass of curd on a cutting board. Cut the curd into 3-inch slices. Put the pot into a sink full of 100°F water. Place the slices in the pot and cover the pot. Maintain the curds at 100°F, turning them every 15 minutes for 2 hours.

9. The curd slices should be tough and have a texture similar to that of chicken meat. Break the slices into ½-inch cubes and put them into the covered pot. Put the pot back into a sink full of 100°F water. Stir the curds with your fingers every 10 minutes for 30 minutes. Do not squeeze the curds; merely stir them to keep them from matting.

10. Remove the pot from the sink. Add the salt and stir gently.

11. Line a 2-pound cheese mold with cheesecloth. Place the curds in the mold. Press at 10 pounds of pressure for 15 minutes.

12. Remove the cheese from the mold and gently peel away the cheesecloth. Turn over the cheese, re-dress it, and press at 40 pounds of pressure for 12 hours.

13. Repeat the process but press at 50 pounds of pressure for 24 hours.

14. Remove the cheese from the mold. Peel away the cheesecloth. Air-dry the cheese at room temperature for 2–5 days, or until it is dry to the touch.

15. Wax the cheese (see page 57).

16. Age it at 50 to 55°F for 3–12 months. This cheese develops a sharper flavor as it ages.

YIELD: 2 pounds

FIT FOR A QUEEN

For Queen Victoria's wedding celebration in 1840, the farmers in Somerset, England, made a Cheddar cheese weighing 1,100 pounds and measuring more than 9 feet wide.

sage cheddar

For a delicious variation, try adding sage to the Stirred-Curd Cheddar (see page 106).

1–3 tablespoons chopped fresh or dried sage

½ cup water

Ingredients for Stirred-Curd Cheddar (see page 106)

1. Boil the sage in the water for 15 minutes, adding more water to cover the herbs as needed.

2. Strain the flavored water into a small bowl and let cool; reserve the boiled sage.

3. Heat the milk and flavored water according to step 1 of the Stirred-Curd Cheddar recipe.

4. Follow steps 2 through 8 of the Stirred-Curd Cheddar recipe. Gently stir the boiled sage into the curds.

5. Follow steps 9 through 16 of the Stirred-Curd Cheddar recipe.

YIELD: 2 pounds

caraway cheddar

Here's another tasty way to make Stirred-Curd Cheddar (see page 106).

½–2 tablespoons caraway seeds

½ cup water

Ingredients for Stirred-Curd Cheddar (see page 106)

1. Boil the caraway seeds in the water for 15 minutes, adding more water to cover the seeds as needed.

2. Strain the flavored water into a small bowl and let cool; reserve the boiled seeds.

3. Heat the milk and flavored water according to step 1 of the Stirred-Curd Cheddar recipe.

4. Follow steps 2 through 8 of the Stirred-Curd Cheddar recipe. Gently stir the boiled seeds into the curds.

5. Follow steps 9 through 16 of the Stirred-Curd Cheddar recipe.

YIELD: 2 pounds

jalapeño cheddar

This variety can be quite spicy.

½–4 tablespoons chopped jalapeño chiles

½ cup water

Ingredients for Stirred-Curd Cheddar (see page 106)

1. Boil the chiles in the water for 15 minutes, adding more water to cover the chiles as needed.

2. Strain the flavored water into a small bowl and let cool; reserve the boiled chiles.

3. Heat the milk and flavored water according to step 1 of the Stirred-Curd Cheddar recipe.

4. Follow steps 2 through 8 of the Stirred-Curd Cheddar recipe. Gently stir the boiled chiles into the curds.

5. Follow steps 9 through 16 of the Stirred-Curd Cheddar recipe.

YIELD: 2 pounds

RECIPE FROM A HOME CHEESE MAKER

american cheese

Combine 1 gallon of whole milk and ½ cup of milk powder. Add 1 cup of cultured buttermilk at 86°F. Let set for 1–2 hours. Dissolve ¼ tablet of rennet in ¼ cup of cooled, sterilized water and add it to the milk. When the curd gives a clean break, cut it into ½-inch cubes. Hold at 86°F for 30 minutes. Over the next 30 minutes, raise the temperature to 104°F, stirring often. Hold for at least 60 minutes at 104°F. When it is ready, remove from the heat, wash, drain, and salt to taste. Place the curds into a mold while very warm and press with moderate pressure.

derby cheese

Derby originated in Derbyshire, England. It is very similar to Cheddar but has a higher moisture content and ages more quickly.

2 gallons whole milk

1 packet direct-set mesophilic starter or 4 ounces prepared mesophilic starter

½ teaspoon liquid rennet (or ½ rennet tablet) diluted in ¼ cup cool, unchlorinated water

2 tablespoons cheese salt

Cheese wax

1. Heat the milk to 84°F. Add the starter and stir well. Cover and allow the milk to ripen for 45 minutes.

2. Make sure the milk's temperature is 84°F. Add the diluted rennet and stir gently with an up-and-down motion for 1 minute. If using farm-fresh cow's milk, top-stir for 1 minute longer. Cover and allow to set at 84°F for 50 minutes.

3. Cut the curds into ½-inch cubes.

4. Heat the curds to 94°F, increasing the temperature no more than two degrees every 5 minutes. Stir gently to keep the curds from matting. When the temperature reaches 94°F, stir the curds for 10 minutes.

5. Place the mass of curd on a draining board and cut it into 2-inch slices. Lay the slices on the draining board and cover them with a clean towel, which should occasionally be placed in a bowl of 94°F water, then wrung dry. (Never use a towel that has been used during bread making. The yeast can cross contaminate the cheese, making it spongy.) The aim is to keep the temperature of the curd slices at 94°F. Turn over the slices every 15 minutes. Let them drain for 1 hour.

6. Break the curd slices into quarter-size pieces. The curd should be tough and tear when pulled apart. Add the salt and stir gently.

7. Place the curds in a cheesecloth-lined mold. Press at 15 pounds of pressure for 10 minutes.

8. Remove the cheese from the mold and gently peel away the cheesecloth. Turn over the cheese, re-dress it, and press at 30 pounds of pressure for 2 hours.

9. Repeat the process but press at 50 pounds of pressure for 24 hours.

10. Remove the cheese from the mold, peel away the cheesecloth, and air-dry at room temperature for 2–5 days, or until the cheese is dry to the touch.

11. Wax the cheese (see page 57).

12. Age it at 50 to 55°F for 3 months.

YIELD: 2 pounds

THE BIG CHEESE

In 1801, the townspeople of Cheshire, Massachusetts, worked together to create a mammoth cheese, which was presented to Thomas Jefferson in honor of his recent presidential victory. The curd was produced on individual farms from 1 day's milk (900+ gallons) and then transported to the village green, where it was placed in a cider press. The 1,200-pound cheese was then moved by sled, boat, and wagon to the White House.

leicester

A mild, hard cheese similar to Cheddar, Leicester ripens somewhat more quickly. It originated in Leicester County, England, and is traditionally made from cow's milk and colored.

2 gallons whole milk

1 packet direct-set mesophilic starter or 4 ounces prepared mesophilic starter

2 drops cheese coloring per gallon of milk, diluted in ¼ cup water

½ teaspoon liquid rennet (or ½ rennet tablet) diluted in ¼ cup cool, unchlorinated water

2 tablespoons cheese salt, plus a pinch for dusting

Cheese wax

1. Heat the milk to 85°F. Add the starter and mix well. Cover and allow the milk to ripen for 45 minutes.

2. Add the coloring, stirring to distribute evenly.

3. Make sure the milk's temperature is 85°F. Add the diluted rennet and stir gently with an up-and-down motion for several minutes. If using farm-fresh cow's milk, top-stir for several minutes longer. Cover and allow to set at 85°F for 45 minutes.

4. Cut the curd into ¼-inch cubes. Stir them occasionally, and gently, for 15 minutes.

5. Heat the curds to 95°F, increasing the temperature no more than two degrees every 5 minutes. Stir gently to avoid matting. Maintain the curds at 95°F for 30 minutes, stirring gently to keep the curds from matting.

6. Pour the curds into a colander and let them drain for 20 minutes.

7. Place the mass of curd on a draining board. Cut it into 2-inch-long slices to drain. Lay the slices on the draining board and cover them with a clean towel, which should occasionally be placed in a bowl of 96°F water, then wrung dry. (Never use a towel that has been used during bread making. The yeast can cross contaminate the cheese, making it spongy.) Turn the slices every 20 minutes for 1 hour.

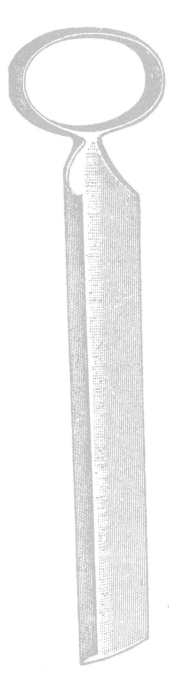

CHEESE TRIER.

8. Break the slices into nickel-size pieces and put them in a bowl. Stir them for several minutes. Add 2 tablespoons of the salt and gently stir several minutes longer.

9. Place the curds in a cheesecloth-lined mold and press at 15 pounds of pressure for 30 minutes.

10. Remove the cheese from the mold and gently peel away the cheesecloth. Turn over the cheese, re-dress it, and press at 30 pounds of pressure for 2 hours.

11. Repeat the process but press at 50 pounds of pressure for 24 hours.

12. Remove the cheese from the mold and peel away the cheesecloth. Dust the cheese with the remaining salt and shake off any excess. Air-dry the cheese at room temperature for 2–5 days, or until it is dry to the touch.

13. Wax the cheese (see page 57).

14. Age the cheese at 55°F. If you want, you can eat it in 12–16 weeks, but it will mature at 9 months and develop a very subtle, individual flavor.

YIELD: 2 pounds

gouda

Gouda originated in the Dutch town of Gouda, near Rotterdam. It is a washed-curd, semi-hard cheese with a smooth texture and a deliciously tangy taste. It looks particularly distinctive when covered with traditional red cheese wax (though that is not done in Holland).

2 gallons whole milk

1 packet direct-set mesophilic starter or 4 ounces prepared mesophilic starter

½ teaspoon liquid rennet (or ½ rennet tablet) diluted in ¼ cup cool, unchlorinated water

2 pounds cheese salt, for brine

1 tablespoon calcium chloride, for brine

1 gallon cold water, for brine

Cheese wax

1. Heat the milk to 90°F. Add the starter and mix well. Cover and allow the milk to ripen for 10 minutes.

2. Add the diluted rennet and stir gently with an up-and-down motion for 1 minute. If using farm-fresh cow's milk, top-stir 1 minute longer. Cover and let the milk set at 90°F for 1 hour, or until it gives a clean break.

3. Cut the curd into ½-inch cubes. Let them set for 10 minutes.

4. Drain off one-third of the whey. Stirring continuously, slowly add just enough 175°F water to raise the temperature of the curd to 92°F.

5. Let the curd settle again for 10 minutes. Drain off the whey to the level of the curd.

6. Once again, while stirring constantly, slowly add just enough 175°F water to bring the temperature of the curd to 100°F. Keep the curd at 100°F for 15 minutes, stirring often to keep the curds from matting.

7. Allow the curds to set for 30 minutes.

8. Pour off the remaining whey.

TROUBLESHOOTING If, after removing your cheese from the mold, it has no closed rind (the curds have not properly knit together), dip it in 100°F water and press for 30 minutes.

9. Quickly place the warm curds in a 2-pound cheese mold lined with cheesecloth, breaking them as little as possible. Press at 20 pounds of pressure for 20 minutes.

10. Remove the cheese from the mold and gently peel away the cheesecloth. Turn over the cheese, re-dress it, and press at 40 pounds of pressure for 20 minutes.

11. Repeat the process but press at 50 pounds of pressure for 12 to 16 hours. Remove from the press.

12. Make a saturated brine solution by combining the salt, calcium chloride, and water in a noncorrosive (glass or stainless-steel) container. Soak the cheese in the brine for 12 hours.

13. Remove the cheese from the brine and pat dry. Refrigerate the brine solution for other recipes (see page 53). Air-dry the cheese at 50°F for 3 weeks.

14. Wax the cheese (see page 57).

15. Age it at 50°F for 3–4 months, turning it 3 or 4 times a week. For a real treat, keep one around for 6–9 months.

YIELD: 2 pounds

WASHED-CURD CHEESES

Gouda and Colby are washed-curd cheeses. During cooking, the whey is removed from the pot and replaced with water. This washes the milk sugar, or lactose, from the curd and lowers the acid level to avoid souring the cheese. This process gives these cheeses their typical smooth texture and mild flavor. Such cheeses cure somewhat faster than other varieties and are ready for eating in 12 weeks.

caraway gouda

Here's a tasty variation to Gouda.

> 1 tablespoon caraway seeds
>
> ½ cup water
>
> Ingredients for Gouda (see page 116)

1. Boil the caraway seeds in the water for 15 minutes, adding more water to cover the seeds as needed.

2. Strain the flavored water into a small bowl and let cool; reserve the seeds.

3. Heat the milk and flavored water according to step 1 of the Gouda recipe.

4. Follow steps 2 through 8 of the Gouda recipe. Gently stir the boiled caraway seeds into the curds. Blend thoroughly and quickly. You do not want the curds to cool before they are placed in the cheese mold.

5. Follow steps 9 through 15 of the Gouda recipe.

YIELD: 2 pounds

hot pepper gouda

Try this recipe as a spicy alternative to Gouda.

> 1 teaspoon dried jalapeño chiles
>
> ½ cup water
>
> Ingredients for Gouda (see page 116)

1. Boil the chiles in the water for 15 minutes, adding more water to cover the chiles as needed.

2. Strain the flavored water into a small bowl and let cool; reserve the chiles.

3. Heat the milk and flavored water according to step 1 of the Gouda recipe.

4. Follow steps 2 through 8 of the Gouda recipe. Gently stir the boiled chiles into the curds. Blend thoroughly and quickly. You do not want the curds to cool before they are placed in the cheese mold.

5. Follow steps 9 through 15 of the Gouda recipe.

YIELD: 2 pounds

Paula Lambert, The Mozzarella Company
Dallas, Texas

Cheese maker and cookbook author Paula Lambert once lived in Italy, where she loved to eat fresh mozzarella. Back in Texas in the early 1980s, bereft of anything resembling her beloved mozzarella, she did what any sensible person would do: She started her own cheese factory, deep in the heart of Dallas. "I found farmers with cows and goats to buy milk from and built a small factory," she recalls. "At first, no one knew what fresh mozzarella was! It took a lot of education."

Paula has gone from making one kind of mozzarella to producing about 20 kinds of cheese, including chèvre, ricotta, crème fraîche, mascarpone, queso fresco, and Caciotta (an aged cheese similar to Monterey Jack). She sells her cheeses to fine restaurants, gourmet shops, and directly to individuals throughout the United States. She and her nine cheese makers (all women) have won many awards from the American Cheese Society. Amazingly, they make everything by hand. The only mechanical device in the entire place is a pump that carries milk to the 60-gallon vat.

Does Paula have any advice for the novice cheese maker? "Yes. Don't give up. When you are developing a cheese, change only one variable at a time, and keep meticulous records of times, temperatures, and other factors every single day. Most of all, be patient." In addition to the fine recipes on the company's Web site (www.mozzco.com), Paula features many of her cheeses in her book, *The Cheese Lover's Cookbook and Guide.* (Three of her recipes using cheese are featured on pages 218, 234, and 250.)

How re-creating the tastes of Italy led to a successful business

colby

A type of Cheddar in which the curds are washed during the cooking stage, colby is an American cheese named after the township in southern Wisconsin where it was first made. It has a more open texture than Cheddar, contains more moisture, has a pleasantly mild flavor, and can be aged from 2 to 3 months.

2 gallons whole milk

1 packet direct-set mesophilic starter or 4 ounces prepared mesophilic starter

4 drops cheese coloring, diluted in ¼ cup water (or 2 drops per gallon of milk)

½ teaspoon liquid rennet (or ½ rennet tablet) diluted in ¼ cup cool, unchlorinated water

2 tablespoons cheese salt

Cheese wax

1. Heat the milk to 86°F. Add the starter and mix thoroughly. Cover and allow the milk to ripen for 1 hour.

2. Add the coloring and stir.

3. Make sure the milk's temperature is 86°F. Add the diluted rennet and stir gently with an up-and-down motion for 1 minute. If using farm-fresh cow's milk, top-stir 3 minutes longer. Cover and let set for 30 minutes, or until the curd gives a clean break.

4. Cut the curd into ⅜-inch cubes. Stir gently. Let the curds set for 5 minutes.

5. Heat the curds by two degrees every 5 minutes until the temperature reaches 102°F. Stir gently to keep the curds from matting. Maintain the temperature of the curds at 102°F for 30 minutes, stirring gently.

6. Drain off the whey to the level of the curds. While stirring, add 60°F water until the temperature of the curds and water reaches 80°F. Maintain the curds at 80°F for 15 minutes. Stir to prevent matting. (The temperature of the additional water controls the moisture content of the cheese. If a drier cheese is desired, keep the curd-water mixture a few degrees higher than 80°F. For a moister cheese, keep the temperature below 80°F.)

7. Pour the curds into a colander. Allow the curds to drain for 20 minutes.

8. Break the curds into thumbnail-size pieces. Add the salt and mix gently but thoroughly.

9. Place the curds into a cheesecloth-lined mold. Press at 20 pounds of pressure for 20 minutes.

10. Remove the cheese from the mold, gently peel away the cheesecloth, turn over the cheese, re-dress it, and press at 30 pounds of pressure for 20 minutes.

11. Repeat the process but press at 40 pounds of pressure for 1 hour.

12. Repeat the process but press at 50 pounds of pressure for 12 hours.

13. Remove the cheese from the mold and peel away the cheesecloth. Air-dry at room temperature for several days, or until the cheese is dry to the touch.

14. Wax the cheese (see page 57).

15. Age the cheese at 50°F for 2–3 months.

YIELD: 2 pounds

traditional swiss

Warning: Longer aging of this cheese may transport you to the Alps . . .

2 gallons whole milk

1 packet direct-set thermophilic starter or 4 ounces prepared thermophilic starter

⅛ teaspoon *Propionic shermanii* powder

½ teaspoon liquid rennet (or ½ rennet tablet) diluted in ¼ cup cool, unchlorinated water

2 pounds cheese salt, for brine, plus a pinch

1 gallon cold water, for brine

1. Heat the milk to 90°F. Add the starter and mix well.

2. Remove ¼ cup of milk from the pot and add the *Propionic shermanii* to it. Mix thoroughly to dissolve the powder. Add the mixture to the milk and stir. Cover and allow the milk to ripen for 10 minutes.

3. Make sure the milk's temperature is 90°F. Add the diluted rennet and stir gently with an up-and-down motion for 1 minute. If using farm-fresh cow's milk, top-stir for several minutes longer. Cover and let the milk set at 90°F for 30 minutes.

4. Using a curd knife and a stainless-steel whisk, cut the curd into ¼-inch cubes.

5. Keeping the curd temperature at 90°F, gently stir the curds for 40 minutes. This is called *foreworking* and helps expel whey from the curds before they are heated.

6. Heat the curds by one degree every minute until the temperature is 120°F (this will take 30 minutes). Maintain the temperature at 120°F for 30 minutes, stirring often. The curds must be cooked until they reach a stage called *the proper break.* To test for this, wad together a handful of curds and rub it gently between your palms. If the ball readily breaks apart into individual particles, the curds are sufficiently cooked. (If they are not sufficiently cooked, they will be too soft to hold together.) Let the curds set for 5 minutes.

7. Pour off the whey (reserve it for other recipes).

8. Line a 2-pound mold with cheesecloth and place it in the sink or over a large pot. Quickly ladle the curds into the mold. You do not want the curds to cool. Press at 8–10 pounds of pressure for 15 minutes.

9. Remove the cheese from the mold and gently peel away the cheesecloth. Turn over the cheese, re-dress it, and press at 14 pounds of pressure for 30 minutes.

10. Repeat the process but press at the same pressure (14 pounds) for 2 hours.

11. Repeat the process but press at 15 pounds of pressure for 12 hours.

12. Make a saturated brine bath by combining the salt and water in a noncorrosive pot; stir well. Remove the cheese from the mold, peel away the cheesecloth, and soak the cheese in the brine. Sprinkle the remaining pinch of salt on the surface of the floating cheese. Refrigerate the brine and let the cheese soak for 12 hours.

13. Remove the cheese from the brine and pat dry. Reserve the brine for other recipes (see page 53). Place on a clean cheese board and store at 50 to 55°F and 85 percent humidity. Turn the cheese daily for 1 week, wiping it with clean cheesecloth dampened in salt water. Do not wet the cheese.

14. Place the cheese in a warm, humid room, such as the kitchen, with a temperature between 68 and 74°F. Turn it daily and wipe it with a cheesecloth dampened in salt water. Do not wet the surface of the cheese. Let the cheese set for 2–3 weeks, until eye formation is noticeable. (The cheese will swell somewhat and become slightly rounded.)

15. Age the cheese at 45°F and 80 percent humidity for at least 3 months. Turn the cheese several times a week. Remove any surface mold with cheesecloth dampened in salt water. A reddish coloration on the surface of the cheese is normal and should not be removed.

YIELD: 2 pounds

caraway swiss

Try this tasty variation to the Traditional Swiss recipe; the caraway seeds impart their own distinct flavor to the cheese.

> 2 tablespoons caraway seeds
>
> ½ cup water
>
> Ingredients for Traditional Swiss (see page 122)

1. Boil the caraway seeds in the water for 15 minutes, adding more water to cover the seeds as needed.

2. Strain the flavored water into a small bowl and let cool; reserve the seeds.

3. Heat the milk and flavored water according to step 1 of the Traditional Swiss recipe.

4. Follow steps 2 through 7 of the Traditional Swiss recipe. Gently stir the boiled caraway seeds into the curds. Blend thoroughly and quickly. You do not want the curds to cool before they are placed in the cheese mold.

5. Follow steps 8 through 15 of the Traditional Swiss recipe.

YIELD: 2 pounds

SWISS CHEESES

Swiss types of cheese have been known since the time of the Romans. They were made in the Alpine regions and are characterized by their fragrant, sweet, nutty flavor and the holes (eyes) throughout them. Contrary to popular lore, the holes are not the result of mice; they are caused by *Propionibacterium,* which produce carbon dioxide gas.

   The thermophilic bacterial starter for Swiss cheese consists of a 50/50 mix of *Lactobacillus bulgaricus* and *Streptococcus thermophilus.* During cooking, the temperature of the curds may go as high as 120°F, and thus heat-loving bacteria are needed to develop the lactic acid. The thick rind is a result of soaking in brine prior to aging. The cheese is usually aged at least 5 months. During the early part of the aging process, store the cheese for 2 to 3 weeks in a warm room (70°F) with fairly high humidity (80 percent) so that the *Propionibacterium* can grow and produce gas. A customer recommends using yogurt with *Propionic shermanii* for a starter in the traditional Swiss recipe; his cheese came out tasting just like Jarlsberg.

emmental

This famous Swiss cheese owes its name to the Emmental valley near Bern, Switzerland.

2 gallons whole milk

1 packet direct-set thermophilic starter or 4 ounces prepared thermophilic starter

1 teaspoon *Propionic shermanii* powder

½ teaspoon liquid rennet (or ½ rennet tablet) diluted in ¼ cup cool, unchlorinated water

2 pounds cheese salt, for brine

1 gallon cold water, for brine

1. Heat the milk to 90°F. Add the starter and mix well.

2. Remove ¼ cup of the milk from the pot and add the *Propionic shermanii* to it. Mix thoroughly, making sure the powder is dissolved. Add it to the milk in the pot and stir. Cover and allow the milk to ripen for 10 minutes.

3. Make sure the milk's temperature is 90°F. Add the diluted rennet and stir gently with an up-and-down motion for 1 minute. If using farm-fresh cow's milk, top-stir for several minutes longer. Cover and let the milk set at 90°F for 30 minutes.

4. Cut the curd into ¼-inch cubes using a curd knife and a stainless-steel whisk. Keeping the curd temperature at 90°F, gently stir the curds for 20 minutes. This foreworking helps expel whey from the curds before they are heated.

5. Heat the curds no more than two degrees every 5 minutes, until the temperature reaches 100°F (this should take about 30 minutes).

6. Heat the curds one degree every 2 minutes, until the temperature reaches 114°F (this should take 30 minutes). Maintain this temperature for 30 minutes, stirring often. The curds must be cooked until they reach the proper break. To test for the proper break, wad together a handful of curds. Rub the wad gently between your palms. If the ball of curds readily breaks apart into individual curd particles, the curds are sufficiently cooked. Allow the curds to set for 5 minutes.

7. Follow steps 7 through 15 for Traditional Swiss (see page 122).

YIELD: 2 pounds

monterey jack

Created in 1892 in Monterey County, California, this cheese may be made with skim, part-skim, or whole milk. If you use whole milk, the cheese will be semisoft; if you use skim milk, it will be hard enough to grate.

2 gallons whole milk

1 packet direct-set mesophilic starter or 4 ounces prepared mesophilic starter

½ teaspoon liquid rennet (or ½ rennet tablet) diluted in ¼ cup cool, unchlorinated water

1 tablespoon cheese salt

Cheese wax

1. Heat the milk to 90°F. Add the starter and stir thoroughly. Cover and allow the milk to ripen at 90°F for 30 minutes.

2. Add the diluted calcium chloride, if necessary.

3. Add the diluted rennet and stir gently with an up-and-down motion for 1 minute. Cover and let set at 90°F for 30–45 minutes, or until the curd gives a clean break.

4. Cut the curd into ¼-inch cubes and let set for 40 minutes.

5. Heat the curds to 100°F, increasing the temperature by two degrees every 5 minutes (this will take about 35 minutes). Stir gently but frequently to keep the curds from matting.

6. Maintain the curds at 100°F for 30 minutes, stirring occasionally to keep the curds from matting. Let the curds set for 5 minutes.

7. Carefully pour off the whey to the level of the curds. Allow the curds to set 30 minutes longer, stirring every 5 minutes to prevent matting. Maintain the temperature at 100°F.

8. Line a colander with cheesecloth and place it in a sink. Ladle the curds into the colander. Sprinkle the salt over the curds, mixing gently, and let drain.

9. Place the curds in a cheesecloth-lined mold. Press the cheese with a 3-pound weight for 15 minutes.

10. Remove the cheese from the mold and gently peel away the cheesecloth. Turn over the cheese, re-dress it, and press at 10 pounds of pressure for 12 hours.

11. Remove the cheese and place it on a clean surface at room temperature to air-dry. Turn twice a day until the surface is dry to the touch. Drying may take 1–3 days, depending on the temperature and humidity.

12. Wax the cheese (see page 57).

13. Age the cheese at 55°F for 1–4 months, turning it over at least once a week. (If you used raw milk, your cheese must be aged for at least 60 days.) The flavor will become sharper as the cheese ages.

YIELD: 1 pound

"*Ken-no: This was a large rich cheese, made by the women of the family with a great affectation of secrecy, and was intended for the refreshment of the gossips who were in the house at the 'canny minute' of the birth of a child. Called* Ken-no *because no one was supposed to know of its existence — certainly no male being, not excepting the master of the house. After all had eaten their fill on the auspicious occasion, the rest was divided among the gossips and taken home.*"

—*Brewer's Dictionary of Phrase and Fable,* 1898

manchego

This cheese originated in Spain near the plains of Toledo and was made from the milk of manchego sheep. It has a rich, mellow taste and is available in four stages of ripeness. Manchego fresco is aged for 5 days or fewer; manchego curado is aged for 3–12 weeks; manchego viejo is aged for 3–12 months; and manchego aceite is aged in olive oil for more than 1 year. In Latin America today, manchego is made almost entirely from cow's milk.

2 gallons whole milk

½ packet direct-set mesophilic starter or 3 ounces prepared mesophilic starter

½ packet direct-set thermophilic starter or 1 ounce prepared thermophilic starter

¼ teaspoon lipase powder diluted in ¼ cup of water and allowed to sit for 20 minutes before using, for stronger flavor (optional)

½ teaspoon liquid rennet (or ½ rennet tablet) diluted in ¼ cup cool, unchlorinated water

2 pounds cheese salt, for brine

1 gallon cold water

1. Heat the milk to 86°F. Add both starters and mix well. Cover and allow the milk to ripen at 86°F for 45 minutes.

2. Add the lipase, if desired. Add the diluted rennet and stir gently with an up-and-down motion for 1 minute. Cover and let set at 86°F for 30 minutes, or until the curd gives a clean break.

3. Cut the curd into ½-inch cubes and let set for 5 minutes.

4. Cut the cubes into rice-size pieces by slowly stirring them with a stainless-steel whisk for 30 minutes.

5. Heat the curds to 104°F, increasing the temperature two degrees every 5 minutes (this will take about 45 minutes). Stir gently to prevent the curds from matting.

6. Let the curds set for 5 minutes, then pour off the whey.

7. Line a mold with cheesecloth and ladle the curds into it. Press lightly at 15 pounds of pressure for 15 minutes.

8. Remove the cheese from the mold and gently peel away the cheesecloth. Turn over the cheese, re-dress it, and press again at 15 pounds of pressure for 15 minutes.

9. Repeat the process and press again at 15 pounds of pressure for 15 minutes.

10. Repeat the process but press at 30 pounds of pressure for 6 hours.

11. Make a saturated brine solution by combining the salt and water in a noncorrosive container. Remove the cheese from the mold and place it in the brine. Let it soak at 55°F for 6 hours.

12. Remove the cheese from the brine and pat dry. Reserve the brine for other recipes (see page 53). Age at 55°F, turning daily. Age for any length of time (see above), depending on the type of cheese you want, and coat with olive oil to keep the cheese from drying out. Remove unwanted mold with cheesecloth dampened in salt water.

YIELD: 2 pounds

haloumi

Made in Cyprus, Haloumi is a firm, pickled (brined) cheese. It is a good hot-weather cheese: The salt inhibits the growth of mold and unwanted bacteria, which usually thrive in temperate conditions.

2 gallons whole milk

1 packet direct-set mesophilic starter or 4 ounces prepared mesophilic starter

½ teaspoon liquid rennet (or ½ rennet tablet) diluted in ¼ cup cool, unchlorinated water

¼ cup plus 2 pounds cheese salt, for brine

1 gallon cold water, for brine

1. Heat the milk to 86°F. Add the starter and mix well.

2. Add the diluted rennet and stir gently with an up-and-down motion for 1 minute. Cover and allow to set at 86°F for 30–45, minutes or until the curd gives a clean break.

3. Cut the curd into ½-inch cubes.

4. Increase the temperature two degrees every 5 minutes, until the curds reach 104°F (this will take about 45 minutes), stirring gently to keep the curds from matting. Maintain the curds at 104°F for 20 minutes, stirring gently every few minutes.

5. Ladle the curds into a cheesecloth-lined colander. Drain the whey into a pot and reserve.

6. Pack the curds into a cheesecloth-lined mold and press at 30 pounds of pressure for 1 hour.

7. Remove the cheese from the mold and gently peel away the cheesecloth. Turn over the cheese, re-dress it, and press at 50 pounds of pressure for 30 minutes.

8. Remove the cheese from the mold and cut into 3-inch-square blocks.

9. Bring the reserved whey to 176 to 194°F. Place the curd blocks in the whey and soak for 1 hour, at which time the cheese will have a texture similar to that of cooked chicken breast and will rise to the surface.

10. Strain the curds into a colander and let cool for 20 minutes.

11. Sprinkle the curds with ¼ cup of the salt and let cool for 2–4 hours

12. Combine the remaining 2 pounds of salt and the cold water to make a saturated brine solution. Soak the cheese in the brine for up to 60 days. The flavor increases with age, but the cheese may be eaten fresh at any time during the 60-day period.

YIELD: 2 pounds

"The Groaning Cheese: This was a large cheese, so called from its being in old days supplied by the husband against the time of his wife's delivery. At the birth of the child, it was cut in the center in such a way that by degrees a ring was formed through which the child was ceremonially passed on the day of christening."

—John Brand, *Observations on the Popular Antiquities of Great Britain,* 1841

Abe Madey, Hawthorne Valley Farm
Ghent, New York

Hawthorne Valley Farm was one of the first dairies in the United States to be certified as organic. The farm is operated according to biodynamic principles and is licensed to sell raw milk. Cheese maker Abe Madey helps make yogurt, quark, and a variety of artisan cheeses, which are sold at the farm and in natural-food groceries throughout the Northeast.

Reflecting on how he got started in cheese making, Abe says, "I grew up around the farm. I learned the fundamentals here, and have talked to lots of other cheese makers along the way."

Abe makes cheese in a 200-gallon Swiss copper vat, which is unusual in the United States. Copper vats are part of traditional cheese making in Europe, and Abe believes that the copper influences the cheese through its superior heat conductivity and other, more subtle ways. It can't be cleaned with harsh chemicals, but Abe likes to keep it shiny, so he gently cleans it with whey.

A special copper vat, biodynamic dairying, and a philosophy of cheese

What has cheese making taught him? "First of all, it can be very humbling," Abe says. "What goes on is so complex, yet so simple. To govern and lead the process takes experience. It's nice just to let the cheese 'happen,' but ultimately you have to impose discipline on it and on yourself to achieve proficiency and consistency. Everything in cheese making has consequences, including your mood and what you are thinking about."

Abe is always tinkering, but right now he's happy with the farm's yogurt and quark, likes the Alpine (a rinded Swiss), and wants to make the Cheddars better, with a closer texture. He suspects the copper may not be right for the Cheddars. The farm also makes Edamer, a German variant of Edam. "Cheese making is a life process, not just a technique," he says. "I've only been doing it for five years; it probably takes at least twenty years to be really good at it. And each 'generation' of cheese will be different."

CHAPTER 6

ITALIAN CHEESE

The cheeses in this chapter include mozzarella, provolone, Parmesan, Romano, and montasio. Most of these cheeses use a thermophilic (heat-loving) starter in their preparation. The basic steps in the production of Italian cheeses are the same as those used to make hard cheese (chapter 5).

For a thorough review of the techniques, see chapter 3.

Mozzarella and provolone are soft, unripened, pulled-curd cheeses. The curds are heated to a very high temperature (170°F), which gives the cheese its stretchy texture. Parmesan, Romano, and montasio are hard cheeses, called *grana* because of their granular textures. They are made with low-fat milk (2% butterfat) and are usually aged for at least 10 months. If you wish, they may be aged longer and used as a grating cheese. Of course, if you can't wait (and I wouldn't blame you), you may try them at 3 months and use them as a slicing cheese. (If you have the patience to wait and save one wheel for 12 months, both you and your lucky friends will be smiling all day when you taste it.)

30-minute mozzarella

Mozzarella was first made by the monks of San Lorenzo di Capua, Italy, from sheep's milk. In the 16th century, when water buffalo were introduced to Naples, the rich milk of those animals started to be used. The following recipe is a quick and easy way to make fresh mozzarella at home in less than 30 minutes! (Make sure the milk you use for this cheese is NOT "ULTRA"-pasteurized. The protein is damaged in the process and will leave you with ricotta rather than mozzarella.)

For a party treat, slice the mozzarella and arrange it alternately with ripe tomato slices. Then drizzle with fresh pesto, scatter with sun-dried tomatoes, and top with a smattering of pine nuts. Serve with crusty bread and wine. Heaven!

1½ level teaspoons citric acid dissolved in ½ cup cool water

1 gallon pasteurized whole milk (see Note in step 1)

⅛–¼ teaspoon lipase powder (see Note in step 1), dissolved in ¼ cup cool water and allowed to sit for 20 minutes, for a stronger flavor (optional)

¼ teaspoon liquid rennet (or ¼ rennet tablet) diluted in ¼ cup cool, unchlorinated water

1 teaspoon cheese salt (optional)

---

1. While stirring add the citric acid solution to the milk at 55°F and mix thoroughly. (If using lipase, add it now.)

Note: You may use skim milk, but the yield will be lower and the cheese will be drier. If you add lipase to this cheese, you may have to use a bit more rennet, as lipase makes the cheese softer. Try the recipe without it first and experiment later.

2. Heat the milk to 90°F, stirring constantly. Remove the pot from the heat and slowly stir in the diluted rennet with an up-and-down motion for about 30 seconds. Cover the pot and leave undisturbed for 5 minutes.

3. Check the curd. It should look like custard, with a clear separation between the curd and the whey. (If the curd is too soft or the whey is too milky, let set for a few more minutes.) Cut the curd with a knife that reaches all the way to the bottom of your pot.

4. Place the pot back on the stove and heat the curds to 105°F, gently moving the curds around with your spoon. (Note: If you will be stretching your curds in water instead of in the microwave, heat the curds to 110°F in this step.) Remove from the heat and continue to stir slowly for 2 to 5 minutes. (Stirring for 5 minutes will result in a firmer cheese.)

USING DRY MILK POWDER

If all your store has is "ULTRA"-pasteurized, a very delicious option is to use dry milk powder and cream. Reconstitute enough non-fat instant milk powder overnight to make 1 gallon of milk. When making mozzarella use 7 pints of this with 1 pint of light cream or half and half. (Because of the ratio the cream may be "ULTRA"-pasteurized.

NO MICROWAVE?

If you don't have a microwave, you may want to put on heavy rubber gloves at this point. Heat the reserved whey to at least 175°F. Add ¼ cup of cheese salt to the whey. Shape the curd into one or more balls, put them in a ladle or strainer, and dip them into the hot whey for several seconds. Knead the curd with spoons between each dip and repeat this process several times until the curd is smooth and pliable.

5. Scoop out the curds with a slotted spoon and put into a 2-quart microwavable bowl. Press the curds gently with your hands, pouring off as much whey as possible. Reserve the whey.

6. Microwave the curds on HIGH for 1 minute (see box at left). Drain off all excess whey. Gently fold the cheese over and over (as in kneading bread) with your hand or a spoon. This distributes the heat evenly throughout the cheese, which will not stretch until it is too hot to touch (145°F inside the curd).

7. Microwave two more times for 35 seconds each; add salt to taste after the second time (optional). After each heating, knead again to distribute the heat.

8. Knead quickly until it is smooth and elastic. When the cheese stretches like taffy, it is done. If the curds break instead of stretch, they are too cool and need to be reheated.

9. When the cheese is smooth and shiny, roll it into small balls and eat while warm. Or place them in a bowl of ice water for ½ hour to bring the inside temperature down rapidly; this will produce a consistent smooth texture throughout the cheese. Although best eaten fresh, if you must wait, cover and store in the refrigerator.

YIELD: ¾–1 pound

TROUBLESHOOTING If the curds turn into the consistency of ricotta cheese and will not come together, change the brand of milk: It may have been heat-treated at the factory to too high a temperature.

mozzarella: the traditional method

Originally, mozzarella was made from buffalo's milk (it is now typically made from cow's milk). This recipe involves a number of techniques unique to this type of cheese. For example, the curds are heated to a very high temperature (170°F) to produce the stretch for which mozzarella is famous. Have a pair of rubber gloves and wooden spoons handy for working the mozzarella curd in hot water (steps 7 and 8). This recipe is more flavorful than the 30-Minute Mozzarella, it can be stored in brine, and it keeps longer — up to several months in the freezer.

2 gallons farm-fresh milk

A pH meter or any other means to test ph

1 packet direct-set thermophilic starter, or 4 ounces prepared thermophilic starter

¼ teaspoon lipase powder, dissolved in ¼ cup cool water and allowed to set for 20 minutes, for stronger flavor (optional)

½ teaspoon liquid rennet (or ½ rennet tablet) diluted in ¼ cup cool, unchlorinated water

2 pounds cheese salt, for brine

1 tablespoon calcium chloride, for brine

1 gallon cold water, for brine

1. Heat the milk to 90°F. The pH should be 6.8. If it isn't, wait and test again. Add the starter; mix well. Add the lipase, if desired. Cover and let ripen for 30 minutes.

2. Add the diluted rennet and gently stir with an up-and-down motion for 1 minute. Top-stir for several additional minutes. Cover and let set at 90°F for 75 minutes, or until the milk has set into a soft curd.

3. Once it has set, it will most likely have the texture of soft to firm yogurt. Very gently cut the curd into ⅜-inch cubes. Let set, undisturbed, for 20 minutes.

4. You will see whey floating on the surface. The pH should be about 6.5, which means that the acidity is increasing. If it isn't, wait a bit longer and test again.

5. Slowly heat the curds to 100°F, raising the temperature no more than two degrees every 5 minutes. Gently stir the curds. As you heat them, they will slowly shrink and become firmer. Once they have reached 100°F, let them set, undisturbed, for 5 minutes.

6. Drain the whey from the curds. (If desired, save the whey for other recipes.) Fill a sink with 102°F water, then place the pot of curds in the water. Let the curds acidify at this temperature for up to 2½ hours. Every

20 minutes, drain off the whey and flip over the curd mass. At the end of 2½ hours, check the acidity of the whey. The pH should be 5.2–5.3. If it isn't, wait a bit longer and test again.

7. Once the curds have reached a pH of 5.2, place them on a draining board or another convenient spot where they can be cut and still drain some whey. To see whether the curds are ready to be worked, cut off a ½-inch slice and cut it into ½-inch cubes. Place the cubes in a stainless-steel bowl and cover them with 170°F water. Using two wooden spoons, work the cubes by pressing them together until they meld into a ball. The surface will become shiny and the cheese will readily stretch like taffy when gently pulled apart.

8. Continue working the sample with wooden spoons, pressing out whey into the hot water, which will become cloudy. When the cheese starts to develop small blisters on the surface, stop working. If it does not give a proper stretch, check the acidity. If there is no stretch or the pH is above 5.2–5.3, place the cheese back into a warm-water bath until the pH is at the proper level, then test again. When the pH reaches the correct level, repeat the process with the remaining curds.

9. Put the cheese into a bowl of cool water to firm. For a salty cheese, combine the 2 pounds of salt, the calcium chloride, and the cold water to make a brine solution. Soak the cheese for 1 hour. Remove it from the brine and pat dry. Reserve the brine for other recipes (see page 53). At this point, the cheese may be eaten fresh. If you prefer a melting cheese for pizza, put it into a resealable bag and store in the refrigerator for up to 1 week.

YIELD: About 2 pounds

provolone

Provolone is a pasta filata *(pulled) type of cheese. According to tradition dating back to Roman times, provolone is ripened and smoked. Today, a more mild variety with a delicate, light taste is widely produced. Provolone, from the Italian for "large oval" or "large sphere," may be molded into a variety of shapes and tied with a cord to leave an impression in the rind.*

1 gallon pasteurized whole or partially skim milk

1 packet direct-set thermophilic starter

¼ teaspoon lipase powder, dissolved in ¼ cup cool water and allowed to set for 20 minutes

¼ teaspoon liquid rennet (or ¼ rennet tablet) diluted in ¼ teaspoon cool, unchlorinated water

2 pounds cheese salt (for brine)

1 gallon cold water

1. Heat the milk to 97°F. Add the starter and mix thoroughly. Cover and allow the milk to ripen for 60 minutes, while maintaining the temperature at 97°F.

2. Add the lipase and stir well. Let set for 10 minutes.

3. Add the diluted rennet, stirring gently with an up-and-down motion for 1 minute. Let set for 20 minutes.

4. Cut the curds into ⅜-inch cubes. Let set for 10 minutes.

5. Heat and stir the curds gently to 144°F, taking 45 minutes and increasing by 2-3°F every 5 minutes. Let set for 15 minutes.

6. Remove curds from the whey, put into a bowl or colander, and let sit for 30 minutes, keeping the heat at least 105°F. (Cover the colander and let it sit in the pot over the warm whey.)

7. Now start your stretch test by taking a small piece of curd and dipping it into 180°F water. If it does not stretch, try again at 15 minute intervals. This process can take up to 90–120 minutes. Once you have a smooth and shiny stretch, you are ready to slice your curd into 1 inch slices and start dipping them into your hot water. Let sit in water until entire mass stretches easily.

8. Working with gloved hands, stretch the curd, forming it into one large ball as you go. Holding this ball in your hands, form it into a bag- or jug-shaped cheese. Making a depression in the top surface with your thumb while pushing the excess curd into the center, shape it by pulling up on the curd mass from the bottom to the top and working it back down into the center hole. (If the curd cools down too much to stretch, dip the ball into the hot water again. As the curd stretches and becomes shiny, begin forming the "jug neck" by squeezing the opening.

9. Once your cheese is completed, place it into a bowl of ice water for 30 minutes. Combine the 2 pounds of salt and the cold water to make a brine solution. Transfer the cheese to the brine and soak for 2 hours.

10. Remove the cheese from the brine and pat dry. Reserve the brine for other recipes (see page 53). Tie each ball with a cord to hang.

11. Hang the cheese for 3 weeks at 50°F. To age the cheese, hang at 40 to 45°F for 2–12 months, depending on the desired sharpness. (It also may be cold-smoked at 40°F after brining and before hanging to age.)

YIELD: About 1 pound

NOTE: Final streching pH is 5.2–5.3.

parmesan

Parmesan is a hard grating cheese that is usually made from low-fat (2% butterfat) cow's milk. The cheese originated in the region around Parma, Italy. It is usually aged for at least 10 months to develop a sharp flavor that is often described as piquant. When using Parmesan, grate only the amount needed. The cheese will lose much of its flavor if it is grated, then stored. For a sharper-flavored Parmesan, use 1 gallon of cow's milk and 1 gallon of goat's milk, or add lipase powder.

2 gallons low-fat milk (2% butterfat)

1 packet direct-set thermophilic starter or 4 ounces prepared thermophilic starter

¼ teaspoon lipase powder, dissolved in ¼ cup cool water and allowed to set for 20 minutes, for stronger flavor (optional)

½ teaspoon liquid rennet (or ½ rennet tablet) diluted in ¼ cup cool, unchlorinated water

2 pounds cheese salt (for brine)

1 gallon water

1 teaspoon olive oil

1. Heat the milk to 90°F. Add the starter and mix well. Add the lipase, if desired. Cover and let ripen for 30 minutes.

2. Make sure the milk's temperature is 90°F. Add the diluted rennet and stir gently with an up-and-down motion for 2 minutes. You may need to top-stir several additional minutes. Cover and let set at 90°F for 30 minutes, or until the curd gives a clean break.

3. Cut the curd into ¼-inch cubes.

4. Heat the curds to 100°F, raising the temperature two degrees every 5 minutes. Stir often.

5. Raise the temperature of the curds three degrees every 5 minutes, until the temperature of the curds reaches 124°F. Stir often. The curds should now be about the size of a grain of rice, and they will squeak when chewed. Allow the curds to set for 5 minutes.

6. Carefully pour off the whey without losing any of the curd particles. Line a 2-pound cheese mold with cheesecloth. Pack the curds into the mold and press lightly at 5 pounds of pressure for 15 minutes.

7. Remove the cheese from the mold and gently peel away the cheesecloth. Turn the cheese, re-dress it, and press at 10 pounds of pressure for 30 minutes.

8. Repeat the process but press at 15 pounds of pressure for 2 hours.

9. Remove the cheese from the mold, line it with a fresh cloth, and put the cheese back into the mold. Press at 20 pounds of pressure for 12 hours.

10. Remove the cheese from the press. Peel away the cheesecloth. In a large, noncorrosive container, combine the salt and water to make a saturated solution. Soak the cheese in the brine for 24 hours at room temperature.

11. Remove the cheese from the brine and pat dry. Reserve the brine for other recipes (see page 53). Age at 55°F and 85 percent relative humidity for at least 10 months. Turn over the cheese daily for the first several weeks, then weekly after that. Remove any mold with a cloth dampened in vinegar or salt water. After the cheese has aged for 2 months, rub the surface with olive oil to keep the rind and cheese from drying out.

YIELD: About 2 pounds

“ *Cheeseparer: A skinflint; a man of small savings; economy carried to excess — like one who pares or shaves off very thinly the rind of his cheese instead of cutting it off.*”

—Brewer's Dictionary of Phrase and Fable, 1898

romano

Romano is one of the most popular Italian hard cheeses. It was first produced near Rome and originally was made with ewe's milk. It is now made with both cow's and goat's milk in regions of southern Italy and in Sardinia. If it is aged for 5 to 8 months, it may be used as a table cheese. Longer aging (usually more than 1 year) produces a piquant grating cheese. For a sharper-flavored Romano, use 1 gallon of low-fat cow's milk (2% butterfat) and 1 gallon of goat's milk, or add lipase powder (see ingredients).

2 gallons low-fat milk (2% butterfat)

6 ounces heavy cream

1 packet direct-set thermophilic starter or 4 ounces prepared thermophilic starter

¼ teaspoon lipase powder, dissolved in ¼ cup cool water and allowed to set for 20 minutes, for stronger flavor (optional)

½ teaspoon liquid rennet (or ½ rennet tablet) diluted in ¼ cup cool, unchlorinated water

2 pounds cheese salt (for brine)

1 gallon water

1–2 tablespoons olive oil

1. Heat the milk to 88°F. Add the cream. Add the starter and mix well. Add the lipase, if desired. Cover and allow the milk to ripen for 10 minutes.

2. Add the diluted rennet, stirring gently with an up-and-down motion for several minutes. Cover and allow to set at 88°F until the curd gives a clean break.

3. Using a curd knife and a stainless-steel whisk, cut the curd into ¼-inch cubes.

4. Heat the curds to 116°F over the course of 45 minutes, raising the temperature two degrees every 5 minutes at first, then gradually increasing to one degree per minute. Maintain the curds at 116°F for 30 minutes, or until they become firm enough that they retain their shape when squeezed.

5. Drain off the whey. (Reserve for other recipes.)

6. Line a 2-pound cheese mold with cheesecloth. Place the curds into the mold. Press at 5 pounds of pressure for 15 minutes.

7. Remove the cheese from the mold and gently peel away the cheesecloth. Turn over the cheese, re-dress it, and press at 10 pounds of pressure for 30 minutes.

8. Repeat the process but press at 20 pounds of pressure for 2 hours.

9. Repeat the process but press at 40 pounds of pressure for 12 hours.

10. Remove the cheese from the mold. Peel away the cheesecloth. In a large, noncorrosive container, combine the salt and water to make a saturated brine solution. Soak the cheese in the brine for 12 hours in the refrigerator.

11. Remove the cheese from the brine and pat dry. (Reserve the brine for other recipes.) Age the cheese at 55°F and 85 percent relative humidity. Turn over the cheese frequently and remove any mold with a cloth dampened in vinegar or salt water.

12. After 2 months, lightly rub the cheese with olive oil to keep the rind and cheese from drying out. Age for 3–10 months longer.

YIELD: About 2 pounds

RECIPE FROM A HOME CHEESE MAKER

caccio cavallo

This cheese is made in southern Italy using naturally ripened raw milk. Heat the milk to 95°F and add the rennet. After the curd has set, break it into pieces. Drain and reserve the whey. Heat the whey to boiling, then pour it over the curd. Let the curd set for 8–14 hours, depending on the air temperature. Cut the curd into pieces and submerge in boiling water, then knead the curds and form the mass into the desired shape. Soak in cold water for 2 hours and in brine for 30 hours. Air-dry the cheese, then smoke it until it attains a fine golden color. Eat it on bread or with pasta.

montasio

Traditionally made in monasteries, montasio is a hard cheese that is used as a table cheese when aged for 3 months and as a grating cheese when aged for 1 year or longer. Usually, the grating cheese is made with skimmed milk. For a sharper flavor, use 1 gallon of low-fat cow's milk and 1 gallon of goat's milk in place of the 2 gallons of whole milk.

2 gallons whole milk

1 packet direct set thermophilic starter or 2½ ounces prepared thermophilic starter

½ packet direct set mesophilic or 1 ounce prepared mesophilic starter

1 teaspoon liquid rennet (or ¼ rennet tablet) diluted in ¼ cup cool, unchlorinated water

2 pounds cheese salt, for brine

1 gallon water, for brine

1. Heat the milk to 88°F. Add both starters and mix well. Cover and allow the milk to ripen for 60 minutes.

2. Make sure the milk's temperature is 88°F. Add the diluted rennet and stir gently with an up-and-down motion for several minutes. Cover and allow the curds to set at 88°F for 30 minutes, or until the curd gives a clean break.

3. Cut the curds into ¼-inch cubes using a curd knife and a stainless-steel whisk.

4. Heat the curds to 102°F, raising the temperature two degrees every 5 minutes and stirring often to keep the curds from matting. Maintain the temperature at 102°F for 60 minutes and continue to stir.

5. Drain off the whey to the level of the curds. Add hot water until the curd-whey mixture reaches 110°F. Maintain that temperature for 10 minutes. Stir the curds to keep them from matting. Drain off the whey.

6. Line a 2-pound cheese mold with cheesecloth. Quickly place the curds into the mold. Press at 5 pounds of pressure for 15 minutes.

7. Remove the cheese from the mold and peel away the cheesecloth. Turn over the cheese, re-dress it, and press at 5 pounds of pressure for 30 minutes.

8. Repeat the process but press at 10 pounds of pressure for 12 hours.

9. In a large, noncorrosive container, combine the salt and water to make a saturated brine solution. Soak the cheese in the brine for 6 hours at room temperature. Remove the cheese from the brine and pat dry. Reserve the brine for other recipes (see page 53).

10. Age the cheese at 55 to 60°F for 2 months. The relative humidity should be close to 85 percent.

YIELD: About 2 pounds

guido's cheese

With a bit of honey on top, this cheese is perfect as an after-dinner treat. It goes well with a nice glass of Chianti.

2 gallons farm-fresh milk

1 packet direct-set thermophilic starter, or 2½ ounces prepared thermophilic starter

1 tablet vegetable rennet, dissolved in ½ cup cool water

1 pound cheese salt (for brine), plus more for seasoning

1 gallon water

1. In a double boiler, heat the milk to 90°F. Turn off the heat and add the starter. Stir thoroughly and let set for 25–30 minutes.

2. Add the rennet, stir, and let set for about 15 minutes.

3. Make cuts with a long knife in the solidifying milk. The curd is ready when it shows a clean cut, like pudding. Cut the curd into small pieces.

4. Stirring frequently, slowly heat the curds to 120°F over a period of 30–40 minutes.

5. Line a mold with cheesecloth and ladle in the curds. Press the cheese with your hands. Put the mold with the cheese into a bowl to collect the draining whey. Put a weight of about 2–3 pounds on the cheese. Turn over the cheese and rewrap it in the cheesecloth; this ensures a good shape. Turn the cheese frequently at first, then every few hours, keeping the cheese at 90°–95°F for 4–6 hours total. Remember to rewrap the cheese each time.

6. Let it set for 24 hours with a 2-pound weight on top.

7. Combine 1 pound of the salt and the water to make a brine solution. Remove the cheese from the mold, remove the cheesecloth, and put the cheese into the brine. Let set for 24 hours.

8. Remove the cheese from the brine and pat it dry with paper towels. (Reserve the brine for future uses.) Sprinkle with additional salt to taste.

9. Line a dish with paper towels, put the cheese into the dish, and age in a dry, cool place for at least 3 weeks.

10. For the first week, turn it 2 or 3 times a day. After the first week, turn it once a day.

Guido Giuntini, Home Cheese Maker
Collingdale, Pennsylvania

When Guido and his American wife, Margot, moved from Italy to Pennsylvania in 1999, he discovered to his dismay that it was hard to find good Italian cheese that tasted the way it did at home in Florence. He decided to make his own, found New England Cheesemaking Supply on the Internet, and ordered rennet and a recipe for Parmesan. He was hooked.

To make Christmas presents for December 2001, Guido and Margot drove two hours to Amish country to buy 24 gallons of milk still warm from the cows. Every night for a week, they made cheese in their kitchen and aged it in the cellar. "We used a recipe that's a blend of different hard cheeses," Guido says. Family and friends loved the cheese.

When he can, Guido obtains raw milk, which he believes tastes better and works better for cheese. "We pasteurize it so we won't die," he says cheerfully, "and we also age the cheese a bit. If we die, at least we die with good cheese." While the cheese is aging, Guido turns it frequently, two or three times a day for the first week, once a day thereafter. He also loves to smell his cheese, an aroma he regards as "one of the best smells on earth." In fact, he adds, "When a deodorant is made with a cheese smell, I will buy it."

Guido and Margot's favorite way to eat their cheese is also a traditional way that cheese (usually sheep's-milk cheese) is enjoyed in Italy. After a meal, they drizzle slices of their cheese with honey and enjoy the contrasting sweet and sour tastes along with a glass of Chianti. Guido admits that the combination of cheese and Chianti always makes him homesick. His dream is to live in the country and make cheese for a living. In the meantime, he teaches Italian in an inner-city high school by day and makes his beloved Italian cheese by night. See page 146 for Guido's cheese recipe.

> *Making cheese that reminds him of his native Tuscany*

CHAPTER 7

WHEY CHEESE

*"Little Miss Muffet
Sat on a tuffet,
Eating some curds and whey."*

When you make cheese, there is usually a large amount of whey left over. The whey is separated by cooking and draining the curds. It contains milk sugar (up to 5 percent), albuminous protein, and minerals. Although the temperatures used in hard-cheese making are not high enough to separate

out the albuminous proteins, the higher temperatures necessary to make whey cheeses allow that process to take place.

Whey may also be used in cooking; in this case, it can be refrigerated for up to 1 week. It is particularly delicious as a liquid substitute in bread making. It can also be used as a soup stock, and it makes a refreshing summer drink when served with ice and crushed mint leaves. I have heard that if you feed it to pigs, you can reduce your grain bill by one third.

A number of cheeses can be made with the clear, fresh whey left over from hard-cheese making (when making cheese with whey, it must not be more than 3 hours old). As with regular-cheese making, the freshest whey will produce the sweetest cheese. Also note that whey may be warmed over a direct heat source.

The techniques used in this chapter are fairly straightforward, so I will not recap them; see chapter 3 to review them, as needed.

ziergerkase

This cheese originated in Germany. It may be eaten fresh or aged for several weeks.

2 gallons fresh whey, no more than 3 hours old

1 quart whole milk, for increased yield (optional)

¼ cup vinegar (I like apple cider)

1 quart water

1 quart red wine

¼ cup cheese salt

Herbs (optional)

1. Pour the whey into a large pot. Add the milk, if desired. Heat the mixture to 200°F.

2. Slowly add the vinegar. Turn off the heat.

3. Allow the mixture to set for 10 minutes. You will see white flakes of protein floating in it.

4. Carefully pour the mixture into a colander lined with butter muslin and allow it to drain.

5. When the muslin is cool enough to handle, tie the corners into a knot and hang the bag over the sink to drain for several hours, or until the curds stop dripping whey. Allow the curds to cool.

6. Line a 1-pound cheese mold with butter muslin. Add the curds and press at 20 pounds of pressure for 24 hours.

7. Remove the cheese from the press and gently peel away the cheesecloth.

8. In a large bowl, combine the water, wine, and salt; add the herbs, if desired. Add the cheese and cover. Place the bowl in the refrigerator for 4 days and turn the cheese twice a day.

9. Remove the cheese from the soaking liquid. Drain on paper towels and cover with cheese wrap. The cheese may be eaten fresh or aged for several weeks in the refrigerator before serving. It will keep for 3–4 weeks.

YIELD: About 1 pound

mysost

Made from the whey of cow's milk, mysost originated in Scandinavia. It has a unique sweet-sour flavor and is often sliced and served on hot toast for breakfast. The color ranges from light to dark brown, depending on the degree of sugar caramelization and whether cream has been added. For a more spreadable consistency, shorten the boiling time. If you would like a cheese that can be sliced, heat the mixture to a thicker consistency before pouring it into the molds. As a variation, add crushed walnuts to the thickened whey just before it is cooled. Using a wood cookstove is an economical way to make this cheese, because many hours of boiling are involved.

Fresh whey, no more than 3 hours old, from making cheese with 2 gallons of cow's milk

1–2 cups heavy cream (optional)

1. Pour the whey into a pot and bring to a boil. Watch the pot carefully. As soon as the whey begins to boil, foam will appear on the surface. Skim off the foam with a slotted spoon and place it in a bowl. Reserve in the refrigerator. (If you don't remove the foam, the whey will boil over.)

2. Let the whey boil slowly, uncovered, over low heat. When it boils down to 75 percent of its original volume (this can take 6–12 hours), start stirring often to prevent sticking. Add the reserved foam. At this point, the whey will begin to thicken.

3. Add the cream, if desired. The amount you add will determine the final texture of the cheese.

4. Once thickening is taking place, remove the mixture from the pot and put it into a blender. Use caution! Because the whey is very hot, you must hold the cover with a potholder while blending or the cover will pop off and scald you. Blend the mixture at medium speed for 1 minute, until the consistency is smooth and creamy. This step prevents your cheese from becoming gritty.

5. Pour the mixture back into the pot and cook over low heat, stirring constantly. The mixture will continue to thicken.

6. When the mixture approaches a fudgelike consistency, place the pot in a sink full of cold water and stir continuously until it is cool enough to be poured into molds (traditionally rectangular). If the whey is not stirred, the cheese may become grainy.

7. Once cool, remove the cheese from the molds, cover, and store in the refrigerator. This cheese will keep for 4 weeks in the refrigerator and may be frozen for up to 6 months.

YIELD: 1½ pounds

GJETOST

This cheese is made with the whey from goat's milk. Goat's cream may be added to the whey for a smoother consistency. Follow the directions for making mysost (see page 150), then add goat's cream in step 3. The cheese is tan and has a unique sweet-sour flavor.

Yield: 1½ pounds

whey ricotta

Originally from Italy, ricotta is a delicious, soft, fresh curd cheese used extensively in Italian cooking. It is made from ewe's-milk whey, but this recipe is a variation for those of us who don't have a milking sheep in our backyard. You must use fresh whey. This recipe has a low yield.

2 gallons fresh whey, no more than 3 hours old

1 quart whole milk, for increased yield (optional)

¼ cup cider vinegar

4 ounces prepared mesophilic starter, to improve flavor (optional)

½ teaspoon cheese salt (optional)

Herbs (optional)

2 tablespoons light or heavy cream (optional)

1. Pour the whey into a large pot. Add the milk, if desired. Heat the mixture to 200°F.

2. While stirring, turn off the heat and add the vinegar. You will notice tiny white particles of precipitated albuminous protein.

3. Carefully ladle the curds into a colander lined with butter muslin. Allow it to drain. If desired, fold in the mesophilic starter. When the muslin is cool enough to handle, tie the corners into a knot and hang the bag over the sink to drain for several hours.

4. When the cheese stops draining, untie the muslin and place the cheese in a bowl. Add the salt and the herbs, if desired. For a richer, moister cheese, add a small amount of cream.

5. Cover the bowl and refrigerate for up to 1 week.

YIELD: 1–2 cups

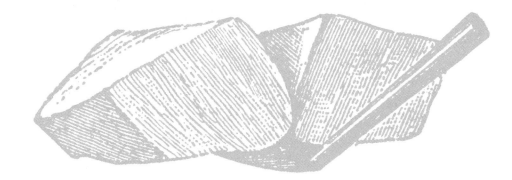

ricotta from heaven

The sweet aroma and the delicious, delicate flavor truly make this a heavenly treat.

Fresh whey, no more than 3 hours old, left over from making hard cheese

1. Heat the whey in a pot until foam appears. This usually happens just prior to boiling; if the mixture boils, it will taste burned.

2. Turn off the heat; let the whey set for 5 minutes.

3. Gently skim off the foam and place the whey in a colander lined with butter muslin.

4. Let drain for 15 minutes, then refrigerate. This ricotta will keep for up to 1 week in the refrigerator, but I doubt you will have any left by then!

YIELD: About ½ pound per gallon of whey

RECIPE FROM A HOME CHEESE MAKER

a tang to the whey

Ten months ago we bought a Guernsey cow. Since that time, we have really enjoyed the fresh milk and the pretty good Gouda cheese my wife produces. I didn't like to see all that whey going to the dogs, chickens, cats, and turkeys, and then found that when you add Kool-Aid, Tang, or other powdered fruit drink mix, the result is a very refreshing beverage. The kids really like it, and we now have a gallon jar in the refrigerator at all times. With the proteins and minerals left in the whey, nutritionally it sure beats soda beverages.

CHAPTER 8

BACTERIA- AND MOLD-RIPENED CHEESE

Bacteria- and mold-ripened cheeses owe much of their flavor and texture to specific bacteria and molds that are added to the milk and/or applied to the surface of the cheese. White molds and red bacteria grow on the surface of cheeses, and blue molds can grow both on the surface and throughout the cheese. Bacteria-ripened cheese, such as Limburger, originated in Belgium and Germany; mold-ripened cheese, including Camembert and blue cheese, were first produced in France.

In places where bacteria- and mold-ripened cheeses have been produced for hundreds of years, the specific bacteria and molds are in the air and on the shelves of the caves and rooms in which the cheeses are aged, automatically inoculating the freshly made cheeses. In those cases, new bacteria and molds must be added only periodically to the milk or the cheese. However, this will not be true for beginning cheese makers, who will need to purchase bacteria and molds from cheese-making supply houses.

If you are making only one variety of cheese within this group, you don't have to worry about cross contamination. I recommend aging each type of bacteria- and mold-ripened cheese in a separate storage area and away from any nonbacterial- and mold-ripened cheeses, because these microorganisms can rapidly spread in your kitchen to other aging cheeses.

The following pages provide an overview of the basic steps involved in the production of bacteria- and mold-ripened cheeses; for a more thorough review, see chapter 3.

Ripening

For most soft mold-ripened cheeses, a fairly large amount of starter is added, and the ripening time can be rather lengthy, as a significant increase in acidity is required.

Renneting

A comparatively small amount of rennet is used to set most mold-ripened cheeses. It may take 1 hour or more for the milk to coagulate, and the curd is slightly softer than that produced in hard cheeses.

Cutting the Curd

The curd is usually cut into ½-inch cubes, or sometimes into thin slices, and gently ladled into a cheese mold.

Cooking

The cooking temperature is quite low, usually around 90°F. Some recipes omit this step.

Molding and Draining

The curds are placed into cheese molds, most of which have traditional shapes and sizes. Many cheeses are placed into molds that are sandwiched between two boards and two mats. (See the illustration of a mold sandwich on page 52.) In a mold sandwich, the mold is placed on a cheese mat, which rests on a cheese board that is situated in a sink or pan to facilitate drainage. The mold is filled to the top with curd. Drainage begins immediately. A second cheese mat is placed on top of the mold and a wooden cheese board is placed on the mat. Because these are unpressed cheeses, the curd sinks under its own weight. After a period of draining, the cheese is flipped over. The cheese mat that is now on the top is gently peeled off the cheese to allow the cheese to fall to the bottom of the mold. The turning process continues as the cheese drains for 24 to 36 hours.

Salting

Once the cheese has sufficiently drained and assumed the shape of the mold, it is removed from the mold and salted on all surfaces. The salt helps retard the growth of unwanted organisms but does not interfere with the desired mold growth. Salting also draws out some of the moisture and is helpful in preserving the cheese.

Applying Bacteria and Molds

Carefully following a recipe's recommendations for proper aging, temperature, and humidity is of the utmost importance: Optimal growth of desirable bacteria and molds is dependent on very specific conditions.

Penicillium candidum (White Mold)

This mold is used to age Camembert, Brie, and related cheeses. It may be added directly to the milk (enhancing early growth) or sprayed onto the surface of the cheese.

Geotrichum candidum (White Mold)

This is added to cheese in the same way as *P. candidum.*

Penicillium roqueforti (Blue Mold)

This mold, which is cultivated on rye bread, is used for making blue cheeses. The liquid is added to the milk before renneting and grows throughout the cheese. Another technique is to pierce a cheese with a needle to create air holes. The mold, which requires oxygen, can then penetrate the surface and continue growing within the interior.

Brevibacterium linens (Red Bacteria)

This reddish brown bacterium is sprayed onto cheese, then smeared on the surface by hand.

Spraying mold onto the surface of cheese.

Aging

Bacteria- and mold-ripened cheeses need to be aged in a rather cool, moist setting in order to allow the bacterium or mold to grow. The temperature is usually 45°F and the relative humidity is 85 to 95 percent. Creating this environment in the home is a challenge. A secondhand refrigerator may be useful. A camping or dorm-size refrigerator is great because it's small, and the more cheese, the more humidity. Place a tray of water on the bottom of the refrigerator for moisture and keep the setting at 45°F. Age the cheeses on mats, so that air can circulate freely underneath them.

If an extra refrigerator will not fit into your budget, you may try to age these cheeses in your regular refrigerator. (The drawback to using the household refrigerator is that at such low temperatures, bacteria and mold will not have the ideal conditions for reproducing and it may be far too cold for mold to develop properly.) If you do attempt this method, place the cheese on a cheese mat and put it in a closed container in which you have placed a bowl of water for moisture.

White mold–ripened cheese develops a furry, thick white coat within 14 days. Then the cheese is wrapped in cheese wrap and aged 6 weeks longer. Blue mold–ripened cheese develops mold within 10 days. At that time, the cheese must be pierced with holes so that oxygen will reach the interior and aid mold growth (see illustration on page 45). In red bacteria–ripened cheese, bacteria will appear in 2 weeks and look like a reddish brown smear on the surface of the cheese.

Note: Be careful when making bacteria- and mold-ripened cheeses. Bacteria and mold will cross contaminate other cheeses in close proximity.

CHEESE CAVES

No one knows for sure how someone figured out that molds and other organisms could improve the flavor of cheese. We'll just give credit to serendipity. Those who make Roquefort cheese tell the story of a young shepherd who left his lunch in a cave near the village of Roquefort; when he returned 2 weeks later, the bread had crumbled away and his cheese had veins of green growing through it. The hungry boy nibbled on the cheese and *voilà!* He shared his discovery with the villagers, and a new cheese was born.

You can still visit the Roquefort caves in France, where wheels and wheels of cheese are aged on racks in arched caverns, as well as cheese caves in England (where cheese has been ripened in the caves around Cheddar since the 12th century), Italy, Spain, Canada, the United States, and other countries. In Sogliano al Rubicone, Italy, the opening of the Fossa caves on St. Catherine's Day in late November is the occasion of an annual festival and a tasting party for the cheeses aged in the caves since August.

Because not all cheese-making areas are blessed with the proper geological upbringing that creates caves, cheese makers have learned to build their own that mimic the steady temperatures and high humidity of natural caves. Natural stone, cast concrete, large cement culverts, and even straw bales have been used to build caves. If you tour cheese caves, you can see cheeses in various stages of finishing. And if you're lucky, you may be offered a taste.

---

white mold–ripened cheese

The cheeses that use white molds are soft white cheeses, and their curds are typically not cooked or pressed. Instead, they are salted and usually sprayed with mold spores, though mold may also be added to the milk to produce a rich white "bloom" on the surface of the cheese. Today, these cheeses are sought after as delicacies and savored throughout the world.

camembert

Camembert cheese originated in the French village of the same name. It was discovered in 1791 by Marie Fontaine and became one of the most prized cheeses in the world. Penicillium candidum grows on the surface during curing. The mold develops the sharp taste of the cheese and aids in creating its runny consistency. The cheese is difficult to make because of the exacting conditions required during curing. It must be stored at 45°F with a relative humidity of 85 to 95 percent.

One-half gallon of milk will make enough curd to fill a standard Camembert mold. Once the cheese has been opened, it stops aging; therefore, make several at a time so you can periodically test for ripeness. This recipe makes approximately four cheeses.

2 gallons whole milk

½ teaspoon direct-set Flora Danica* starter or 4 ounces prepared Flora Danica starter

Penicillium candidum white mold, rehydrated according to package directions 10–15 hours before using

¼ teaspoon liquid rennet diluted in ¼ cup cool, unchlorinated water

Cheese salt, for sprinkling

*Note: Flora Danica may be used as either a direct-set or a reculturable starter (see page 20)

1. Heat the milk to 90°F. Add the starter, stirring to combine. Cover and let the milk ripen for 90 minutes. If adding mold directly to the milk, do so now, following package directions, and mix well.

2. Add the diluted rennet and gently stir with an up-and-down motion for several minutes. Cover and let the milk set at 90°F for 60 minutes, or until the curd gives a clean break.

3. Cut the curd into ½-inch cubes. Gently stir the curds for 15 minutes.

4. Let the curds set for 15 minutes at 90°F. Meanwhile, sterilize in boiling water four Camembert molds, eight reed cheese mats, and eight cheese boards (6" x 6"). Place everything in a convenient spot to drain.

5. Place a mat on a cheese board and a mold on the mat (the start of a mold sandwich).

6. Pour off the whey to the level of the curds. Ladle the curds gently into the mold until full. Place a reed mat on top of the mold and a cheese board on top of the mat (the finished mold sandwich). Repeat this process with the remaining molds.

7. Let drain for 1 hour. Very carefully lift a mold and its cheese boards and quickly flip it over. Make sure the cheese is not sticking to the top mat by gently peeling the mat from the top of the mold. You do not want to tear the surface of the cheese, which will happen if you briskly lift the mat. Turn at hourly intervals for 5 hours, or until the cheeses are about 1–1½ inches high and have shrunk away from the sides of the molds.

8. When they have sufficiently drained, remove from the molds and sprinkle salt over the entire surface of each. Let set for 10 minutes so the salt can dissolve.

9. If spraying on the mold, lightly spray all surfaces using an atomizer. Cheeses should not appear wet.

10. Place the cheeses on plastic or reed cheese mats and age at 45°F and 95 percent relative humidity. After 2 days, you may want to spray the cheeses lightly once more with mold. Let them age 3 days longer, until the first whiskers of mold appear on the surface. When white mold appears, turn them over and let age for 7–9 days. After 10–14 days of aging, a profuse white mold will have developed. Wrap the cheeses in cheese wrap and store at 45°F for 4–6 weeks. The cheeses are ready to eat when there is a runny consistency throughout when brought to room temperature.

YIELD: More than 2 pounds

TROUBLESHOOTING If blue mold develops on the cheese, your curing room is too humid or you are allowing too much moisture to remain in the cheese during its production. Reduce the humidity in the curing room and thoroughly clean and disinfect all shelves to eliminate blue mold. If you see a black furry mold starting to develop, dab it carefully with salt to remove it and prevent it from spreading. That mold is called *poil de chat* (cat's hair) and you do not want it on your cheese!

petit brie

Known to some as the queen of cheeses, Brie is truly one of the most delicious and highly regarded cheeses in the world. It is also one of the most troublesome to make. The ripening of Brie is a very delicate matter and must be done under optimum conditions. Due to its low acidity and high moisture content, it is very susceptible to problems in handling, curing, and salting. The shape is a flat disk measuring 5½ inches wide by 1½ inches high. (We use our Camembert mold.) The better Bries have a reddish brown mottling caused by Brevibacterium linens (red bacteria) and a pale yellow interior that when truly ripe is almost like custard. (Traditionally, red bacteria are present in the aging room; however, if you are making this at home for the first time, you may add a small amount of the bacterium to the milk during cheese making.) The following recipe is one that has been adapted for home use. Your patience with this process will be greatly rewarded.

2 quarts whole milk (3.25–3.50% butterfat)

⅛ teaspoon Flora Danica* starter or 1 ounce prepared Flora Danica starter

White mold, rehydrated according to package directions 10–15 hours before using

8 drops liquid rennet diluted in ¼ cup cool, unchlorinated water

Cheese salt, for sprinkling

*Note: Flora Danica may be used as either a direct-set or a reculturable starter (see page 20)

1. Heat the milk to 86°F (84°F, if using goat's milk). Add the starter and stir well. Cover and allow the milk to ripen for 15 minutes. If adding mold directly to the milk, do so now, following package directions, and stir well.

2. Add the diluted rennet and stir gently with an up-and-down motion for 1 minute. Cover and leave undisturbed at 84 to 86°F for about 3 hours. It will coagulate slowly. (As with all recipes that use small amounts of rennet, the quantity may need to be adjusted if the cheese is too hard or the curds fail to set properly.)

3. Cut the curd into ½-inch cubes.

4. Sterilize in boiling water one mold, two cheese mats, and two cheese boards (6" x 6"). Place everything in a convenient spot to drain.

5. Place a mat on a cheese board and a mold on the mat (the start of a mold sandwich).

6. Carefully pour off the whey. Gently ladle the curds into the mold. Place a mat on top of the mold and a cheese board on top of the mat (the finished mold sandwich). Repeat the entire process with the remaining molds.

7. Drain overnight at a room temperature of 68 to 70°F. When the curds have settled to half their original volume, very carefully lift a mold and its cheese boards with both hands and quickly flip over the cheese. If the curd is stuck to the mat, gently peel it back and the cheese will drop down in the mold. You do not want to tear the surface of the cheese, which will happen if you briskly lift the mat.

8. When the cheese is firm enough to retain its shape (usually after setting 1 day longer), gently rub salt on the top and sides of the cheese. After a few hours, turn and gently rub salt on the bottom.

9. If spraying on the mold, lighly spray all surfaces using an atomizer. Allow the cheese to dry at 55 to 57°F for about 1 week. When white mold appears, let the cheese age at 50°F and 85 percent humidity for 3–5 months.

YIELD: 12 ounces

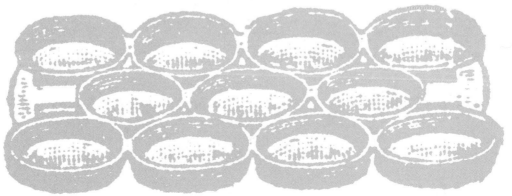

coulommiers

A soft, white mold–ripened cheese, Coulommiers is in the same family as Camembert. It has a long tradition in both England and France. The English version is consumed fresh, is soft and spreadable, and is not mold-ripened. The French recipe is for a soft, runny cheese like Camembert.

The customary mold for Coulommiers is a two-piece affair consisting of two stainless-steel hoops, one of which fits inside the other. *Coulommiers* is French for "columns," and that is what the mold looks like. The assembled hoops are 6 inches in height and 4¾ inches in diameter. They are filled with curd, and once it sinks below the level of the top hoop, that hoop is removed and the cheese is flipped over. If the cheese mold were not in two sections, the draining cheese would splatter when turned over in the tall mold. One Coulommiers mold is enough to make cheese from ½ gallon of whole milk. As an alternative, you may use a Camembert mold.

english-style coulommiers

½ gallon whole milk

¼ teaspoon direct-set Flora Danica* starter or 1 ounce prepared Flora Danica starter

3 drops liquid rennet diluted in 2 tablespoons cool, unchlorinated water

Cheese salt, for sprinkling

Note: Flora Danica may be used as either a direct-set or a reculturable starter (see page 20)

1. Heat the milk to 90°F. Add the starter, stirring well. Cover and allow the milk to ripen for 20 minutes.

2. Add the diluted rennet and gently stir with an up-and-down motion for several minutes. Cover and let set at 90°F for 45 minutes.

3. Sterilize in boiling water one mold, two cheese mats, and two cheese boards. Place a cheese mat on a board and place the mold on the mat. Set it in an area where the whey can drain freely.

4. Using a stainless-steel ladle, skim thin layers of curd from the pot and gently lower them into the mold, using one hand to steady the mold. Continue to ladle thin slices of curd into the mold until it is filled. Be careful not to tip the mold or all the curd will rush out the bottom. The thinner you slice the curd, the faster the cheese will drain. Place the second cheese mat on top of the filled mold and place a cheese board on top of the mat. Let the cheese set at 72°F for 6–9 hours.

5. When the curd has sunk below the level of the top hoop, remove the hoop and place the cheese mat and board on top of the remaining hoop. If you are using a Camembert mold, do this when the curds have sunk halfway down into the mold. Very carefully lift the mold and cheese boards with both hands and quickly flip over the cheese. Set down the mold and gently remove the top mat, making sure not to tear the cheese, which may be sticking to it. Clean the cheese mat and replace it on top of the hoop. Replace the board.

6. Allow the cheese to drain for up to 2 days, flipping over the mold several times a day. The cheese is done when it stands 1–1½ inches in height and has pulled away from the sides of the mold.

7. Salt the cheese lightly on all surfaces. Eat right away or wrap in cheese wrap and age for 1–2 weeks.

YIELD: 12 ounces

herbed english-style coulommiers

This is a delicious variation of English-Style Coulommiers. For a tasty combination, try a clove of finely diced garlic, a few sprigs of chopped chives, a pinch of freshly ground black pepper, and a dash of paprika.

Ingredients for English-Style Coulommiers (see page 162)

Herbs

1. Follow steps 1 through 5 for English-Style Coulommiers (page 162).

2. As you ladle the curd slices into the mold, sprinkle the herbs between them.

3. Continue steps 6 through 8 for English-Style Coulommiers.

YIELD: 12 ounces

french-style coulommiers

Ingredients for English-Style Coulommiers (see page 162)

White mold, rehydrated according to package directions 10–15 hours before using

1. Follow steps 1 through 7 for English-style Coulommiers (page 162).

2. Remove the cheese from the mold and lightly salt it. Spray lightly with white-mold powder using an atomizer.

3. Age the cheese for 5 days at 45°F and a relative humidity of 85–95 percent. After 5 days, small whiskers of white mold will appear on the surface of the cheese.

4. Turn over the cheese and age it 9 days longer. At that time, the cheese will be covered with a thick growth of white mold.

5. Wrap it in cheese wrap and age it for 4–6 weeks at 45°F. (If you see a black furry mold starting to develop, dab it carefully with salt to remove it and prevent it from spreading. This mold is called *poil de chat* [cat's hair], and you do not want it near your cheese!)

YIELD: 12 ounces

Alyce Birchenough, Sweet Home Farm
Elberta, Alabama

Alyce Birchenough and her husband, Doug Wolbert, moved from chilly Michigan to balmy 'bama in 1984 to start a home-based business. They studied soil maps, talked to local farmers, and bought a parcel of flat land dotted with pine and pecan trees about 10 miles from the Gulf Coast. Their land is on a good section of clay loam, perfect for grazing their small herd of Guernsey cows and growing winter cover crops of rye, clover, and barley. (*Winter* is a relative term at Sweet Home Farm, where an average year has 300 frost-free days and 75 to 100 inches of rain.)

Sweet Home Farm was licensed as a Grade A dairy in 1987, and Alyce and Doug became the first licensed farmstead cheese makers in the state. Their cheese is made solely from the milk of their own cows, which eat only lush, homegrown grass and hay plus regionally grown grain. Sweet Home uses no herbicides, pesticides, or growth hormones on the farm, and no preservatives or coloring in the cheese. The cheeses (all made from raw milk and aged for at least 60 days) are sold in a shop on the farm.

A mom-and-pop cheese operation in the sunny South

Alyce and Doug make cheese twice a week, usually about 150 gallons at a time. The original (and still most popular) variety, Elberta, is a semisoft, buttermilky cheese. They've added more than a dozen other varieties, including 'Bama Jack, Gouda, feta, a baby Swiss, and several Italian types of which Alyce is particularly proud, such as Montabella (firm, sharp, and aged five months or longer) and Pepato Asiago (seasoned with whole peppercorns and aged at least six months). Sweet Home Farm's blue cheese (available plain or with garlic flavor) gets rave reviews for its taste and texture. The couple also burns herbs and uses the ash to flavor their Terra Strata. Alyce advises novice cheese makers to "start small. See if you enjoy it, and figure out what you like to eat, because you'll be making a lot of it!"

blue mold–ripened cheese

Blue cheeses have been made since the time of the Romans. The term *Roquefort* first appeared in 1070 and referred to a blue-veined cheese made from ewe's milk. Blue cheeses are usually not pressed; they take their shape as the curds sink under their own weight in the mold. Salt is used for curing and to inhibit undesirable molds.

Blue cheeses are not for beginners. In many ways, a good homemade blue cheese is like a child: easy and fun to produce but difficult to bring to proper maturity. They must be aged in very damp, cool places for several months. If the proper environment is not maintained, they can dry out and develop undesirable surface molds. The three recipes that follow — blue, Stilton, and Gorgonzola — are presented in order of difficulty.

blue cheese

This is made with whole milk. Cow's milk makes a light yellow cheese; goat's milk, a white one. The flavor comes from the mold growing on the surface and inside the cheese.

2 gallons whole milk

⅛ teaspoon *Penicillium roqueforti* (blue mold)

1 packet direct-set mesophilic starter or 4 ounces prepared mesophilic starter

1 teaspoon liquid rennet (or ¼ rennet tablet) diluted in ¼ cup cool, unchlorinated water

2 tablespoons cheese salt, plus a pinch for sprinkling

1. If using cow's milk, heat it to 90°F (86°F for goat's milk). Add the mold, then starter; mix well. Cover and let ripen at 90°F (86°F for goat's milk) for 60 minutes.

2. Add the diluted rennet; gently stir with an up-and-down motion for 1 minute. Cover and let the milk set at 90°F (86°F for goat's milk) for 45 minutes, or until the curd gives a clean break.

3. Cut the curd into ½-inch cubes. Let set for 5 minutes. (If using goat's milk, let set for 10 minutes.)

4. Gently stir the curds every 5 minutes to keep them from matting. Do this for 60 minutes.

5. Let the curds set, undisturbed, for 5 minutes.

6. Pour off the whey. Put the curds in a colander and let drain for 5 minutes. Put the curds back into the pot and gently mix them by hand so they are not matted.

7. Add 2 tablespoons of the salt and mix well. Let set for 5 minutes. Meanwhile, sterilize in boiling water a 2-pound cheese mold, two cheese mats, and two cheese boards (6" x 6"). Let everything drain.

8. Place a mat on a cheese board and the mold on the mat. Fill the mold with curds. Cover with a cheese mat and a cheese board. Turn over the mold every 15 minutes for the first 2 hours, then once an hour for the next 2 hours. Let drain overnight.

9. Remove the cheese from the mold; sprinkle with the remaining salt on all surfaces. Shake off excess salt. Let set at 60°F and 85 percent humidity. (Many basements meet those requirements.) Set the cheese on a cheese mat or board. Turn it over each day for 3 days, salting it and shaking off the excess each time.

10. Using a sterilized ice pick or $\frac{1}{16}$-inch-diameter knitting needle, poke 40 holes from top to bottom. Age at 50°F and 95 percent humidity. (An extra refrigerator with a pan of water on the bottom works well.) It's best to store the cheese on its side in a wooden cradle. Every 4 days, give it a quarter turn on its side to keep it from becoming misshapen. Mold appears within 10 days.

11. After 30 days, the surface of the cheese will be covered with blue mold and a reddish brown smear. Gently scrape them off with a long-bladed knife.

12. Scrape off the mold and smear every 20–30 days.

13. After 90 days, scrape the cheese and wrap in foil. Lower the refrigerator's temperature to between 34 and 38°F and age 60 days longer, turning the cheese weekly. For a milder cheese, sample after 3 months. Ideally, it's ready to eat after 6 months.

YIELD: 2 pounds

stilton-style cheese

This English cheese was first mentioned in the early part of the 18th century. It is made from milk enriched with cream and combines the subtle flavor of Cheddar with the sharp taste of blue cheese.

2 gallons whole milk

2 cups light cream or half-and-half

⅛ teaspoon *Penicillium roqueforti* (blue mold)

1 packet direct-set mesophilic starter or 2 ounces mesophilic starter

¼ teaspoon liquid rennet diluted in ¼ cup cool, unchlorinated water

2 tablespoons cheese salt

1. In a large pot, thoroughly combine the milk and cream. Heat the mixture to 86°F. Add the mold. Add the starter and mix well. Cover and allow the mixture to ripen for 30 minutes.

2. Add the diluted rennet and stir gently with an up-and-down motion for 1 minute. Top-stir for several more minutes. Cover and let set at 86°F for 90 minutes.

3. Using a slotted spoon, transfer the curds into a cheesecloth-lined colander resting in a bowl. When the curds are in the colander, they should be surrounded by whey in the bowl. Let the curds set in the whey for 90 minutes.

4. Tie the corners of the cheesecloth into a knot and hang the bag to drain for 30 minutes.

5. When the bag has stopped dripping, place it on a cheese board where it can drain. Place a board on top of the bag and place 8 pounds of weight on the board. Press the cheese overnight in a kitchen that has a temperature of 68 to 70°F.

6. Remove the curds from the bag. Break into 1-inch pieces and put them in a bowl.

7. Add the salt and mix thoroughly but gently.

8. Sterilize in boiling water a 2-pound cheese mold, two cheese mats, and two cheese boards. Put everything in a convenient spot to drain.

9. Place a mat on a cheese board and the mold on the mat (the start of a mold sandwich). Ladle the curds gently into the mold. Place a mat on top of the mold and a cheese board on top of the mat (the finished mold sandwich).

10. Carefully flip over the mold every 15 minutes for 2 hours. Keep the kitchen at 70°F and let set overnight.

11. Flip the cheese several times a day for the next 4 days.

12. Using a sterilized ice pick or knitting needle with a diameter of ¹⁄₁₆ inch, poke 25 holes from the top to the bottom of the cheese. Let the cheese set on a cheese mat at 50 to 55°F and a relative humidity of 90 percent.

13. Turn the cheese several times a week. Scrape off mold and slime once a week. Age the cheese for 4 months.

YIELD: 2 pounds

gorgonzola

First produced in Italy, Gorgonzola is named after a village outside of Milan. It has been made for at least 1,000 years and was initially matured in caves in the valley of Valassina, which were no doubt ideal for the formation of Penicillium *mold growth. Gorgonzola is a rich, creamy cheese with a flavor enhanced by blue mold. This recipe calls for making two batches — one in the evening and one the following morning. The ingredients below are for one batch. You will need to double the ingredients but maintain the same measurements and proportions for each batch.*

2 gallons whole milk

1 pinch (1/64 teaspoon) *Penicillium roqueforti* (blue mold)

1 packet direct-set mesophilic starter or 4 ounces mesophilic starter

1/2 teaspoon liquid rennet (or 1/4 rennet tablet) diluted in 1/4 cup cool, unchlorinated water

2 tablespoons cheese salt, plus a pinch for sprinkling

*Note: To rehydrate blue mold, take 1/4 cup milk at room temperature and sprinke mold on milk. Let rehydrate for 1 minute, stir, and let set 15–30 minutes.

1. Heat the milk to 86°F. Add the rehydrated mold. Add the starter and stir to distribute evenly. Cover and allow the milk to ripen for 30 minutes.

2. Add the diluted rennet and stir gently with an up-and-down motion for 1 minute. Cover and let the milk set at 86°F for 45 minutes.

3. Cut the curds into 1/2-inch cubes. Let set for 10 minutes.

4. Pour the curds into a cheesecloth-lined colander. Tie the corners of the cheesecloth into a knot and hang the bag to drain overnight in the kitchen at a temperature of 68 to 70°F.

5. In the morning, repeat steps 1 through 4 to make a second batch of curds from 1 gallon of milk and the same amounts and proportions of ingredients. Drain these curds in a cheesecloth bag for 1 hour.

6. Cut the first batch of drained curds (from the previous evening) into 1-inch cubes. Place in a bowl. Cut the second batch of drained curds (from this morning) into 1-inch cubes and place in another bowl.

7. Add 2 tablespoons of the salt to each bowl of curds and mix in thoroughly but gently.

8. Sterilize in boiling water one 2-pound cheese mold, two cheese mats, and two cheese boards. Put everything in a convenient spot to drain.

9. Place a mat on a cheese board and the mold on the mat (the start of a mold sandwich). Place half the morning curd on the bottom and around the perimeter of the mold. Place the evening curd mostly in the center of the mold. Cover the top with the remaining morning curd. Place a cheese mat on top of the mold and a cheese board on top of the mat. Put the mold in a room where the temperature is 55 to 60°F. Flip over the mold every 15 minutes for the first 2 hours.

10. Flip over the cheese several times a day for the next 3 days.

11. Remove the cheese from the mold and sprinkle salt over all surfaces. Shake off excess salt. Age the cheese at 55°F and a relative humidity of 85 percent.

12. Rub the cheese with salt each day for the next 4 days.

13. Using a sterilized ice pick or knitting needle with a 1/16-inch diameter, poke 25 holes from the top to the bottom of the cheese.

14. After 30 days at 55°F, age the cheese at 50°F and a relative humidity of 85 percent for 60 days longer. (A second refrigerator with a pan of water on the bottom works well.) Every few weeks, scrape the cheese clean of all mold and any smear with a long-bladed knife.

15. Age the cheese 3 months longer. It is now ready to eat, or it can be aged several months longer, if desired.

YIELD: 2 pounds

red bacteria–ripened cheese

These cheeses are known for their strong smell, which is caused by red bacteria, and their mild taste, due to the washed-curd method of production. The degree of flavor development varies with the length of aging, which will depend on your personal taste.

muenster

Muenster dates back to the Middle Ages. It originated in the Alsace region of France. It is traditionally made with whole cow's milk, but you may use goat's milk. This semisoft bacteria-ripened cheese develops a tasty flavor in a relatively short amount of time.

2 gallons whole milk

1 packet direct-set or 4 ounces prepared mesophilic starter

4–8 drops cheese coloring diluted in ¼ cup water (optional)

½ teaspoon liquid rennet (or ½ rennet tablet) diluted in ¼ cup cool, unchlorinated water

2 pounds cheese salt, for brine, plus a pinch for sprinkling

1 gallon cold water, for brine

½ teaspoon *Brevibacterium linens* (red bacteria) diluted in ½ cup cool, sterile water

Cheese wax

1. Heat the milk to 90°F (88°F for goat's milk). Add the starter; mix well. Cover and let ripen at 90°F (88°F for goat's milk) for 15 minutes. Add coloring, if desired.

2. Add the diluted rennet and stir gently with an up-and-down motion for 1 minute. Cover and let set at 90°F (88°F for goat's milk) for 40 minutes, or until the curd gives a clean break.

3. Cut into ⅜-inch cubes and let set for 5 minutes.

4. Raise the heat by two degrees every 5 minutes, until the curds reach 100°F (98°F for goat's milk), about 25 minutes. Stir gently to keep curds from matting.

5. Maintain the curds at 100°F (98°F for goat's milk) for 30 minutes, stirring gently every few minutes. Let the curds set for 5 minutes.

6. Sterilize in boiling water one cheese mold, two cheese mats, and two cheese boards. Let drain. Place a mat on a cheese board and the mold on the mat.

7. Drain the whey until the curds are visible. Ladle the curds into the mold. Place a mat on top of the mold and a cheese board on top of the mat.

8. Let drain for 30 minutes. Carefully lift the mold and cheese boards and quickly flip over the cheese. Gently peel off the top mat, rinse it, and return it to the cheese.

9. Repeat the process five more times, every 20 minutes.

10. Let the cheese rest at room temperature overnight.

11. Make a saturated brine solution with 2 pounds of salt and the water. Remove the cheese from the mold and soak it in the brine at 50°F for 12 hours. Sprinkle the remaining salt on the exposed surface of the soaking cheese. Flip it over several times during the brine soak.

12. Remove from the brine and pat dry with a paper towel. Reserve the brine for other recipes (see page 53).

13. Place the diluted bacteria in an atomizer and lightly spray the surface of the cheese.

14. Flip the cheese and lightly spray the other side.

15. Let the cheese ripen at 60°F and 85–95 percent humidity for 10–14 days.

16. Check it every other day and gently wipe the surface clean with cheesecloth dampened in lightly salted water. This helps spread the bacteria evenly over the surface and inhibits unwanted bacteria, yeast, and mold. The cheese will develop a reddish brown color due to the bacteria. The longer the bacteria develop, the stronger the flavor of the cheese will be.

17. Air-dry the cheese at 50°F and 95 percent humidity for several days.

18. Wax the cheese (see page 57) and age it at 45 to 50°F for 6 weeks longer.

YIELD: 2 pounds

brick cheese

Developed in the United States, brick cheese has a characteristic rectangular shape that is about 10 by 5 by 3 inches. It can be made in the traditional rectangular mold or in any mold that allows adequate drainage. A reddish brown bacterium (Brevibacterium linens) grows on the surface and gives the cheese its mild, nutty flavor. Because the flavor is in large measure a result of the bacterial growth, the cheese cannot be thicker than the previously stated dimensions or the bacterial enzymes and flavor components will not penetrate the interior of the cheese. Brick has a mildly sharp flavor and is affectionately known as "the married man's Limburger" because it is not as strong as the real Limburger.

2 gallons whole milk

1 packet direct-set or 4 ounces mesophilic starter

Brevibacterium linens (red bacteria) diluted in 1 quart cool water according to package directions

Geotrichum candidum (white mold), rehydrated according to package directions 10–15 hours before using (optional)

2 drops cheese coloring per gallon milk, diluted in ¼ cup water (optional)

½ teaspoon liquid rennet (or ½ rennet tablet) diluted in ¼ cup cool, unchlorinated water

2½ pounds cheese salt, for brine

2 gallons water, for brine

Cheese wax

1. Heat the milk to 86°F. Add the starter, stirring to combine. If adding mold(s) directly to the milk, add them now and stir thoroughly. Cover and allow the milk to ripen for 10 minutes.

2. Add the diluted cheese coloring, if desired, and stir thoroughly.

3. Add the diluted rennet and stir gently with an up-and-down motion for 3 minutes. Cover and let set at 86°F for 30 minutes, or until the curd gives a clean break.

4. Cut the curd into ¼-inch cubes. Stir gently for 10 minutes.

5. Increase the temperature of the curds by one degree during the first 5 minutes, until it reaches 87°F.

6. Increase the temperature by two degrees during the next 5 minutes, until it reaches 89°F.

7. Increase the temperature by three degrees during the next 5 minutes, until it reaches 92°F.

8. Increase the temperature by four degrees during the next 5 minutes, until it reaches 96°F.

9. Allow the curds to set, undisturbed, for 5 minutes.

10. Noting the level of the whey, drain the whey to 1 inch above the level of the curds. Add enough water at 103°F to replace the whey that was drained off.

11. Stir the curds for 20 minutes, maintaining the temperature at 96 to 103°F.

12. Let the curd set undisturbed for 5 minutes, then drain off the diluted whey.

13. Sterilize in boiling water one 2-pound hard cheese mold, two cheese mats, and two cheese boards. Put everything in a convenient spot to drain.

14. Place a mat on a cheese board and the mold on the mat (the start of a mold sandwich).

15. Gently ladle the curds into the mold. Place a mat on top of the mold and a cheese board on top of the mat (the finished mold sandwich).

16. After 15 minutes, carefully lift the mold and cheese boards with both hands and quickly flip over the cheese. Add a follower to the mold.

17. After 30 minutes, turn over the cheese, replace the follower, and press with a 5-pound weight. Turn over the cheese every hour for the next 3 hours, replacing the follower and the 5-pound weight each time. After the last turn, leave the cheese in the mold with the follower and the weight for 2½ hours.

18. Combine 2 pounds of the salt and 1 gallon of the water to make a brine bath (see page 53). Remove the cheese from the mold and soak in the brine solution for 24 hours at room temperature. Sprinkle a pinch of salt on the exposed surface of the cheese.

(recipe continued on next page)

19. Remove the cheese from the brine and dry it with a paper towel. If spraying on the mold(s), lightly spray all surfaces using an atomizer.

20. Store the cheese at 60°F and a relative humidity of 90 percent for 14 days. Combine the remaining ½ pound of salt and 1 gallon of water to make a light saltwater solution. Store the saltwater solution in the refrigerator. Each day for 14 days, stir the saltwater solution and remove 1 cup of the salt water to use for washing the cheese. Wearing sterilized gloves, gently wash the cheese by wetting the palm of one hand with the salt water and dampening all surfaces of the cheese (this is called smearing). After 14 days, the cheese will have a reddish brown color due to bacterial growth. Rinse the cheese in cool water and gently dry it with paper towels. If a stronger flavor is desired, do not rinse the cheese before wrapping or waxing it.

21. Wax the cheese (see page 57) or wrap it in cheese wrap and age it at 45°F for 6–10 weeks. Turn it several times a week.

YIELD: 2 pounds

Marjorie Susman & Marian Pollack
Orb Weaver Farm
New Haven, Vermont

In 1981, Marjorie Susman and Marian Pollack were living in Massachusetts, working at other occupations but dreaming of running a small diversified organic farm that would include a market garden and dairy cows. Marjorie had completed a two-year program at the Stockbridge School of Agriculture at the University of Massachusetts in Amherst, and the plan began to come together when the two women found a 100-acre farm in the Lake Champlain valley. They started selling milk from their small herd of Jerseys and established a four-acre organic garden.

Then they discovered cheese making, and became the first farmhouse cheese makers in Vermont. Orb Weaver Farmhouse Cheese, their signature product, is a slightly tangy, buttery colby-style cheese that is moister than Cheddar. Marjorie and Marian age their cheese in wax for eight months. In 2001, they built a domed cheese cave (straight out of *Lord of the Rings,* with a red door and hinges shaped like a shepherd's crook) to age 2-pound and 10-pound

Seven Jerseys, a cheese cave to please a Hobbit, and a happy life in the hills of Vermont

unwaxed wheels, which are washed and turned twice a week. The 52°F cave has a fountain to add humidity.

Twice a week from November through May, Marjorie and Marian set 1,000 pounds of milk, enough to make 130 pounds of cheese. In late spring, they dry off the cows, put them out to pasture, and turn their attention to gardening and producing the sweetest hay for next winter. "By late spring," says Marjorie, "we're so ready to stop making cheese and get outside, but then come fall we can't wait to start again." She offers several thoughts to would-be cheese makers:

"Don't be afraid to get started. Cheese is really a great way to store milk! Even after all these years, it's amazing and exciting to see the milk coagulate. It's important to stay in touch with all parts of cheese making, from the hay and grass we feed the cows to the way we stir, form, wax, and date-stamp each wheel by hand. We love our cows and call them by their names. We even play them classical music at night."

limburger

Limburger is a soft, surface-ripened cheese with a strong flavor and aroma. It was first produced in Luttich, Belgium, and is named for the province of Limbourg. It was made later in the United States by Swiss and German immigrants. Limburger is made from pasteurized milk in a process similar to that of brick cheese but is softer bodied and has a higher moisture content. Like brick cheese, it is rectangular in shape but is somewhat smaller (about 2½ by 2½ by 5 inches), which accounts, in part, for the more pronounced flavor: There is more surface area for bacterial growth in relation to volume.

2 gallons pasteurized whole milk

1 packet direct-set mesophilic starter or 2 ounces mesophilic starter

Brevibacterium linens (red bacteria) diluted in 1 quart cool water according to package directions

Geotrichum candidum (white mold), rehydrated according to package directions 10–15 hours before using (optional)

2 drops cheese coloring per gallon of milk, diluted in ¼ cup water (optional)

¾ teaspoon liquid rennet (or ¼ rennet tablet) diluted in ¼ cup cool, unchlorinated water

2½ pounds cheese salt

2 gallons water

1. Heat the milk to 86°F. Add the starter, stirring to combine. If adding the bacteria (and mold, if desired) directly to the milk, do so now and stir to combine. Cover and allow the milk to ripen for 10 minutes.

2. Add the diluted cheese coloring, if desired, and stir to distribute evenly.

3. Add the diluted rennet and stir gently with an up-and-down motion for 3 minutes. Cover; let set at 86°F for 30 minutes, or until the curd gives a clean break.

4. Cut the curd into ¼-inch cubes. Limburger curds have a jellylike consistency and are softer than the curds of brick cheese. Stir gently for 10 minutes.

5. Increase the temperature of the curds by one degree during the first 5 minutes, until it reaches 87°F.

6. Increase the temperature by two degrees during the next 5 minutes, until it reaches 89°F.

7. Increase the temperature by three degrees during the next 5 minutes, until it reaches 92°F.

8. Stir the curds for 20 minutes, maintaining the temperature at 92°F.

9. Let the curds set undisturbed for 5 minutes, then drain off the whey.

10. Sterilize in boiling water one 2-pound hard-cheese mold (or a rectangular Limburger mold), two cheese mats, and two cheese boards. Let everything drain.

11. Place a mat on a board and the mold on the mat.

12. Gently ladle the curds into the mold. Place a mat on top of the mold and a board on top of the mat.

13. After 1 hour, carefully lift the mold and cheese boards with both hands and quickly flip over the cheese.

14. Continue to flip the cheese once an hour for the next 6 hours.

15. Leave the cheese in the mold for 17 hours longer (this brings it to a total of 24 hours in the mold).

16. Remove the cheese from the mold.

17. Combine 2 pounds of the salt and 1 gallon of the water to make a brine bath (see page 53) and soak the cheese in the brine solution for 8–12 hours at room temperature. Sprinkle a pinch of the remaining salt on the exposed surface of the cheese.

18. Remove the cheese from the brine and pat dry with a paper towel. If spraying on the bacteria (and mold, if desired), lightly spray all surfaces using an atomizer.

19. Age the cheese at 60°F and a relative humidity of 90 percent for 10 days. Combine the remaining ½ pound of salt and 1 gallon of water to make a light salt solution. Store the saltwater solution in the refrigerator. Every other day for 10 days, stir the solution and remove 1 cup to use for washing the cheese. Wearing sterilized gloves, gently wash the cheese with the salt water by wetting the palm of one hand and dampening all surfaces of the cheese (this is called smearing).

(recipe continued on next page)

20. Store the cheese 10 days longer at 60°F, smearing it every 3–4 days with the salt solution. To allow more time for bacterial growth, age the cheese at 60°F for 1 week longer.

21. Limburger is not waxed and the surface bacterial growth is not removed prior to wrapping the cheese. Traditionally, Limburger is wrapped in parchment paper and then wax paper or foil and aged for at least 3 weeks longer at 40 to 50°F.

YIELD: 2 pounds

RECIPE FROM A HOME CHEESE MAKER

port du salut

Trappist monks created this type of cheese in their monasteries in France. It is a member of the Limburger family but has a rather mild flavor. The cheese is usually round, 3 pounds, and 1½ inches thick.

Ripen and heat whole milk to between 90 and 95°F. Add enough rennet to curdle the milk in 30–40 minutes. Cut the curd into small cubes and dip out excess whey. Stirring constantly, heat the curds to between 100 and 105°F over the course of 20–30 minutes, then let set for a few minutes. Drain most of the remaining whey while constantly stirring the curds to prevent matting. The curds are ready for pressing when they are the size of wheat and do not stick together when squeezed by hand but crumble easily between the fingers.

Place the hot curds into a cheesecloth-lined mold without letting them cool. Apply 3–4 pounds of pressure, gradually increasing the pressure to 50–70 pounds. At the end of the first hour, turn the cheese, re-dress it, and turn several more times during a 12-hour pressing period. Rub salt by hand on the surface in the amount of 1.2 to 2 percent of the weight of the cheese after pressing. After 2 days, age the cheese at 55°F and 95 percent humidity. After 2 more days, place the cheese in a saturated brine bath to which a very small amount of color has been added. When the cheese comes out of the bath, it will be yellowish and greasy or slimy.

Return it to the shelf and rub every day with cheesecloth dampened in salt water. After 1 week, put the cheese into the brine bath again to ensure a firm rind. Then rub it by hand with brine during the remainder of the aging period. After 6 weeks, it is ready to eat. The cut surface is creamy in color and may show some small holes. The texture is soft enough to spread without losing its shape in handling.

CHAPTER 9

GOAT'S-MILK CHEESE

Although nearly all of the cheeses in this book may be made with goat's milk, this chapter is dedicated to the goat lovers out there who are looking for a few extra "wheys" to use their own milk. You can also use cow's milk

for any of the recipes in this chapter, but it won't produce the "goaty" flavor that comes from the fatty acids capric, caproic, and caprylic present in goat's milk. These cheeses combine the techniques used for hard, soft, and mold-ripened cheeses; to review those techniques, see chapter 3.

Goat's-milk curd is softer than that of cow's milk, so it must be treated very gently. After cutting the curd, you may have to let the cubes settle for 10 minutes so they firm up enough to begin the cooking

process. I recommend using calcium chloride for making hard cheeses with goat's milk. Remember that because goat's milk doesn't contain carotene, it produces a white cheese. You may add cheese coloring to the milk if serving a white Cheddar troubles you. It will not change the flavor or the texture of the cheese.

Note: Flora Danica starter is an excellent fresh goat-cheese starter for any of the soft-cheese recipes. It may be used either as a direct-set or as a reculturable starter (see page 20).

chèvre

Chèvre is the French word for "goat." This fresh, creamy cheese is easy to make. It is an excellent spread, and you can add herbs and spices for variety. It may also be used by itself as a substitute for cream cheese or ricotta in cooking. When made with whole milk, it has the consistency of cream cheese. Chèvre made with skim milk has a lower yield and a drier consistency.

1 gallon pasteurized whole goat's milk

1 packet direct-set chèvre starter

1. Heat the milk to 86°F. Add the starter, stirring to combine.

2. Cover and let set at a room temperature not below 72°F for 12 hours. (I like to make this cheese at night, so I can drain it when I get up in the morning.)

3. Line a colander with butter muslin. Gently ladle the curds into the colander. Tie the corners of the muslin into a knot and hang the bag over the sink to drain for 6–12 hours, or until the curds reach the desired consistency. (A shorter draining time produces a cheese spread; a longer draining time produces a cream cheese–type consistency.) A room temperature of at least 72°F will encourage proper draining.

4. Store in a covered container in the refrigerator for up to 1 week.

YIELD: 1½ pounds

soft goat cheese

This delicious soft cheese is a very basic goat cheese for beginners. You may want to experiment with various sizes and shapes of soft-cheese molds from a cheese-making supply house. It makes a great spread for sandwiches, bagels, and crackers.

½ gallon pasteurized whole goat's milk

1 ounce prepared fresh starter

1 drop liquid rennet diluted in 5 tablespoons cool, unchlorinated water

1 teaspoon cheese salt (optional)

1. Heat the milk to 76°F. Add the starter, stirring to combine.

2. Add 1 tablespoon of the diluted rennet and stir with an up-and-down motion for 1 minute.

3. Cover and allow the milk to set for 12–18 hours, or until it coagulates. The room temperature should not exceed 72°F.

4. Scoop the curds into individual goat-cheese molds (approximately 3¼ inches in height). When the molds are full, put them in a convenient place to drain. Drain for 2 days.

5. After 2 days of draining, the cheese will have sunk to about 1 inch in height and will maintain a firm shape. Unmold the cheese. If desired, lightly salt the surface to taste immediately after unmolding. Eat the fresh cheese now or wrap it in cheese wrap and store up to 2 weeks in the refrigerator.

YIELD: About 1 pound

"*Many's the long night I've dreamed of cheese — toasted, mostly.***"**
—Robert Louis Stevenson

herbed soft goat cheese

For a delicious variation, try adding herbs to goat cheese. Chopped garlic, onion, and ground paprika make a tasty combination. Or try adding dill seeds, caraway seeds, or freshly ground black pepper separately or in various combinations.

Ingredients for Soft Goat Cheese (see page 183)

Herbs

1. Follow steps 1 through 4 for Soft Goat Cheese.

2. As you scoop the curds into the cheese molds, sprinkle in layers of herbs.

3. Follow step 5 for Soft Goat Cheese.

YIELD: About 1 pound

saint maure

This is a soft, mold-ripened goat cheese. The white mold grows on the surface of the cheese and helps produce a pungent flavor.

Ingredients for Soft Goat Cheese (see page 183)

Penicillium candidum (white mold), rehydrated according to package directions 10–15 hours before using

1. Follow steps 1 through 5 for Soft Goat Cheese.

2. When you remove the cheeses from their molds, lightly salt all surfaces, then lightly spray with the white-mold powder using an atomizer.

3. Let the cheese age for 14 days at 50 to 55°F and a relative humidity of 95 percent. By that time, the cheese will have developed a thick coat of white mold. Wrap in cheese wrap and store in the refrigerator for up to 2 weeks. (For a further discussion of the application of white-mold powder, see page 45.)

YIELD: About 1 pound

feta

Feta is a heavily salted cheese that originated in Greece. It is made from sheep's milk or goat's milk and is often crumbled into small pieces for salads. Goat's milk naturally contains lipase enzyme, which imparts a stronger flavor. If you are making this recipe with a different type of milk, you may want to add lipase for a stronger-flavored cheese.

1 gallon pasteurized whole goat's milk

¼ teaspoon lipase powder diluted in ¼ cup water and allowed to sit for 20 minutes (optional)

1 packet direct-set mesophilic starter or 4 ounces prepared mesophilic starter

½ teaspoon liquid rennet (or ½ rennet tablet) diluted in ¼ cup cool, unchlorinated water

2–4 tablespoons cheese salt

⅓ cup cheese salt, for brine (optional)

1 teaspoon calcium chloride, for brine (optional)

½ gallon water, for brine (optional)

1. Combine the milk and the diluted lipase, if desired. Heat the milk to 86°F. Add the starter, stirring to combine. Cover and allow the milk to ripen for 1 hour.

2. Add the diluted rennet and gently stir with an up-and-down motion for several minutes. Cover and allow to set at 86°F for 1 hour.

3. Cut the curd into ½-inch cubes. Allow to set, undisturbed, for 10 minutes.

4. Gently stir the curds for 20 minutes.

5. Pour the curds into a colander lined with cheesecloth. Tie the corners of the cheesecloth into a knot and hang the bag over the sink to drain for 6 hours.

6. Untie the bag and cut the curds into 1-inch slices, then cut the slices into 1-inch cubes. Sprinkle the cubes with the salt to taste. Place in a covered bowl and allow to age for 4–5 days in the refrigerator.

7. For a stronger flavor, make a brine solution by combining the ⅓ cup of salt, the calcium chloride, and the water. Place the cheese in the solution and store in the refrigerator for 30 days. (Use this method only if your goat's milk comes from a farm; store-bought goat's milk tends to disintegrate in brine.)

Note: If your curds are not setting firmly enough for you to cut easily, next time add the diluted calcium chloride to the milk before adding the starter.

YIELD: 1 pound

goat's-milk cheddar

This stirred-curd variety of Cheddar has a sharp, peppery flavor and can be consumed after aging for 4 weeks but improves with flavor if aged up to 12 weeks.

2 gallons whole goat's milk

1 packet direct-set mesophilic starter or 4 ounces prepared mesophilic starter

½ teaspoon liquid rennet (or ½ rennet tablet) diluted in ½ cup cool, unchlorinated water

Cheese salt

Cheese wax (optional)

⅛ teaspoon calcium chloride diluted in ¼ cup water (optional)

1. Heat the milk to 85°F. Add the starter; mix well. Cover and allow the milk to ripen for 30 minutes.

2. Add diluted rennet; gently stir with an up-and-down motion for several minutes. Let set at 85°F for 1 hour.

3. Cut the curd into ½-inch cubes. Allow the curds to set, undisturbed, for 10 minutes.

4. Gradually heat the curds to 98°F, raising the heat no more than two degrees every 5 minutes. Stir gently to keep the curds from matting. Maintain the temperature at 98°F for 45 minutes, stirring gently. Drain off the whey and add 2 tablespoons of the salt to the curds and mix well.

5. Line a 2-pound cheese mold with cheesecloth. Quickly place the curds into the mold. Press the cheese at 20 pounds of pressure for 15 minutes.

6. Remove the cheese from the mold; gently peel away the cheesecloth. Turn it over, re-dress it, put it back into the mold, and press at 30 pounds of pressure for 1 hour.

7. Repeat the process but press at 50 pounds of pressure for 12 hours.

8. Remove from the press. Gently peel away the cheesecloth. Rub salt on all surfaces. Place on a cheese board.

9. Rub salt on it once a day for 2 days. Turn daily. When the surface is dry, you may wax it (see page 57).

10. Age the cheese at 50 to 55°F for 4–12 weeks.

YIELD: 2 pounds

whole goat's-milk ricotta

Ricotta *means "to recook." Although ricotta is traditionally made by reheating the whey from hard-cheese making, you can make it using this simple variation. The end result has a lot of flavor and a large yield.*

1 gallon whole goat's milk

¼ cup vinegar (I use apple cider vinegar)

3 tablespoons butter, melted

½ teaspoon baking soda

1. Heat the milk to 195°F. (Do not boil; this will result in a "cooked" flavor.)

2. Slowly stir in the vinegar a little at a time, watching for the clear separation of the whey. If the whey is still milky when you have added all the vinegar, increase the heat to 205°F. (Adding too much vinegar will impart an acidic, or sour, taste to your cheese.)

3. With a slotted spoon, gently ladle the curds into a colander lined with butter muslin.

4. Drain for 1 minute. Place the curds into a bowl.

5. Add the butter and baking soda and mix well. Store in a covered container in the refrigerator for up to 1 week.

YIELD: About 2 pounds

goat's-milk cottage cheese

Here is a delicious variation on cottage cheese that is made from whole goat's milk. You may use nonfat milk; however, you will need a cream separator to remove the cream from goat's milk. A small amount of rennet must be added to the milk, as the solid content of goat's milk is not sufficient to allow starter bacteria to adequately coagulate the curd. Fresh fruit, such as chopped pineapple, may be mixed into the final cheese.

2 gallons pasteurized whole goat's milk

1 packet direct-set mesophilic starter or 4 ounces prepared mesophilic starter

4 drop liquid rennet diluted in ¼ cup cool, unchlorinated water

2 tablespoons heavy cream (optional)

Cheese salt (optional)

Herbs (optional)

⅛ teaspoon calcium chloride diluted in ¼ cup of water (optional)

1. Heat the milk to 72°F. Add the starter, stirring to combine.

2. Add the diluted rennet and stir gently with an up-and-down motion for 1 minute.

3. Cover and let the milk set at 72°F for 12–18 hours, until coagulated. The curd will be quite soft.

4. Cut the curd into ½-inch cubes. Allow them to settle for 15 minutes.

5. Gradually increase the temperature three degrees every 5 minutes for the next 30 minutes, until the temperature reaches 90°F.

6. Increase the temperature one degree per minute for the next 12 minutes, until the temperature reaches 102°F. Cook the curds at 102°F for 30 minutes, or until they are firm and no longer have a custardlike interior.

7. Let the curds set for 5 minutes at 102°F.

8. Pour off the whey. Pour the curds into a colander lined with cheesecloth. Allow them to drain for several minutes. (For a less sour cottage cheese, dip the bag of curds several times into a bowl of cool water, then let it drain for several minutes.) Rinse the bag of curds in a bowl of ice water to cool them, then place the bag in a colander to drain for 5 minutes.

9. Place the curds in a bowl and break up any pieces that have matted. For a creamier texture, add the heavy cream. Add the salt and herbs to taste, if desired. Store in a covered container in the refrigerator up to 2 weeks.

Note: If your curds are not setting firmly enough for you to cut easily, next time add the diluted calcium chloride to the milk before adding the starter.

YIELD: 2 pounds

cajeta (mexican caramelized candy)

The consistency of this candy is that of caramel and it has a rich, dark color. Try it on ice cream or use it as a dip for fresh, crisp autumn apples.

2 tablespoons cornstarch

¼ teaspoon baking soda

3 quarts whole goat's milk

3 cups sugar

1. Dissolve the cornstarch and baking soda in 1 cup of the milk and stir to dissolve any lumps.

2. Add the remaining milk and the sugar. Bring the mixture to a boil, stirring constantly, and cook until it is the consistency of caramel sauce.

3. Pour into clean jars, cool, and enjoy.

goat's-milk provolone

The stage of lactation at which goat's milk is produced has a significant effect on whether the curd stretches as it is supposed to. Milk produced early in a doe's lactation makes a curd that stretches beautifully; later in the season, however, the curd will stop stretching. Therefore, varying amounts of citric acid are added to milk produced at different times during lactation. Too much citric acid makes a curd that stretches like a dream but never quite becomes solid — this happens with early-lactation milk. Too little citric acid makes a curd that is unstretchable — this happens with late-lactation milk. Early in the lactation season, add 1 teaspoon of citric acid per gallon of milk. As lactation progresses, increase it in ⅛-teaspoon increments up to 2 teaspoons per gallon. For flavor, the following recipe uses a thermophilic culture, as well as citric acid. Do not use calcium chloride in this recipe, because it will prevent your cheese from stretching.

---

4 gallons whole goat's milk

1 packet direct-set thermophilic starter or **5 ounces** prepared thermophilic starter

½–1 teaspoon lipase powder dissolved in ¼ cup cool water

4 teaspoons citric acid dissolved in ¼ cup cool water

1 teaspoon liquid rennet (or ½ rennet tablet) diluted in ¼ cup cool, unchlorinated water

2 pounds cheese salt, for brine

1 gallon water, for brine

1 teaspoon vegetable oil

Cheese wax

---

1. In a very large pot, warm 2 gallons of the milk to 86°F. Add the starter and diluted lipase; mix well. Cover and allow the milk to ripen for 45 minutes.

2. In a separate container, chill the remaining milk to 35°F. Add the diluted citric acid to the chilled milk, stirring to combine.

3. Add the chilled milk to the warm milk and bring the temperature back up to 86°F.

4. Add the diluted rennet to the milk and stir gently with an up-and-down motion for 1 minute. Let set for 15 minutes, or until the curd gives a clean break.

5. Cut the curd into ½-inch cubes. Allow them to set for 5 minutes.

6. Gradually increase the temperature to 118°F over the next 30 minutes (approximately one degree per minute), stirring to keep the curds from matting. Allow them to set for 15 minutes.

7. Drain the curds in a colander for 15 minutes. Cut them into 1-inch cubes.

8. Put a handful of the cubes into 145°F water. Let the curds soak in the hot water until their temperature reaches 130°F.

9. Using your hands, stretch the handful of curds with upward motions until it is smooth and shiny. Work quickly, but if it loses its stretch, dip it again into hot water. Shape it into a ball or pear or use a mold, then put it into a bowl of ice water until firm. Repeat with the remaining curds.

10. Combine the salt and water to make a brine solution. Soak the cheese balls in the brine at 50 to 55°F for 1–3 days, depending on their size.

11. Remove the cheese balls from the brine and pat dry. Reserve the brine for other recipes (see page 53). Rub the surfaces with vegetable oil to prevent mold and cracking, then tie them with heavy twine. Leave a length of twine so you can hang them up. If desired, smoke them for 3–4 hours at no hotter than 40°F.

12. Hang them up to dry at 50 to 55°F and 85 percent humidity for 3 weeks.

13. Clean the surfaces with lightly salted water, let them dry, then wax them (see page 57). Hang them up to age at 40 to 45°F for between 3 months (mild) and 12 months (sharp).

YIELD: 3½–4 pounds

goat's-milk mozzarella

This recipe makes a tender, fresh mozzarella. Do not use calcium chloride, because it will prevent your cheese from stretching.

4 gallons whole goat's milk

1 packet direct-set thermophilic starter or 5 ounces prepared thermophilic starter

½–1 teaspoon lipase powder dissolved in ¼ cup cool water

4 teaspoons citric acid dissolved in ¼ cup cool water

1 teaspoon liquid rennet (or ½ rennet tablet) diluted in ¼ cup cool, unchlorinated water

1. Follow steps 1 through 5 for Goat's Milk Provolone (see page 190).

2. Continue with steps 7 through 9 (skip step 6; you do not cook the curd). It is best to salt the curd to taste as you are stretching it.

YIELD: 3½–4 pounds

" *In Wensleydale, when cows were released for the first bite [in spring], the alder growing by the stream — often breaking into bud while melted snow still netted the fields — gave the special flavor to Wensleydale cheese, which could only be made to perfection in the early spring. Even today in Wensleydale they disparage winter-made cheese, calling it 'hay cheese.' "*

—Dorothy Hartley, *Lost Country Life*

Cydne Propis, Home Cheese Maker
Fort Lauderdale, Florida

Cydne Propis and her husband live on 2½ acres on the outskirts of Fort Lauderdale. When Cyd saw an ad in *Countryside* magazine for a cheese-making kit, she thought it would be the perfect solution to her husband's lactose intolerance.

She soon found that no one in the area would sell her raw milk, so she made cheese from store-bought milk and bottled goat's milk sold in specialty markets. Somewhere along the line, she bought a pair of emus and some chickens.

Cyd loves to make mozzarella, shaping the cheese into tiny balls for dessert trays and flavoring them with cinnamon, allspice, or almonds. She also keeps fresh mozzarella in the refrigerator in a marinade of Italian herbs, sun-dried tomatoes, and olive oil.

A magazine ad led to a cheese-making kit, which led to cheese, which led to emus (really), which led back to goats and cheese

"I take my cheese-making equipment, especially rennet and a thermometer, along when we travel so I can make cheese from local milk," Cyd says. "I've made cheese in California, New Jersey, New York, Paris, and Rome. As long as we can get a suite with a kitchen, I can make cheese." Because Cyd and her husband love goat's-milk cheese the most, four Nubian goats are soon to set up housekeeping in their backyard. "I'll be able to milk them and have cheese-making parties," says Cyd.

CHAPTER 10

OTHER DAIRY PRODUCTS

The following dairy products are easy to produce at home. They make a nice addition to your cheese repertoire and will really impress your friends at a party. These recipes can be made with almost any type of milk, including dried milk powder, nonfat milk, whole milk, light cream (25%), and half-and-half. Of course, the higher the butterfat content, the higher the yield and the creamier the finished product. Don't forget: The fresher the milk, the fresher your product!

Feel free to experiment by adding fresh or dried herbs, a variety of spices, and various sweeteners to any of these dairy products after they are done.

The recipes in this chapter are not at all complicated, and the techniques used to produce them are very straightforward; see chapter 3 to review any of the techniques, as needed.

buttermilk

Traditionally, buttermilk is the liquid that remains after butter has been separated from milk or cream. Its composition is 90 percent water, 5 percent lactose, 4 percent milk proteins, and 1 percent butterfat. Buttermilk obtained this way is not the type you use for cheese making. This recipe uses a culture and may itself be used as a culture in recipes for soft cheese. The length of setting time alters the viscosity and amount of acidity in the final product; experiment with this for variations in thickness and flavor.

> 1 quart pasteurized whole or skim milk
>
> 1 packet direct-set buttermilk starter

1. Heat the milk to 86°F.

2. Add the starter; let the milk set undisturbed at room temperature (72°F) for 12 hours, or until coagulated.

3. It is now ready to use, and will keep for up to 1 week stored in the refrigerator.

YIELD: 1 quart

sour cream

In the "old days," all you had to do to get sour cream was leave milk on the back of the woodstove to sour. Today, because of the high-heat treatments that store-bought milk goes through, all you would get is spoiled milk. Sour cream's tangy taste may be made more or less acidic with the length of setting time. (Longer setting produces a tangier product.) For a low-calorie sour cream, substitute nonfat milk for the light cream.

> 1 quart pasteurized light cream or half-and-half (25–40% butterfat)
>
> 1 packet direct-set sour cream starter culture

1. Heat the cream to 86°F.

2. Add the starter; let set undisturbed at room temperature (72°F) for 12 hours, or until coagulated.

3. It is now ready to use, and will keep for up to 1 week stored in the refrigerator.

YIELD: 1 quart

kefir from live grains

Because kefir has bubbles and contains about 2½ percent alcohol, it is often referred to as the "champagne of milk." This light, tangy, cultured milk drink has been enjoyed in the Caucasus region of Russia for thousands of years. The name means "good feeling" or "pleasure," and the mountain people believed it had healing properties and was a gift from God. Traditionally, it is made with live grains, and its unique flavor comes from the combination of bacterial acidification and alcohol produced by yeast during the fermentation process. With proper care, you will be able to pass down the cauliflower-like grains to your grandchildren. This recipe is surely just as deliciously effervescent as that enjoyed long ago.

1 container (about 3 tablespoons) kefir grains

3 cups fresh pasteurized milk (whole or nonfat)

1. Place the grains in a clean, 1-quart glass jar and pour the milk over them.

2. Cover the jar loosely and let set at room temperature for 24 hours, agitating the jar from time to time.

3. After 24 hours, gently stir the mixture with a spoon.

4. Place a nonmetal strainer over a bowl and pour the kefir through it. *Gently* stir until most of the kefir falls through into the bowl. Refrigerate and enjoy!

5. To save the grains for next time, do not rinse them. Leave some curds clinging to them, and do not try to remove every last drop of kefir. Gently scoop the grains with the clinging curds into a clean glass jar. In a week or two, you will notice that they have expanded.

TROUBLESHOOTING Depending on how mild or strong you like your kefir, pour more or less milk over the grains. Experiment by using anywhere between a 5:1 ratio of milk to kefir grains (2 cups of milk to 3 tablespoons of grains) and a 25:1 ratio (10 cups of milk to 3 tablespoons of grains). When you have too many grains to use up, slow kefir production by culturing it in the refrigerator. When making kefir in the refrigerator, you must strain the grains once a week.

6. For your next batch of kefir, pour 3–4 cups of fresh milk over 3 tablespoons of grains and repeat steps 1 through 5.

YIELD: 3–4 cups

RECIPE FROM A HOME CHEESE MAKER

soda cheese I (cup cheese)

Cup cheese is an old Amish and Mennonite recipe still made in Pennsylvania. The sour (already curdled) milk must come from your own animal; store-bought sour milk will not work.

1 gallon sour milk (let stand at room temperature until thickened)

3 tablespoons butter

½ teaspoon baking soda

1 cup cream

1 egg, beaten

1 teaspoon cheese salt

1. Heat the milk to 115°F. With a knife, cut both ways through the curdling milk.

2. Line a colander with butter muslin. Pour in the milk. Tie the corners of the muslin into a knot, hang up the bag, and let drain overnight.

3. Crumble the curds and stir in the butter and baking soda. Let set for 5 hours.

4. Place the mixture in a double boiler and heat until it melts. Add the cream and stir until smooth.

5. Add the egg and salt and bring the mixture to a boil. Pour into dishes. Serve with homemade bread and butter.

kefir from starter culture

This recipe uses a powdered form of kefir starter and is slightly less fermented than the kefir made from live grains.

> 1 quart pasteurized whole milk
>
> 1 packet kefir starter culture

1. Heat the milk to 86°F.

2. Add the starter and let the milk set undisturbed at room temperature (72°F) for 12–15 hours, or until coagulated.

3. It is now ready to use, and will keep for up to 1 week stored in the refrigerator.

YIELD: 1 quart

RECIPE FROM A HOME CHEESE MAKER

soda cheese II

2 gallons thick sour milk

1 cup milk

3 tablespoons butter

1 tablespoon cheese salt

1 teaspoon baking soda

1. Combine the milks and heat, stirring occasionally, over low heat until hot but not boiling. Let set at that temperature for 2 hours.

2. Line a colander with butter muslin. Pour in the milk. Tie the corners of the muslin into a knot, hang up the bag, and let drain overnight.

3. Remove to a bowl. Work the curds with your hands. Cover and let set. Continue to work with your hands several times a day for 4 days. Do not refrigerate.

4. On the fifth day, stir in the butter, salt, and baking soda and let set for 1 hour.

5. Put the mixture into a double boiler and melt it. Pour into a bowl. The cheese will harden into a spreadable consistency if refrigerated. Serve with lettuce or jelly sandwiches.

crème fraîche  or

This fresh, heavy cream is wonderfully rich in flavor and takes only a few minutes of your time. After you make it, you may want to drain it for a really creamy base for use in dips and spreads. Crème Fraîche has a deliciously rich sour cream tang to it and, when drained, is a real hit with a hot loaf of sweet bread or stuffed into figs.

1 quart pasteurized light
   cream or half-and-half
   (25–40% butterfat)

1 packet crème fraîche
   starter culture

1. Heat the cream to 86°F.

2. Add the starter and let the cream set undisturbed at room temperature (72°F) for 12 hours, or until coagulated.

3. It is now ready to use, and will keep for up to 1 week stored in the refrigerator.

YIELD: About 1 pound

yogurt

Yogurt was eaten in the ancient world from the Arab nations and throughout the Middle East to central Asia and southern Europe. A Russian professor named Ilya Metchnikoff was the person most responsible for bringing yogurt to the West. It's one of the easiest milk products to make, and some claim it is beneficial for a healthy and long life.

1 quart milk (any type)

¼ cup dry milk powder, for a thicker product (optional)

1 tablespoon thickener; such as carrageenan, pectic, or gelatin (optional; use as a substitute for or in addition to dry milk powder

1 packet yogurt starter or 2 tablespoons yogurt with live cultures

1. Combine the milk, milk powder (if using), and thickener (if using). Heat the mixture to 180°F.

2. Let the milk cool to 116°F. Add the starter; mix well.

3. Keep covered, at 116°F, for at least 6 hours, or until set to the consistency of thick cream.

4. Refrigerate and serve cold. This will keep, refrigerated, for up to 2 weeks.

5. If desired, save 2–3 tablespoons of the yogurt to make your next batch. When it stops working, open a new packet of yogurt culture powder and start again.

Note: You can use a few tablespoons of store-bought yogurt with live cultures in place of powdered yogurt culture, but be aware that there may be additives in it and the culture may not be as strong as that made from the powdered culture. If using goat's milk, mix 1 drop of rennet in 4 tablespoons of cool, unchlorinated water, then add 1 tablespoon of the diluted rennet to the goat's milk; this will help the yogurt thicken nicely.

YIELD: 1 quart

TROUBLESHOOTING If your yogurt is not firm enough, it is probably due to one of several reasons. Your starter may be weak or you may have added the starter when the milk was too hot. Your starter may have been killed by detergent residue. The yogurt may have been at too low a temperature during setting. If you used farm-fresh milk, there may have been antibiotics in the milk (allow at least 3 days after all antibiotic treatment is completed to use the milk from that animal).

soy yogurt 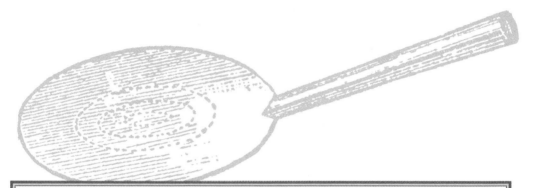 or

Soy yogurt is higher in protein than yogurt made with cow's milk.

---

1 quart soy milk

1 packet direct-set yogurt starter (contains no milk products)

---

1. Heat the milk to 110°F and add the starter.

2. Cover and keep in a warm spot of at least 100°F until it reaches the desired thickness.

3. If desired, save 2–3 tablespoons of the soy yogurt for your next batch. When it stops working, use a new packet of yogurt culture powder and start again.

YIELD: About ¾ pound

COOKING WITH YOGURT

When cooking with yogurt, as with all high-protein products, spare the heat. Low temperatures and short heating times are best. Keep the temperature below 120°F if you want to keep the active cultures alive. It is best to stir in yogurt toward the end of the cooking process — for example, to thicken soup just before serving.

When exposed to a few hours of cooking time, however, yogurt will invariably separate. If you must cook it for any length of time, you can avoid separation or curdling by adding a stabilizing mixture. Combine ½ tablespoon of flour or cornstarch and 1 tablespoon of milk or water and blend into a paste, then mix into 1 pint of yogurt. While stirring continuously, in one direction only, heat the mixture over medium heat until it comes to a boil. Lower the heat and let simmer, uncovered and without further stirring, until it thickens. This will take about 5 minutes. Once thickened, the yogurt may be safely cooked and will not curdle.

butter

Butter was developed as a way of preserving the fat in milk to use during colder seasons. Cream was agitated in a butter churn until the butterfat was released, then the butterfat was washed, salted, and eaten. Today on the farm, butter is still produced using these time-tested methods. Here is a simple way for you to enjoy making your own butter at home. It is not advisable to try this with ultrapasteurized cream, but if it is your only option, let the cream ripen for 12 to 24 hours. Add mesophilic starter and let the cream set overnight to ripen, then follow the directions below, starting with step 2.

1 pint pasteurized heavy
cream or whipping
cream

½ cup cold water

Cheese salt (optional)

1. Let the cream set at room temperature (72°F) for several hours to ripen slightly.

2. Pour into a 1-quart canning jar with a tight-fitting lid and shake vigorously.

3. After 5–10 minutes, when the butter has formed, pour off the liquid buttermilk and spoon the solids into a bowl. (Save the buttermilk for a fresh batch of pancakes; see recipe on page 217.)

4. Add the water and press with the back of a spoon to help expel more buttermilk. Pour off the excess liquid and continue adding cold water and expelling buttermilk until the liquid runs clear.

5. Add salt to taste, if desired, which will help preserve your butter. Refrigerate overnight and enjoy! It will keep in the refrigerator for up to 1 week.

YIELD: About 8 ounces

TROUBLESHOOTING If your butter is not forming, warm up the cream a bit to raise the acidity level. If the butter has a cheesy flavor, it is overly acidic. Sterilize all equipment and next time do not ripen the cream as long. If your butter is rancid, you used dirty equipment or you didn't wash out all the buttermilk with water. Do not eat butter if it is rancid.

ghee (clarified butter)

A highly clarified butter with no milk solids, ghee originated in India. It's better suited to frying, because it doesn't splatter or burn as easily as unclarified butter and imparts a nice flavor to food. During the Middle Ages, butter was always clarified for cooking purposes.

1 stick butter

1. In a heavy saucepan, gently melt the butter over low heat. Allow it to bubble for several minutes, then remove from the heat.

2. Let the butter set for several minutes to allow the milk solids to settle to the bottom of the pot. Skim off the butterfat from the surface, then pour the clear yellow liquid through two layers of butter muslin.

3. Store in the refrigerator. It will resolidify when chilled.

YIELD: About ⅜ cup

RECIPE FROM A HOME CHEESE MAKER

sweet butter

This rich, sweet butter is fabulous, as is the buttermilk. In a glass canning jar, warm 1 quart of cream to 90 to 100°F. Add a scant ¼ teaspoon (or half of a small pack) of direct-set mesophilic culture, stir, and let set overnight. In the morning, chill in the refrigerator until it is 40°F. Scoop it out and beat with a K-beater at a fairly high speed. (Don't whisk or it will thicken too much.) As the butter starts to come, reduce the speed of the mixer. Once the butter has come, drain the buttermilk into a measuring cup. This makes between 1 and 1½ cups of buttermilk. Save it and use it in your baked goods, or just drink it right up — it is so good.

Return the same amount of cold water to the butter and beat it again. Drain and repeat several times until it runs clear. At least for the last wash, use water that is not so cold that it makes the butter hard to work, because you now want to press the butter against the sides of the bowl with a wooden spoon to get out the water. Add salt, if desired. Press the butter into small custard cups, put the cups into small resealable bags, and keep in the refrigerator. The butter keeps for a long time, in or out of the refrigerator.

devonshire clotted cream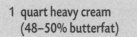

Clotted cream originated in southern England during the summer, when there was an abundance of rich, creamy milk. A shallow pan of milk was placed on a hot stove overnight to allow the cream to rise to the surface. The slow, constant heat caused the cream to thicken and encouraged slight ripening by bacteria. By morning, a wrinkled skin over a layer of thick cream had formed. The following recipe is an adaptation of this traditional method, and it may be made at home using heavy cream. Its distinctly golden brown color and its nutty flavor are caused by partially burnt milk sugar.

1 quart heavy cream
(48–50% butterfat)

1. In a double boiler over medium heat, slowly heat the cream to 175°F. Stir at first to ensure even heating.

2. Without further stirring, raise the temperature to 180 to 190°F. Maintain that temperature for 45 minutes. The surface will develop a thick, wrinkled appearance.

3. Remove from the heat and cool rapidly in a pan of ice water. Cover and place in the refrigerator for 12–24 hours. Skim the clotted cream off the top with a ladle. Store in a covered container in the refrigerator for 1 week.

YIELD: About 1 cup

RECIPE FROM A HOME CHEESE MAKER

skim-milk cup cheese

8½ cups curds from skim milk

2–2½ cups milk (depending on how thick you want it)

2 tablespoons baking soda

2 teaspoons cheese salt

1. Place the curds in butter muslin, tie the corners into a knot, and hang the bag to drain overnight.
2. Place the curds in a stainless-steel double boiler and heat to 200°F. Add 2 cups of the milk and the baking soda. Stir every 5 minutes until the curds melt. This will take 1–2 hours.
3. Once the curds melt, add the salt and the remaining milk. Whip until smooth. Pour into a bowl and let cool.

paskha (russian easter cheese dessert)

This is a Russian recipe that is often made in a 4- to 5-inch-diameter clay flowerpot (clean and sterilized). It is a very rich treat served in small portions as a dessert cake.

5½ cups (2¾ pounds) cream or cottage cheese

2 cups (16 ounces) plain yogurt or sour cream

1–2 sticks (8–16 tablespoons) unsalted butter, softened (1 stick is enough if using homemade cheese)

5 eggs, beaten

2 cups sugar (less 1–2 tablespoons if using homemade cheese)

1–2 tablespoons finely chopped, blanched, and skinned almonds

1 tablespoon currants

1 teaspoon grated lemon peel

Vanilla extract

1. Sieve the cheese into a bowl. Add the yogurt, butter, and eggs and stir with a fork. Pour into a saucepan.

2. On the stovetop, heat to 90°F, stirring constantly. Hold at 90°F until the mixture starts steaming. Do not allow to boil.

3. Remove from the pan, place in a bowl of ice, and let the mixture become quite cold. Add the sugar, almonds, currants, lemon peel, and vanilla to taste. The mixture will be very sweet, but a good deal of sugar drains out.

4. Line a clean, sterilized flowerpot with a large piece of butter muslin. Pack in the mixture and neatly fold the muslin over it. Place a light weight on top.

5. Stand the pot in a dish to catch the whey. Set in a cool place for 12–14 hours, or overnight.

6. Invert onto a serving dish and remove the cloth. Spoon into individual dessert dishes. If not serving immediately, place the dessert dishes on a tray, cover the tray with dampened cheesecloth, and refrigerate for up to 5 days.

YIELD: Ten 4-ounce servings

Lining a flowerpot with butter muslin

Placing a light weight on top of mixture enfolded in butter muslin

Part 3

FOR THE

LOVE OF

CHEESE

CHAPTER 11

SERVING, ENJOYING, AND COOKING WITH CHEESE

"*We have introduced our palate to cheese and come to understand that it is actually our soul that tastes them.***"**

—from *The Story of Cheese Reynolds*

The revival of artisanal cheese making has educated our palates, expanded our menus, and transformed the way we think about cheese. Thanks to the heady variety of cow's-, sheep's-, and goat's-milk cheeses on the market (and being made in our own kitchens), even something as

simple as a cutting board bearing cheese and crackers involves a lot more choice and consideration than it once did.

Steve Jenkins, passionate cheese-monger for The Fairway in New York City, has made a career of studying the great cheeses of Europe and encouraging American cheese makers in their pursuit of excellence. "Twenty-five years ago," he says, "I was happy to sell a good Grafton Cheddar or a Crowley, but there weren't many other choices. We've had a fabulous run since then, and American cheese is finally on par with European cheese."

CUTTING CHEESE

Cutting cheese correctly is just as important as making it correctly. Proper cutting ensures the cheese's attractiveness and presentability and helps preserve its flavor and keeping ability. A cheese sample's flavor and texture vary depending on where it was taken from the cheese, its proximity to the rind, how creamy the portion is, and how much veining is present (as in blue cheese, for example).

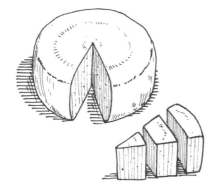

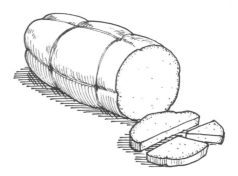

Large, wheel-shaped hard cheeses are cut into triangular wedges from the center out. The larger pieces may then be cut again crosswise.

Large cylinder-shaped cheeses, such as provolone, are sliced crosswise into large rounds. The rounds are then cut into triangular wedges. Small, cylinder-shaped cheeses are sliced crosswise into rounds. Very small cheeses are simply cut in half or served whole.

Pyramid-shaped cheeses are usually cut into quarters or smaller wedges.

Large, wheel-shaped soft cheeses, such as Brie, are also cut into triangular wedges from the center out. The wedges are then cut lengthwise into thin slices.

Proper cutting assures that each portion contains practically the same amount of rind and the same amount of cheese from the center of the wheel or block. This way, all portions are relatively equal in terms of flavor and texture. To accomplish this, each type of cheese is cut differently.

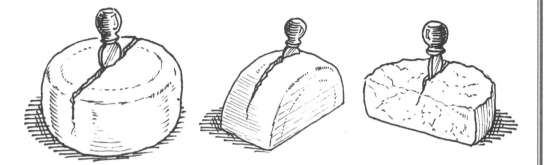

Cutting a whole Parmesan is an art in itself. Use a special almond-shaped knife to preserve the cheese's characteristic granular quality. The cheese is first split in half by making ½- to ¾-inch-deep cuts across the diameter and down the sides. Two knives are then inserted into the cuts and pulled in opposite directions to use lever action to split apart the cheese. This same procedure is then repeated to divide the cheese into smaller portions, always trying to keep a consistent ratio of cheese to rind.

Square or rectangular soft or buttery cheeses are cut in one of two ways. In the first, rectangular pieces are cut from the center of the cheese so that after serving, the two cut faces can be pushed back together to contain the runny center and prevent it from oozing out of the crust. If the entire cheese will be eaten at once, or if the center is not runny, the cheese is cut into triangular wedges.

Serving Cheese

When serving cheese, here are some things to keep in mind:

■ Bring cheese to room temperature (72°F) before serving. Allow about 2 hours per pound to raise the temperature from 40 to 72°F. Leave cheese wrapped while it is warming up.

■ Serve cheese on a sturdy, flat, wooden or marble platter.

■ If guests will cut cheese themselves, provide a strong chef's knife for cutting firm cheeses. Wire cutters or narrow-bladed cheese knives (in which the handle is higher than the blade) are best for soft cheeses. Cheese planes are often used with bars or bricks of hard cheese, such as Cheddar.

■ For a cocktail party or stand-up reception, it will be more convenient for guests if you cut the cheese beforehand. Make sure the cheese doesn't dry out.

Cheese Boards, Flights, Courses, Tastings, and Platters

Cheese hedonists love the sensual pleasures of comparing different types of cheese, serving cheese with other foods (bread, fruit, nuts, honey), and pairing cheese with wine, beer, hard cider, and other beverages. Restaurants and gourmet food shops are happy to provide such presentations, or you can create your own combinations. Several cheese experts weighed in with their ground rules.

Steve Jones, buyer for Provvista Specialty Foods in Portland, Oregon, teaches classes in wine and cheese pairing.

He usually chooses the cheeses first and puts together a cheese board, teaching his students to keep these ideas in mind:

■ Select an odd number of cheeses — presentation is more interesting than with an even number.

■ Leave cheeses whole, if possible.

■ Try for a nice contrast that includes cow's-, goat's-, and sheep's-milk cheeses.

■ Either pick a range of cheeses from soft to firm or select three from the same category (known as a "cheese flight"). For example, three soft cheeses might include Cypress Grove Bermuda Triangle, Old Chatham Camembert, and Westfield Capri.

■ Consider the shapes of the cheeses and how they look on the plate.

■ Choose bread over crackers as an accompaniment. Yeast in the bread marries the cheese and wine. If someone wants crackers, go for a neutral choice, such as Bremer wafers.

■ Grapes are okay, but some fruit can ruin the flavors too much.

■ Walnuts and blue cheese with honey and a big red Italian wine make a nice combination.

Pairing Cheese and Wine

To pair cheese and wine you can go one of three ways:

1. Serve complementary flavors (a big sturdy cheese with a full-bodied wine).

2. Select contrasting flavors, such as champagne and triple-crème cheese, to provide interest and balance.

3. Choose products from the same

region. For example, serve a California dry Jack cheese with a spicy California Zinfandel.

"Usually, I move from lighter to heavier fare; that seems the most natural," Steve says. "For instance, start with a sparkling wine and fresh chèvre. Move through an Alsatian wine served with a true Muenster or a Chardonnay (my least favorite wine to pair with cheese) with a rustic sheep's-milk cheese. Then move to a heavier red with an aged hard cheese, and finish with port or sherry served with blue cheese. Personally, I prefer beer and cheese to wine and cheese. I always choose microbrews, especially oatmeal stout (great with Ig Vella Dry Jack or Old Chatham Shepherd's Wheel) or Belgian-style ales, which I love with several different cheeses. The main rule is this: Eat and drink what you like."

Andrew Fortgang, the manager and cheese director at Gramercy Tavern in New York City, serves 15 or 16 selections on a cheese board. "I try to have a variety," he says, "from lightest to most powerful — goat, soft-ripened, rich double- or triple-crème, hard, stinky. I also want to support our American cheese makers — there's a freshness and vibrancy to our cheeses. Right now we have 5 American cheeses out of 15 on the board." Andrew teaches the Tavern's staff to explain the cheeses they are serving: their name, origin, and style; their flavor and texture; perhaps an anecdote about the cheese or the cheese maker.

When people request cheeses at the end of the meal, the Tavern serves port wine as a default, but Andrew feels it can be horrible with a lot of cheeses. "I encourage our guests to consider the type of cheese first," Andrew explains. "If the cheeses are somewhat similar, you can pick a good wine. But if a cheese board has a lot of variety, it's impossible to pick one wine to suit each one. I try to keep the wine simple, so it doesn't fight with or overshadow the cheese. Beer and/or ale can be the best of all. It goes with most cheese, and it cleanses the palate."

To accompany the cheese, the Tavern serves bread, usually three kinds (currently a plain crusty bread, fennel-raisin, and cranberry-walnut). There is fruit chutney for the cheese plates as well.

"I have a passion, an affinity for cheese," Andrew says. "But in the end, you can't take all the 'rules' about eating cheese too seriously."

Ian Picard, vice president of La Fromagerie Hamel in Montreal, works with his father, mother, and cousin in their shop, which offers 450 cheeses and is the largest cheese shop in Quebec. Ian is the ripener, the affineur, who carefully monitors the cheese "cave" in the basement of the shop. Most of La Fromagerie's cheeses are imported from France; it also stocks many small farmhouse cheeses from Quebec and New Brunswick. Ian and the staff are dedicated to pleasing their customers and will happily let buyers taste from the wheel of cheese they are interested in. "We want each person who eats our cheese to be assured that it is at the very top of its taste and maturity," Ian says.

People come to La Fromagerie Hamel to eat lunch in the tiny café, buy cheese and fine deli meats, choose wine, or participate in one of the shop's cheese and wine tastings. The shop offers tastings for a table of eight, including nine or ten cheeses, charcuterie (pâté or terrine), a variety of breads and crackers, fruit and nuts, and half a bottle of wine per person. Each tasting presentation consists of three or four services, which the shop characterizes in this way:

- Three soft cheeses served with dry white wine.
- Three medium cheeses served with light dry wine or medium red wine.
- Three strong cheeses served with strong wine.
- One or two strong cheeses (blues) served with sweet white wine, port, or grand bourgogne.

Ian is an advocate for the farmhouse cheeses being made in eastern Canada. His favorites include Le Chevalier-Mailloux, an aged cow's-milk cheese made at Ferme Piluma near Quebec City, and two raw-milk cheeses (a cow's-milk cheese, Tomme de Champ Doré, and a sheep's-milk cheese, Le Sieur de Duplessis) from La Bergerie aux Quatres Vents near Monckton, New Brunswick. He describes a good cheese simply as one

that is "long in taste," and looks forward to finding more excellent Canadian farmhouse cheeses for his store.

> **"**Wine and cheese are ageless companions, like aspirin and aches, or June and moon, or good people and noble ventures."
>
> —M. F. K. Fisher

CHEESE TRIER.

breakfasts and breads

cheese dish hancock

■ ■ ■

Perhaps a precursor to toasted cheese, this dish was a favorite of the Shakers in Hancock, Massachusetts. The recipe comes from The Best of Shaker Cooking *by Amy Bess Miller and Persis Fuller (Hancock Shaker Village, 1970). See the profile of Hancock Shaker Village's cheese-making operation on page 216.*

¾ cup shredded Cheddar or Cheshire cheese
2 slices toast
Salt and freshly ground black pepper

1. Scrape or thinly pare some country cheese, a Cheddar or a Cheshire type, into a cup until it is three-fourths full.
2. Fill with boiling water to the rim of the cup and cover with a saucer. Set in a warm place for 10 minutes.
3. Pour off the water and pour the cheese, which will be like thick cream, onto hot toast. Sprinkle with salt and pepper to taste and serve. If the cheese is packed fairly compactly, this amount will be enough for two slices of toast.

YIELD: 1 serving

cheese pudding

■ ■ ■

This baked dish was popular among the Shakers in Hancock, Massachusetts.

1–2 teaspoons butter
6 slices medium-thick bread, well buttered
½ teaspoon prepared mustard
1 pound Yankee cheese (Cheddar-type), thinly sliced
4 eggs
2 cups milk
½ teaspoon salt
¼ teaspoon freshly ground black pepper

1. Preheat the oven to 350°F.
2. Butter a 2-quart baking dish. Cover the bottom with two slices of the bread and spread lightly with the mustard.
3. Cover with one-third of the cheese. Make two more layers with the remaining bread and cheese.
4. Beat together the eggs and milk and pour over the bread and cheese. Season to taste with salt and pepper. Bake for 20 minutes. Serve very hot.

YIELD: 4 servings

A CHEESE-MAKER'S STORY

Hancock Shaker Village

Hancock, Massachusetts

Hancock Shaker Village, home of an active Shaker community from 1783 to 1960, is a beautifully restored history museum dedicated to portraying the Shakers' way of life. Part of that heritage includes cheese making. In order to demonstrate the Shakers' process, cheese makers at Hancock Shaker Village use milk from a small herd of heritage breeds (mostly Durham and Devon cows, which the Shakers preferred) to make cottage cheese, Edam, and Cheddar.

According to museum educator Todd Burdick, the self-sufficient Shakers made their own rennet by slaughtering calves. Although that step is bypassed today at Hancock Shaker Village, the museum's cheese makers make cheese and butter in the restored building — called the Sisters' Dairy and Weave Shop —

Making cheese just the way the Shakers did

first built for cheese making in 1795. Visitors to the museum, including school groups from miles around, help make cheese as part of the museum's Foodways program. They use the Shakers' own antique presses and molds to shape the cheese. As the thrifty Shakers did, they feed the leftover whey to the pigs. And they visit the milking parlor in the beautifully restored, soaring Round Stone Barn, the focal point of the village.

Although the cheese produced at Hancock Shaker Village is not intended for consumption or sale, staffers have been known to taste it. "We wait until we have a batch that is totally sanitary," he said. "Would you eat cheese that 75 fourth-graders just poked their fingers into?" (See page 215 for traditional Hancock Shaker recipes using cheese.)

two-grain pancakes with orange honey topping

■ ■ ■

Try serving these delicious pancakes with warmed preserves and maple syrup, as well as the Orange Honey Topping.

PANCAKES

¾ cup whole-wheat flour
½ cup yellow cornmeal
¼ cup all-purpose flour
3 tablespoons granulated sugar
1½ teaspoons baking powder
1 teaspoon salt
1½ cups buttermilk
1 egg, well beaten
3 tablespoons melted butter, plus additional for the griddle

ORANGE HONEY TOPPING

1 cup (8 ounces) fromage blanc, at room temperature (72°F)
3 tablespoons honey
Zest of 1 orange, finely grated
1 tablespoon half-and-half or milk

1. In a large bowl, mix together the whole-wheat flour, cornmeal, all-purpose flour, sugar, baking powder, and salt.
2. In a separate bowl, mix together the buttermilk, egg, and butter. Stir into the flour mixture until just combined.
3. Warm a griddle over medium heat. Brush with melted butter. Spoon the batter onto the griddle and cook the pancakes until puffed and steam holes appear, 3–4 minutes. Turn and cook until done, about 2 minutes.
4. In a medium-sized bowl, whisk together the ingredients for the topping until smooth.
5. Serve pancakes hot, accompanied by Orange Honey Topping, warmed preserves, and maple syrup.

YIELD: Fourteen 4-inch pancakes

buttermilk pancakes

■ ■ ■

When made with homemade buttermilk, these pancakes are deliciously moist and satisfying. Top them with warm maple syrup and fresh blueberries.

1 egg
1 cup buttermilk
1 cup all-purpose or whole-wheat flour
2 tablespoons vegetable oil
1 tablespoon granulated or brown sugar
1 teaspoon baking powder
½ teaspoon baking soda
½ teaspoon salt
Grease, for the griddle

1. In a medium-sized bowl, beat the egg with a hand beater until fluffy.
2. Add the buttermilk, flour, oil, sugar, baking powder, baking soda, and salt and beat until smooth.
3. Pour ¼ cup of batter at a time onto a hot, greased griddle; cook over medium heat until pancake is dry around the edges. Turn and cook until golden brown.

YIELD: 9 pancakes

ricotta pancakes
with banana pecan syrup

■ ■ ■

Here's a winner from Paula Lambert's The Cheese Lover's Cookbook and Guide. *The ricotta keeps the pancakes moist and makes them puff up as they cook. See the profile of Paula and her business, The Mozzarella Company, on page 119.*

PANCAKES

2 cups unbleached all-purpose flour
1 tablespoon sugar
2 teaspoons baking powder
½ teaspoon baking soda
½ teaspoon salt
2 eggs, separated
2 cups milk
½ cup (4 ounces) ricotta (homemade or store-bought), well drained

BANANA PECAN SYRUP

2 tablespoons unsalted butter
½ cup chopped pecans
2 small bananas, thinly sliced (¾ cup)
1 cup cane or maple syrup

1. Sift together the flour, sugar, baking powder, baking soda, and salt onto a piece of wax paper or a plate.
2. In a medium-sized bowl, with an electric mixer or whisk, beat the egg whites until stiff but not dry.
3. In a large bowl, beat together the egg yolks, milk, and ricotta until well blended and smooth. Add the flour mixture; combine gently with a large spoon.
4. Stir a spoonful of the egg whites into the batter to lighten it, then fold in the remaining egg whites with a rubber spatula.
5. Heat a large nonstick flat griddle or skillet over medium heat. Grease with butter or vegetable oil.
6. Pour ¼–⅓ cup of batter per pancake onto the hot griddle and cook for about 2 minutes, until bubbles form on the surface, then flip the pancakes over using a large wide spatula. Cook on the other side for 2 minutes, or until golden.
7. Transfer the pancakes to a warm platter. Serve immediately or hold in a 200°F oven while you cook the rest of the pancakes.
8. For the syrup, melt the butter in a medium-sized skillet over medium heat. Add the nuts and sauté for about 1 minute, or until fragrant.
9. Add the bananas and cook, stirring, for about 2 minutes.
10. Add the syrup and cook 1–2 minutes longer, until the syrup is hot and slightly thickened. Remove from the heat and set aside in a warm place.
11. Serve pancakes on heated plates topped with warm Banana Pecan Syrup.

YIELD: Sixteen 3-inch pancakes; 4–6 servings

cheese, ham, and potato omelette

■ ■ ■

Try this sizzling treat — it will simply melt in your mouth.

- 4 tablespoons olive oil
- 1 large potato, finely chopped
- 1 medium onion, finely chopped
- 4 eggs, beaten
- ½ teaspoon salt
- ½ cup grated manchego
- ¼ cup chopped ham

1. In a frying pan, heat the oil over low heat.

2. When the pan is hot, add the potato and onion and cook over low heat until the onions start to turn translucent.

3. Add half of the eggs. Sprinkle a little salt over the top and make sure that the eggs run underneath the vegetables.

4. Add the cheese and chopped ham to the remaining eggs, then add the mixture to the frying pan.

5. Allow the omelette to turn golden brown on the bottom, then turn it over. This is easy to do if you are using an omelette pan. If not, place a plate on top of the omelette, turn it onto the plate, then return the omelette to the pan. Cook until lightly browned on the bottom.

YIELD: 2–4 servings

smoked salmon and fromage blanc omelette

■ ■ ■

This is my favorite Saturday-morning treat.

- 3 eggs
- 1 tablespoon water
- Salt and freshly ground black pepper
- 1 tablespoon unsalted butter
- 1 tablespoon minced fresh dill
- ¼ cup (2 ounces) lightly salted fromage blanc
- 1 ounce smoked salmon, finely julienned

1. In a bowl, whisk the eggs. Whisk in the water, salt, and a generous grinding of pepper. Set aside.

2. Warm a 6-inch omelette pan, preferably a nonstick one, over medium heat. When hot, add the butter.

3. When the butter has melted and is foaming, add the eggs. Stir them several times with a rubber spatula, lifting the cooked egg over the uncooked egg. Add the dill and stir to combine.

4. When the eggs are almost set, scatter the cheese and salmon over the top. When the omelette is done to your liking, turn it out of the pan and onto a plate.

YIELD: 2–4 servings

buttermilk cornbread

■ ■ ■

This rustic loaf has always been a hit with the guys when they come in from a long morning in the barn.

 1 teaspoon butter
1⅓ cups flour
 ⅔ cup cornmeal
 ½ cup cornstarch
 ½ cup sugar
 1 tablespoon baking powder
 1 teaspoon baking soda
1⅓ cups buttermilk
5⅓ tablespoons butter, melted and cooled
 1 egg, lightly beaten

1. Preheat the oven to 350°F. Butter an 8-inch square baking pan.
2. In a large bowl, combine the flour, cornmeal, cornstarch, sugar, baking powder, and baking soda.
3. In another bowl, combine the buttermilk, butter, and egg. Pour into the flour mixture and stir until just moistened; do not overstir. Pour immediately into the prepared baking pan.
4. Bake for 55 minutes, or until golden brown. Cut into squares and serve hot.

YIELD: 9 servings

cream cheese muffins

■ ■ ■

These rich and delicious muffins remind me of when I was a little girl on the farm in Jersey.

 2 cups sifted all-purpose flour
 ½ cup sugar
 3 teaspoons baking powder
 ½ teaspoon salt
 ¾ cup (6 ounces) cream cheese, at room temperature (72°F)
 2 eggs
 ⅔ cup milk
 4 tablespoons butter, melted
 1 teaspoon vanilla extract
 ½ cup coarsely chopped dates

1. Preheat the oven to 425°F. Grease 10–12 muffin cups.
2. Combine the flour, sugar, baking powder, and salt in a large mixing bowl. Whisk to blend.
3. In a separate bowl, beat the cream cheese and eggs. Gradually beat in the milk and butter until smooth. Stir in the vanilla.
4. Make a well in the flour mixture and pour in the cream cheese mixture. Blend with a wooden spoon until just moistened. The batter should be lumpy. Add the chopped dates.
5. Spoon into the muffin cups and bake for 20–25 minutes, until a tester inserted near the center comes out clean.

YIELD: 10–12 muffins

buttermilk muffins

■ ■ ■

My kids love to take a dollop of jam and stick it into the middle of these muffins before baking.

4 cups sifted all-purpose flour
2 tablespoons cornmeal
1 teaspoon baking soda
½ teaspoon salt
2½ cups buttermilk
2 eggs, beaten
1 tablespoon sugar

1. Preheat the oven to 400°F. Grease 20 muffin cups.
2. In a large bowl, combine the flour, cornmeal, baking soda, and salt. Set aside.
3. In a separate bowl, combine the buttermilk, eggs, and sugar. Add to the flour mixture, stirring just until moistened.
4. Fill the muffin cups two-thirds full and bake for 20 minutes, or until a tester inserted near the center comes out clean.

YIELD: 20 muffins

yogurt muffins

■ ■ ■

Moist and sweet, these muffins will warm your insides on a snowy winter morning.

1½ cups sifted all-purpose flour
½ cup sugar
1 teaspoon baking soda
1 teaspoon cream of tartar
Pinch of salt
1 cup (8 ounces) yogurt
¼ cup vegetable oil
2 eggs, beaten
1 cup raisins

1. Preheat the oven to 400°F. Lightly grease 8–10 muffin cups.
2. In a medium-sized bowl, combine the flour, sugar, baking soda, cream of tartar, and salt.
3. In a large bowl, combine the yogurt, oil, and eggs. Stir in the raisins. Fold in the flour mixture until just moistened. The batter should be lumpy.
4. Bake for 20–25 minutes, or until a tester inserted near the center comes out clean.

YIELD: 8–10 muffins

RECIPE FROM A HOME CHEESE MAKER

pot cheese

Leave 2 pints of farm-fresh milk in a warm place for 24 hours. The following day, place the soured milk in a saucepan and heat just enough to separate the curds and whey. Drain the whey and hang the curds in a butter muslin bag for a few hours. Work in salt and a little butter to taste. Refrigerate until firm and eat fresh.

black pepper and cheese biscuits

■ ■ ■

A spicy surprise will tickle your taste buds when you bite into one of these exotic biscuits. Topped with a bit of extra fromage blanc or crème fraîche, these biscuits make a great addition to any meal.

1½ cups sifted all-purpose flour
 1 tablespoon baking powder
 2 teaspoons freshly ground black pepper
½ teaspoon salt
¼ teaspoon sugar
½ cup (1 stick) unsalted butter, softened
½ cup (4 ounces) fromage blanc or crème fraîche, at room temperature (72°F)
¼ cup solid vegetable shortening

1. Preheat the oven to 400°F.
2. In a bowl, stir together the flour, baking powder, pepper, salt, and sugar. Set aside.
3. In a medium-sized bowl, cream together the butter, cheese, and shortening. Add the flour mixture to the butter mixture and stir until just combined.
4. Turn the dough onto a floured work surface and roll it to about ¾ inch thick. With a lightly floured 1- to 1½-inch biscuit cutter, cut the dough into biscuits. Transfer them to an ungreased baking sheet. Gather the scraps into a ball, roll out the dough, and cut the remaining biscuits.

5. Bake for 10–12 minutes, or until the biscuits are crisp and the bottoms are lightly gold. Serve warm.

YIELD: 12 biscuits

english muffin bread with whey

■ ■ ■

This bread freezes so well that I like to make four at a time. It's excellent made with milk, but the flavor is even better when you use whey instead.

 2 tablespoons sugar
1⅓ cups warm water
 4 packages or 4 tablespoons active dry yeast
Cornmeal, for sprinkling
12 cups sifted all-purpose flour
½ teaspoon baking soda
 4 cups whey or milk
 4 teaspoons salt

1. Dissolve the sugar in the water.
2. Pour the yeast into a large bowl or plastic container. Add the sugar water and let sit for at least 10 minutes.
3. Meanwhile, grease four loaf pans and sprinkle with the cornmeal.
4. In a large bowl, combine 6 cups of the flour and the baking soda.
5. In a medium-sized saucepan, combine the whey and salt and warm over low heat until just lukewarm. Stir the yeast mixture, then pour the warm whey into it. Stir to combine.

6. Pour the yeast mixture into the flour mixture and stir. Add the remaining flour and combine. (This will take a few minutes, as it makes a very stiff, dry batter. Keep stirring until all of the flour is absorbed.)

7. Preheat the oven to 400°F.

8. Spoon the batter into the prepared loaf pans and press flat. Sprinkle the tops with cornmeal. Let rise in a warm place until the center is 1½ inches above the rim of the pan. (The top of the stove is a good place to do this while the oven preheats.)

9. Bake for 30 minutes.

Note: To bake in the microwave, microwave each loaf on HIGH for 6½ minutes. The crust will be pale. Let it rest for 5 minutes before removing from the pan.

YIELD: 4 loaves

joe castro's kentucky spoon bread with goat cheese and country ham

■ ■ ■

Judy Schad of Capriole Farm (see her profile on page 244) got this recipe from Chef Castro at the notable Brown Hotel in Louisville. Spoon bread is like a cornmeal soufflé; this one is flecked with country ham.

  1 teaspoon butter
  2 medium leeks, cleaned, and white
      sections thinly sliced
2½ cups whole milk
  2 cups half-and-half
  1 cup cornmeal
½ cup all-purpose flour
  1 tablespoon sugar
½ cup (1 stick) butter
  6 eggs, separated
¼ cup heavy cream
½ cup fresh goat cheese, crumbled
¼ cup country ham or prosciutto, diced
    Sorghum, warmed (for drizzling)

1. Preheat the oven to 350°F. Butter a casserole dish and set aside.

2. In a saucepan, cover the leeks with water and simmer until tender. Strain them, squeeze out excess moisture, and set aside. (Save the broth to use in stock or soups.)

3. In a saucepan, combine the milk and half-and-half, scald over medium heat, and gradually whisk in the cornmeal, flour, and sugar until thick. When the mixture is smooth and creamy, remove from the heat and stir in the butter.

4. Beat the egg yolks with heavy cream until light and smooth, then add to the cornmeal mixture.

5. Fold in the leeks, goat cheese, and ham.

6. Whip the egg whites and fold into the cornmeal mixture. Pour into the prepared casserole dish.

7. Bake until the eggs are set, about 20 minutes. Serve warm with a little warm sorghum on the side.

YIELD: 4–6 servings

italian feather bread with whey

■ ■ ■

When served at my workshops, this bread is the hit of the party.

1 cup warm water (100–115°F)
2 packages active dry yeast
1 tablespoon granulated sugar
5⅓ tablespoons butter, cut into small pieces
¾ cup hot whey or milk (120°F)
2 teaspoons salt
5½–6 cups sifted all-purpose flour
1–2 teaspoons butter
Cornmeal, for sprinkling
1 egg white, lightly beaten

1. In a large mixing bowl, combine the water, yeast, and sugar. Let stand until the yeast dissolves and starts to proof (that is, becomes bubbly).

2. Meanwhile, melt the butter in the hot whey and let cool to lukewarm. Add the salt, then combine with the yeast mixture.

3. Stirring vigorously with a wooden spoon, add the flour, 1 cup at a time, until the dough almost comes away from the sides of the bowl. (Don't be afraid if the dough seems rather soft and sticky; it will stabilize during the next step.)

4. Turn out the dough onto a lightly floured surface. Using a baker's scraper or a large spatula, scrape under the flour and the dough, fold the dough over, and press it with your free hand. Continue doing this until the dough has absorbed enough flour from the board and is easy to handle.

5. Knead for 2–4 minutes, being sure to keep your hands well floured, as the dough will still be sticky.

6. When the dough is soft and smooth, let it rest for 5–6 minutes, then divide it in half. Roll each half into a rectangle about 12 by 8 inches. Starting from the wide edge, roll the rectangle quite tightly, pinching the seams as you go.

7. Butter one or two baking sheets and sprinkle with the cornmeal. Place the loaves on the sheets and let them rise in a warm, draft-free place until doubled in bulk, 50–60 minutes.

8. Preheat the oven to 425°F.

9. Brush with the beaten egg white and bake for 30–40 minutes, or until the loaves are a rich, golden color and make a hollow sound when you tap the top with your knuckles.

10. Cool on a rack and slice while fresh.

YIELD: 2 loaves

Jim Wallace, Home Cheese Maker
Shelburne Falls, Massachusetts

Jim Wallace is a Renaissance man in a postmodern world. A former pre-med student and longtime science teacher, Jim turned to fine-art photography for his professional work. At the same time, he embraced both cheese making and home brewing as a way of getting back to a more traditional, preindustrial life.

"I use principles of science in making cheese," Jim explains, "but I also know that science can get in the way of cheese being made in the fine old ways. For example, one of the hardest things about cheese making is to know how the curd should look and feel at different stages. That takes practice. Once you get up to speed by following a few basic steps, once you understand the concepts involved, you can go outside the recipe and experiment."

Jim's first cheese was 30-Minute Mozzarella (see recipe on page 134), which he calls "a great demonstration cheese." He moved to a simple farmstead cheese — "it will age a bit and surprise you" — and now has taken off as a cheese maker, playing with traditional recipes for Parmesan, Romano, Gouda, Cheddar, and mold-ripened French-style cheeses. He ages cheese in his vast 1,500-square-foot cellar. Because Jim also brews beer in the cellar, he admits that sometimes the bacteria fight with each other.

"Overall, I'm thrilled with the cheese I make," Jim says. "I thought my friends would laugh at me, but they're blown away by it." He is working on a traditional bandaged (wrapped) English Cheddar and has made some Parmesan and Gouda that will age for 18 months.

Finding good fresh milk can be a problem, but Jim has located a source from pasture-raised Jerseys. "They are such beautiful animals," he says. "It takes me back to cheese making as it was in the 19th century."

His homemade cheese is a happy marriage of science and art

dips, spreads, and dressings

savory fromage blanc dips

■ ■ ■

Fromage blanc is one of the easiest cheeses to make. Once you produce all you can eat, you will want to figure out new and innovative ways to use it. The Blue Cheese dip is my favorite, and I like to serve it in a beautiful dish surrounded by fresh carrots, celery, radishes, and tomatoes and garnished with sprigs of parsley.

BLUE CHEESE

1 cup (8 ounces) fromage blanc
¼ cup blue cheese
1 tablespoon fresh chopped chives

Combine all ingredients and blend well. Serve slightly chilled.

YIELD: 1¼ cups

GARLIC

1 cup (8 ounces) fromage blanc
2 tablespoons chopped chives
1 clove of garlic, crushed
¼ teaspoon salt

Combine all ingredients and blend well. Serve slightly chilled.

YIELD: 1¼ cups

BASIL

1 cup (8 ounces) fromage blanc
3 tablespoons chopped basil leaves
¼ teaspoon salt
Dash of paprika

Combine all ingredients and blend well. Serve slightly chilled.

YIELD: 1¼ cups

FRESH DILL

1 cup (8 ounces) fromage blanc
2 tablespoons fresh dill leaves
1 scallion
¼ teaspoon salt

Combine all ingredients and blend well. Serve slightly chilled.

YIELD: 1¼ cups

pasta toppings with fromage blanc

■ ■ ■

So you thought making your own pasta was good. Now you can add your own freshly made cheese to this dinnertime special, and just when you thought you had run out of ideas for using fromage blanc. These sauces yield enough topping for 1 pound of cooked pasta.

CRISP VEGETABLES

1–1¼ cups (8–10 ounces) fromage blanc
¼ cup finely diced carrot
¼ cup finely diced red bell pepper
1 large scallion, sliced
1 jalapeño chile, seeded and finely diced (wear gloves when handling chiles)
Salt and freshly ground black pepper

In a bowl, combine the cheese, carrot, bell pepper, scallion, chile, and salt and pepper to taste.

YIELD: 10–14 ounces

PESTO AND WALNUTS

1–1¼ cups (8–10 ounces) fromage blanc
¼ cup chopped walnuts
¼ cup pesto
Salt and freshly ground black pepper

In a bowl, combine the cheese, walnuts, and pesto. Add salt and pepper to taste.

YIELD: 10–14 ounces

HERBS AND PEPPER

1–1¼ cups (8–10 ounces) fromage blanc
2–3 tablespoons herbes de Provence
1 tablespoon extra virgin olive oil
Salt and freshly ground black pepper

In a bowl, combine the cheese, herbs, oil, and salt and pepper to taste.

YIELD: 8–10 ounces

GARLIC AND SUN-DRIED TOMATOES

6–8 large, unpeeled cloves of garlic
2 tablespoons extra-virgin olive oil
1–1¼ cups (8–10 ounces) fromage blanc
8 oil-packed, sun-dried tomatoes, minced
Salt and freshly ground black pepper

1. Preheat the oven to 350°F.
2. In a shallow baking dish, drizzle the garlic with the oil. Bake for 35 minutes, stirring and basting, until garlic is very tender and lightly colored. Cool.
3. Squeeze the garlic from the peels; add the cheese, tomatoes, and oil from the baking dish. Add salt and pepper to taste.

YIELD: 10–14 ounces

ROASTED PEPPER AND ANCHOVIES

1 large red bell pepper
1–1¼ cups (8–10 ounces) fromage blanc
3 or 4 oil-packed anchovy fillets, finely chopped
Salt and freshly ground black pepper

1. On the open flame of a gas burner or under a preheated broiler, roast the bell pepper, turning until the skin is charred.
2. Wearing oven mitts, remove it to a bowl, cover, and let cool.
3. Peel the charred skin, and remove the stem and core; finely chop the pepper.
4. Combine the bell pepper, cheese, anchovies, and salt and pepper to taste.

YIELD: 10–14 ounces

savory cheese spreads

■ ■ ■

For an informal snack, pack these seasoned spreads into crocks and offer them with a loaf of crusty bread, crackers, or sliced raw vegetables.

HERBES DE PROVENCE CHEESE SPREAD

1 cup (8 ounces) fromage blanc, at room temperature (72°F)
1 tablespoon herbes de Provence

1. In a food processor or by hand, blend the cheese into a smooth spread, then add the herbs.
2. Place the cheese in an airtight container and refrigerate until ready to eat.
Note: This spread is best refrigerated for 24 hours; this allows the herbs to flavor the cheese more completely.

YIELD: 8 ounces

CURRIED CREAM CHEESE—CHUTNEY SPREAD

1 cup (8 ounces) cream cheese, at room temperature (72°F)
⅓ cup chopped chutney
1 tablespoon chopped peanuts
1 tablespoon raisins
1 tablespoon chopped scallion
1 egg yolk, cooked and chopped
Curry powder

In a small serving bowl, layer the cheese, chutney, peanuts, raisins, scallion, egg yolk, and the curry powder to taste.

YIELD: 10 ounces

crème fraîche vinaigrette

■ ■ ■

Try this on tender, buttery greens mixed with lots of fresh mushrooms and sprinkled with toasted chopped almonds.

3 tablespoons crème fraîche
4 teaspoons vinegar (your favorite)
1 egg yolk
2 teaspoons Dijon mustard
¼ teaspoon salt
½ cup olive oil
Freshly ground black pepper

1. In a medium-sized bowl, whisk together the crème fraîche, vinegar, egg yolk, mustard, and salt.
2. Slowly add the oil as you continue to whisk. The dressing will thicken slightly.
3. Add the pepper to taste. Use immediately; the dressing does not hold well.
Note: The egg yolk in this recipe is not cooked. See "Egg Information" below.

YIELD: ¾ cup

EGG INFORMATION

Eating eggs, egg whites, or egg yolks that are not completely cooked poses the possibility of salmonella food poisoning. The risk is greater for pregnant women, the elderly and very young, and people with impaired immune systems. You may reduce the risk of salmonella by replacing egg whites with powdered, pasteurized egg-white products. In some areas, you may also be able to purchase pasteurized eggs.

yogurt salad dressings

■ ■ ■

The following dressings may be made with whole or nonfat plain yogurt. They are simple to prepare and make exquisitely creamy dressings for your summer salad enjoyment.

YOGURT AND HERBS

1 cup (8 ounces) yogurt
2 tablespoons finely chopped chives
2 tablespoons finely chopped parsley
2 tablespoons white vinegar
1½ tablespoons lemon juice
⅛ teaspoon freshly ground black pepper
Salt

Combine all ingredients in a bowl, add the salt to taste, and blend until well mixed. Refrigerate in a tightly covered container.

YIELD: 1 cup

YOGURT, GARLIC, AND BLUE CHEESE

1 cup (8 ounces) yogurt
4 tablespoons crumbled blue cheese
2 tablespoons white vinegar
1½ tablespoons lemon juice
2 cloves garlic, finely chopped
⅛ teaspoon freshly ground black pepper
Salt

Combine all ingredients in a bowl, add the salt to taste, and blend until well mixed. Refrigerate in a tightly covered container.

YIELD: 1 cup

HONEY YOGURT

1 cup (8 ounces) yogurt
2 tablespoons honey
2 tablespoons white vinegar
1½ tablespoons lemon juice
⅛ teaspoon freshly ground black pepper
Salt

Combine all ingredients in a bowl, add the salt to taste, and blend until well mixed. Refrigerate in a tightly covered container.

YIELD: 1 cup

MAYONNAISE AND YOGURT

1 cup (8 ounces) mayonnaise
1 cup (8 ounces) yogurt
2 tablespoons finely chopped chives
2 tablespoons finely chopped parsley
2 tablespoons white vinegar
1½ tablespoons lemon juice
⅛ teaspoon freshly ground black pepper
Salt

Combine all ingredients in a bowl, add the salt to taste, and blend until well mixed. Refrigerate in a tightly covered container.

YIELD: 2 cups

appetizers

stuffed cherry tomatoes

■ ■ ■

I always look forward to this early-summer treat, because it is one of the first dishes I can prepare from my garden. These bright, luscious little globes are a feast for the eyes as well as a gastronomic delight for the stomach.

2 pints cherry tomatoes
2 cans (15 ounces each) chickpeas (garbanzo beans), rinsed and drained
1 cup (8 ounces) yogurt
¼ cup olive oil
2 tablespoons sesame seeds, lightly toasted
2 cloves of garlic, minced
2 scallions, minced
Juice of 1 lemon
Salt and freshly ground black pepper
Chopped chives, for garnish

1. Cut the tops from the tomatoes and remove the seeds and membranes with a small spoon or knife. Set aside.
2. In a food processor or blender, process the chickpeas, yogurt, oil, sesame seeds, garlic, scallions, and lemon juice until smooth. Taste and adjust seasoning with salt and pepper.
3. Stuff each tomato with about 1 teaspoon of the mixture and garnish with the chives.

YIELD: About 25

vermont shepherd cheese with apple relish

■ ■ ■

David and Cindy Major prefer to eat their Vermont Shepherd cheese with crackers or French bread and this simple relish. See the profile of David and Cindy on page 30.

6 apples, peeled and finely chopped
2 tablespoons apple cider
1 tablespoon chopped parsley
Juice and grated zest of 1 lemon
½ teaspoon minced crystallized ginger

Mix all ingredients; let sit for 20 minutes. May be prepared ahead; return to room temperature before serving.

broiled pears and vermont shepherd cheese

■ ■ ■

Here's another way the Majors serve cheese.

Pears, sliced
Vermont Shepherd cheese, very thinly sliced
Lemon zest

1. Preheat the broiler.
2. Arrange the pear slices in a single layer on a baking sheet. Sprinkle the pears with the cheese and lemon zest.
3. Broil the pears for 1–2 minutes, until the cheese melts. Serve warm.

gougères (cheese puffs)

■ ■ ■

This recipe, from Mike and Carol Gingrich of Uplands Cheese (see their profile on page 232), is designed for use with their Pleasant Ridge Reserve, a Beaufort type of Gruyère. The gougères are golden brown and crusty, with a soft interior.

1 cup water
6 tablespoons butter, cut into pieces
1 teaspoon salt
⅛ teaspoon freshly ground black pepper
Pinch of nutmeg
1 cup sifted all-purpose flour
4 eggs
1 cup grated Pleasant Ridge Reserve cheese (reserve some for garnish)
1 egg beaten with ½ teaspoon water

1. Preheat the oven to 425°F. In a heavy 1½-quart saucepan, bring the water to a boil. Add the butter, salt, pepper, and nutmeg and boil until the butter is melted.

2. Remove from the heat and add the flour all at once. Beat vigorously with a wooden spatula or spoon to blend thoroughly.

3. Return to the heat and beat over moderately high heat for 1–2 minutes, until the mixture pulls away from the sides of the pan and the spoon, forms a mass, and begins to form a film on the bottom of the pan.

4. Remove from the heat and make a well in the center with a wooden spoon. Immediately break an egg into the well and beat until it has been absorbed.

5. Add the remaining eggs, one at a time. The third and fourth eggs will be absorbed more slowly. Beat for a moment longer to make sure everything is well blended.

6. Beat the cheese into the warm pastry, called choux. Adjust the seasonings, if necessary.

7. On a greased baking sheet, drop by tablespoonfuls or squeeze from a pastry bag into mounds about 1 inch in diameter and ½ inch high.

8. With a pastry brush, paint each puff with the beaten egg mixture (egg wash), taking care not to let the egg drip down onto the baking sheet. Sprinkle each puff with a pinch of grated cheese, if desired.

9. Bake for about 20 minutes, until doubled in size, golden brown, and firm to the touch.

10. Remove from the oven and pierce the side of each puff with a sharp knife. Turn off the oven and place the baking sheet inside, leaving the door ajar, for about 10 minutes. Cool on a wire rack.

YIELD: About 24

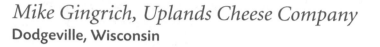

Mike Gingrich, Uplands Cheese Company
Dodgeville, Wisconsin

When Pleasant Ridge Reserve, a Beaufort type of Gruyère, won top honors at the American Cheese Society show in 2001, it was no fluke. Although Mike Gingrich and Dan Patenaude had been making cheese for only two years, many more years of training and research had preceded their endeavor.

In 1994, Mike and Dan, both dairy farmers, sold their small family farms and pooled their resources to buy 300 acres. They wanted to add something to their dairy operation and chose cheese making. They crossbred their Holsteins with Jersey, Ayrshire, French Normandy, Friesian, Brown Swiss, and Tarentaise stock for richer milk. Mike took an apprenticeship as a cheese maker, and the men worked hard to meet Wisconsin's tough regulations for cheese making.

Working with dairy experts, they tried several cheese recipes until they identified the one they liked the most: Beaufort, a style of Gruyère traditionally made in the French Alps from spring milk. Mike and Dan believed that rotational grazing would come closest to mimicking the cows'

Prizewinning cheese made only from "spring milk" in the hills of southwestern Wisconsin

natural grazing rhythms and ensure the best-tasting, sweetest milk and the finest cheese. "The first tasting was exciting," Mike remembers. Pleasant Ridge Reserve went into production.

Today, the farm has 150 milkers. The cows calve in spring, graze and give milk into the fall, are dried off by January, and eat hay until the pastures green up; then the cycle begins again.

"Costs are lower with rotational grazing," Mike reports, "and even though we get a lower milk yield per cow, the cows are healthier and live longer. Grass-fed milk is higher in vitamin E, omega-3 fatty acids, and other nutrients. We believe our grazing system is the way cows evolved and is more consistent with their life processes than the usual practice of confinement and machine-harvested feed."

The proof is in the pudding, or in this case the cheese. Pleasant Ridge Reserve is a superb table cheese. Like French Gruyère, it's excellent in soups, fondues, gratins, and omelettes.

(See pages 231 and 235 for Mike and his wife Carol's recipes using their Pleasant Ridge Reserve.)

westfield farm's fresh goat-cheese appetizer

■ ■ ■

Bob Stetson recommends this recipe as an eye-appealing, easy way to sample Westfield Farm's fresh Capri (or maybe your own home-made version). Serve with crusty French bread or crackers. See the profile of Bob and his wife Debby on page 95.

6 sun-dried tomatoes

8 ounces fresh Capri log

2 cloves garlic

2 tablespoons extra-virgin olive oil

1 tablespoon chopped fresh basil

1 tablespoon chopped fresh parsley

1. Soak the tomatoes in warm water until softened, then slice into thin strips. Set aside.

2. Place the cheese on a serving plate. Crush the garlic into the oil, and pour the mixture over the cheese, allowing some to flow onto the plate. Sprinkle the herbs over and around the log. Press some of the tomato strips onto the log and arrange the rest around it on the serving plate.

YIELD: 4 servings

salads and side dishes

nonfat potato salad

■ ■ ■

If you want something yummy with half the calories, try this delicious potato salad. It hits the spot every time and people will never guess your secret.

1 pound new potatoes, washed and diced

2 tablespoons red wine vinegar

1 cup (8 ounces) plain nonfat yogurt

3 tablespoons chopped walnuts

2 tablespoons capers

½ teaspoon dry mustard or 1 teaspoon prepared mustard

¼ teaspoon celery salt

3 drops hot pepper sauce

½ pound fresh green beans, cut into 1-inch pieces and blanched

½ pound cherry tomatoes, halved

1. Cook the potatoes in salted boiling water until tender. Drain and sprinkle with the vinegar. Let cool.

2. In a medium-sized bowl, combine the yogurt, walnuts, capers, mustard, celery salt, and hot pepper sauce. Set aside.

3. Toss together the potatoes, beans, and tomatoes. Add the yogurt dressing and toss gently. Serve chilled.

YIELD: 4–6 servings

green salad with apples and goat cheese

■ ■ ■

"I love the combination of green apples and toasted nuts," says Paula Lambert, author of The Cheese Lover's Cookbook and Guide, from which this recipe comes. "The apples are so juicy and tart, while the nuts are crunchy and rich. The addition of a creamy, tangy goat cheese seems to even out and intensify the flavors." See the profile of Paula and her business, The Mozzarella Company, on page 119.

SALAD

½ cup pecan halves
1 tart green apple, cored but not peeled
1 teaspoon freshly squeezed lemon juice
½ head red leaf lettuce, washed and dried
½ head romaine lettuce, washed and dried
4 ounces (½ cup) fresh goat cheese, crumbled

BALSAMIC VINAIGRETTE

1 tablespoon balsamic vinegar
1 teaspoon freshly squeezed lemon juice
½ teaspoon salt
 Freshly ground black pepper
⅓ cup extra-virgin olive oil

1. Preheat the oven to 350°F and toast the pecans on a baking sheet for about 5 minutes, until golden brown and aromatic. Do not let them burn. Remove the sheet from the oven, let cool, and coarsely chop the pecans.
2. Cut the apple into thin slices, place in a large salad bowl, and toss with the lemon juice.

3. To make the vinaigrette, Place the vinegar, lemon juice, salt, and pepper to taste in a small bowl and whisk to combine.
4. Slowly drizzle in the oil in a thin stream, whisking constantly until thickened and emulsified. Set aside.
5. Just before serving, tear the lettuce leaves into bite-sized pieces and add to the apple. Add the pecans and vinaigrette and toss to combine well. Sprinkle with the goat cheese and toss again. Arrange on chilled salad plates and serve.

YIELD: 4–6 servings

vermont shepherd cheese, fava bean, and fennel salad

■ ■ ■

This summer salad is wonderful, the perfect thing to make when fava beans are fresh and spicy nasturtiums are in bloom. Cindy Major, proprietor of Vermont Shepherd, says this is an Italian classic that has inspired cheers from those who have sampled it. Use a vegetable peeler to shave the fennel and cheese. See the profile of Cindy, and her husband, David, on page 30.

¼ cup shaved fennel
2 cups shelled fresh fava beans
1 cup shaved Vermont Shepherd cheese
1 tablespoon chopped mint
2 nasturtium flowers, chopped
½ cup extra-virgin olive oil
Salt and freshly ground black pepper

1. Soak the fennel in ice water until ready to serve.

2. Parboil the fava beans in salted water until tender; plunge into ice water and remove the skin from beans.

3. Just before serving, drain the fennel and toss with the fava beans, cheese, mint, and nasturtiums. Toss again with the olive oil and salt and pepper to taste.

YIELD: 4 small servings

scalloped potatoes

■ ■ ■

This classic from Mike and Carol Gingrich of Uplands Cheese Company (see their profile on page 232) really brings out the flavor of their Pleasant Ridge Reserve cheese.

2 pounds potatoes (preferably Yukon Gold), peeled

8 ounces Pleasant Ridge Reserve, finely grated

Salt (optional; cheese supplies enough for most tastes)

Freshly ground black pepper

2 tablespoons butter

1 cup whole milk

1. Preheat the oven to 375°F. Grease a 9-inch square baking dish.

2. Thinly slice the potatoes and place in cold water if you are not assembling the dish immediately. Pat dry before using.

3. Cover the bottom of the prepared baking dish with a thin layer of potatoes.

Add 2 ounces of the cheese; sprinkle with the salt, if desired, and pepper to taste.

4. Make three more layers with the remaining potatoes and cheese, ending with the cheese.

5. Dot with the butter and pour the milk over the top.

6. Bake for 45–60 minutes, until browned on top and bubbling. For best flavor, let the dish sit for ½ hour before serving.

YIELD: 4 servings

mashed sweet potatoes

■ ■ ■

Sweet potatoes are a nice change from regular mashed potatoes, and this dish disappears in no time.

2 pounds sweet potatoes or yams, washed, peeled, and cut into chunks

⅓ cup sour cream

2 tablespoons butter

1 teaspoon grated fresh gingerroot or ½ teaspoon ground ginger

½ teaspoon salt

¼ teaspoon freshly ground black pepper

1. Cook the potatoes in salted boiling water until tender, 20–25 minutes. Drain well.

2. Mash the potatoes, add the sour cream, butter, ginger, salt, and pepper, and blend well.

YIELD: 6 servings

ham, cheese, and potato gratin

■ ■ ■

When the potatoes are ready, I run with my girls into the kitchen to prepare this dish for them. They are so delighted that they do all the washing up after supper.

3½ pounds red-skinned new potatoes, scrubbed and sliced very thin (you may leave the peels on)

10 ounces baked, smoked ham, fat trimmed off

1–1¼ cups (8–10 ounces) fromage blanc

½ cup finely chopped fresh parsley

Freshly ground black pepper

1 cup half-and-half

1 cup whipping cream

2 eggs, well beaten

1. Preheat the oven to 350°F. Butter a 9- by 13-inch baking dish.

2. In a pot of lightly salted cold water, bring the potato slices to a boil. Simmer for 4 minutes, then drain and rinse well under cold water. Set aside.

3. In a food processor, finely mince the ham. In a medium-sized bowl, mash together the ham, cheese, and parsley. Season generously with pepper. Set aside.

4. In a small bowl, whisk together the half-and-half, cream, and eggs.

5. Evenly arrange one-third of the potato slices in the prepared dish. Spread with half the ham mixture. Top with another third of the potatoes and press gently to spread the ham mixture evenly.

6. Pour the cream mixture over the potatoes, lifting the slices slightly with a fork and tilting the dish if necessary to make sure the cream evenly fills the spaces between the potatoes.

7. Bake until the edges are crisply brown and the center is firm, about 1 hour.

8. Let stand on a rack for about 10 minutes before cutting. Serve hot.

YIELD: 6–8 servings

RECIPE FROM A HOME CHEESE MAKER

stink kase

Put about 5 cups of dry curds into a dish. Mix in 1 teaspoon of baking soda and let stand in a warm room until mold begins to form on top. The longer the mixture is aged, the stronger the flavor will be. Add 1 teaspoon of cheese salt and stir with a potato masher. Cook until the mixture is smooth, then add cream or milk until you have achieved the desired thickness. Pour into a bowl and serve.

main courses

prosciutto and cheese calzones

■ ■ ■

*A cold drink and a couple of these little puffs
are just the thing to satisfy a hungry appetite.*

1½ cups grated mozzarella cheese
1½ cups ricotta cheese
½ cup grated Parmesan cheese
1 jar (4 ounces) diced pimientos, well drained
2 ounces thinly sliced prosciutto or salami
2 cloves of garlic, minced or pressed
½ teaspoon dried rosemary, crushed
1 Whey Pizza Dough (see recipe on page 238)
¼ cup extra-virgin olive oil
⅛ cup cornmeal

1. In a medium-sized bowl, combine the
mozzarella, ricotta, Parmesan, pimientos, prosciutto, garlic, and rosemary.
Set aside.
2. Divide the dough into six equal pieces.
Roll each piece into a 7-inch circle.
3. Place a rounded ½ cup of the cheese
mixture on one-half of each circle. Fold
the dough over the filling. Pinch the seam
or press with the tines of a fork to seal.
4. Place the calzones on a large baking
sheet brushed with oil and sprinkled
with cornmeal. With a sharp knife, make
three ¾-inch slits across the top of each
calzone. Brush the tops with oil.
5. Cover and let rise in a warm, draft-free
place until doubled in size, 30–45 minutes.
6. Meanwhile, preheat the oven to 400°F.

7. Bake the calzones for about 25 minutes.
Remove to a serving platter. If desired,
brush with additional oil. Serve warm.

YIELD: 6 servings

stir-fried queso blanco

■ ■ ■

*Serve this dish piping hot over a bed of vermi-
celli or rice.*

2 cups (1 pound) queso blanco, cut into
1-inch cubes
1 cup Marinade (see recipe below)
2 tablespoons extra-virgin olive oil
1 cup French-style green beans or sliced red
and yellow peppers
1 medium onion, sliced and sautéed
½ cup sliced mushrooms
¼ cup slivered almonds

MARINADE

1 cup red wine
1 tablespoon chopped parsley
1 tablespoon soy sauce

1. In a bowl, cover the queso blanco cubes
with the marinade. Marinate for 1 hour.
2. Heat the oil in a wok until hot. Add
the cheese and marinade, beans, onions,
mushrooms, and almonds and stir-fry
for 2–3 minutes over medium-high heat.
3. Cover and cook 5 minutes longer, stirring occasionally to prevent sticking.

YIELD : 8–10 servings

pizza

■ ■ ■

After trying this recipe, calling for pizza delivery will be a thing of the past.

1–2 teaspoons vegetable oil
¼ cup cornmeal

Whey Pizza Dough

3–3½ cups all-purpose flour
   1 package (¼ ounce) or 1 tablespoon rapid-rising yeast
   ¾ teaspoon salt
   1 cup very warm whey or milk (120–130°F)
   2 tablespoons olive oil

Sauce and Toppings

   ¾ cup spaghetti sauce or your favorite pizza sauce
   2 cups thinly sliced fresh vegetables (broccoli, carrots, mushrooms, onions, green bell peppers, and/or zucchini)
   1 jar (2 ounces) sliced pimientos, drained
   2 cups grated mozzarella cheese
   ½ cup grated Parmesan cheese

1. Preheat the oven to 400°F.
2. Lightly oil one 14-inch or two 12-inch pizza pan(s). Sprinkle with cornmeal.
3. For the pizza dough, combine 2 cups of the flour, the yeast, and the salt in a large bowl. Add the whey and olive oil.
4. Add enough of the remaining flour to make a soft dough.
5. Knead on a lightly floured surface until smooth and elastic, 4–6 minutes. Cover and let rest on a floured surface for 10 minutes.

6. Shape the dough into a smooth ball, cover with plastic wrap, and refrigerate until ready to use. If making two pizzas, divide the dough in half and roll it out to fit the pans.
7. Spread with spaghetti sauce. Sprinkle with the vegetables and cheeses. (Fresh mozzarella may be used instead of grated, but it must be added at the last minute, when the pizza is almost done. Otherwise, the moisture in the cheese will seep into the crust.)
8. Bake the pizza at 400°F for 20–25 minutes. The baking time depends on the size and thickness of the crust and the selected toppings.

   YIELD: One 14-inch thick-crust pizza or two 12-inch thin-crust pizzas

easy lasagne

With the combination of mozzarella, ricotta, and Parmesan, this lasagne is a triple treat.

15 ounces (about 2 cups) ricotta cheese
 ½ cup grated Parmesan cheese
 5 cups (40 ounces) spaghetti sauce (do not use a thick or extra-thick variety)
1½ teaspoons dried oregano
12 lasagna noodles (about 12 ounces), prepared according to package directions
 2 cups (16 ounces) shredded mozzarella cheese

1. Preheat the oven to 350°F.

2. Mix the ricotta with ¼ cup of the Parmesan. In a separate bowl, mix the sauce and the oregano.

3. Spread 1 cup of the sauce in an ungreased rectangular 9- by 13-inch baking dish. Top with four of the noodles.

4. Spread 1 cup of the cheese mixture over the noodles, then top with 1 cup of the sauce mixture. Sprinkle with ⅔ cup of the mozzarella.

5. Repeat with four noodles, the remaining cheese mixture, 1 cup of the sauce, and ⅔ cup of the mozzarella. Top with remaining noodles and sauce. Sprinkle with remaining mozzarella and Parmesan.

6. Cover with foil and bake for 30 minutes. Uncover and bake about 15 minutes longer, or until lasagne is hot and bubbly. Let stand for 15 minutes before cutting.

YIELD: 8–10 servings

westfield farm's classic blue log soufflé

■ ■ ■

Debby Stetson developed this memorable entrée using her Classic Blue Log. The soft rind, when baked, has the look and taste of mushrooms. See the profile of Debby and her husband, Bob, on page 95.

 3 tablespoons butter
¼ cup flour
 1 cup milk
 1 Classic Blue Log cheese (4½ ounces), cubed
 3 eggs, separated

1. Preheat the oven to 375°F. Lightly grease a 1-quart soufflé dish (about 8 inches in diameter and 3 inches deep).

2. Melt the butter in a medium-sized skillet over medium heat. Sprinkle in the flour and whisk to make a roux. Cook for 2 minutes, whisking constantly, until the flour turns golden brown.

3. Add the milk and vigorously whisk the mixture until smooth. Turn the heat to low and whisk until thick.

4. Add the cheese and stir until it has melted. Remove from the heat and beat in the egg yolks one at a time.

5. In a clean bowl, whip the egg whites until stiff. Blend a quarter of the egg whites into the cheese mixture to lighten it. Gently fold in the remaining whites and spoon the mixture into the prepared dish.

6. Bake for 30–35 minutes, until the soufflé has puffed 2–3 inches over the rim and the top is golden brown. Serve immediately.

YIELD: 3–4 servings

grilled vegetable stacks with roasted red pepper sauce

■ ■ ■

This dish is great for an outdoor barbecue with chicken or fish and a nice rosé.

1 globe eggplant

1 Japanese eggplant

2 zucchini

2 tomatoes

3 tablespoons extra-virgin olive oil

6 scallions

Salt and freshly ground black pepper

2 large fresh mozzarella balls (about 4 ounces each), sliced

2 tablespoons chopped parsley

ROASTED RED PEPPER SAUCE

2 red bell peppers, grilled, skinned, and seeded

1 large tomato, grilled, skinned, and seeded

2 cups red wine

1 sprig fresh marjoram

1 sprig fresh oregano

1 sprig fresh thyme

Salt and freshly ground black pepper

1. Prepare the grill for medium-high heat.

2. Slice the eggplants and zucchini about ⅛ inch thick on the diagonal. Slice the tomatoes ¼ inch thick and brush with 1 tablespoon of the oil. Toss the eggplants, zucchini, and scallions with the remaining oil and season everything with salt and pepper to taste.

3. Place the vegetables on a grill; cook over medium-high heat. Turn when they start to soften, in about 2 minutes, and then cook for another 2 minutes on the other side.

4. To assemble, alternately layer the eggplant, zucchini, tomatoes, and mozzarella, using two or three slices of cheese per serving. Top each stack with a scallion and sprinkle with parsley. Serve with the Roasted Red Pepper Sauce.

5. TO MAKE THE ROASTED RED PEPPER SAUCE, prepare the grill for medium-high.

6. Finely dice one of the peppers and cut the other one into strips. Roughly chop the tomato.

7. In a sturdy saucepan, combine the diced bell pepper, tomato, wine, marjoram, oregano, and thyme. Cook over a medium-hot area of the grill until the tomato breaks down, about 20–30 minutes. Add the strips of bell pepper and cook 15 minutes more, or until the sauce thickens.

8. Season to taste with salt and pepper.

YIELD: 6 servings

curried panir potato rounds

■ ■ ■

You can cook the panir potato rounds in one of three ways: 1) deep-fry each one separately, 2) lay them on a nonstick pan and bake at 400°F for 10–15 minutes, or 3) broil them for 8–10 minutes. This makes a perfect meal with Fruit Raita (see page 252).

- 6 medium potatoes, cooked, peeled, and mashed
- 1 teaspoon salt
- ¼ teaspoon ground turmeric
- 1 pound frozen peas, thawed and mashed
- 4–5 serrano chiles, finely chopped (optional, wear kitchen gloves when handling chiles)
- 6 tablespoons lemon juice
- ½ teaspoon sugar
- 2 cups (1 pound) panir, cut into 1-inch cubes
- ¾ cup water
- 3–4 tablespoons flour
- 1 cup fine dry unseasoned bread crumbs
- Oil, for deep-frying (optional)
- ½ teaspoon curry powder
- ½ tablespoon diced fresh cilantro
- ½ teaspoon cumin powder

1. Combine the potatoes, ½ teaspoon of the salt, and the turmeric. Cook over medium heat in a large, nonstick skillet, stirring often, for about 4 minutes. Remove to a bowl and reserve.

2. In the same skillet over medium heat, cook the peas, chiles (if desired), lemon juice, the remaining salt, and the sugar, stirring often, for about 4 minutes. Remove from heat.

3. Preheat the deep fryer, oven, or broiler, depending on how you want to cook the panir rounds (see recipe introduction).

4. Place a scoop of the potato mixture in the palm of your hand and flatten it into a 3- or 4-inch-wide round that is ½ inch thick. Repeat with the remaining potato mixture to make 12–14 rounds.

5. Put a panir cube in the center of each round, fold the potato mixture over it, and roll until sealed and rounded. Press firmly to eliminate air pockets.

6. Press the pea mixture around the potato rounds.

7. Whisk together the water and flour to make a smooth, thick paste. Spread the bread crumbs in a shallow pan. Roll the balls in the flour paste, then in the bread crumbs. Set aside.

8. Cook the panir potato rounds as directed above (see step 3).

9. Cut the cooked panir rounds in half, arrange them on a platter, and spoon curry powder around them. Sprinkle with diced fresh cilantro and cumin powder.

YIELD: 8–10 servings

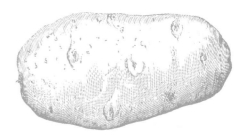

chicken breasts with avocado buttermilk dressing

■ ■ ■

Need another way to prepare chicken? This one's a winner. Serve with brown rice and steamed vegetables.

2 boneless, skinless chicken breasts, halved
2 ripe avocados
¾ cup buttermilk
⅓ cup finely chopped onion
¼ cup mayonnaise
2 tablespoons sour cream
1 tablespoon lemon juice
½ teaspoon salt
¼ teaspoon freshly ground black pepper
3 or 4 drops hot pepper sauce
Dash of ground cumin
Shredded lettuce, parsley sprigs, and sliced
    tomatoes or red bell peppers, for garnish

1. Poach the chicken breasts in boiling water for 20 minutes, or until no longer pink. Refrigerate.
2. Peel and pit the avocados. In a blender or food processor, purée the avocado flesh.
3. Add the buttermilk, onion, mayonnaise, sour cream, lemon juice, salt, black pepper, hot pepper sauce, and cumin and process thoroughly.
4. When ready to serve, arrange the chicken on a serving platter. Garnish with shredded lettuce, parsley sprigs, and sliced tomatoes or red bell peppers. Pour the dressing around the chicken.

YIELD: 4 servings

chilled curried chicken

■ ■ ■

I love curry, and this dish is a favorite when served on a bed of crisp lettuce in summer.

1 tablespoon butter
1 small onion, chopped
⅓ cup red wine
2 teaspoons lemon juice
2 teaspoons tomato sauce
3 dried apricots, chopped
1 teaspoon curry powder
1 bay leaf
⅔ cup fromage blanc
2 tablespoons mayonnaise
2 cups cooked, diced chicken
    (about ½-inch cubes)
½ cup chopped green bell pepper
3 ounces seedless grapes (any type)
Freshly ground black pepper
Cucumber slices, for garnish

1. Melt the butter in a saucepan over medium heat. Sauté the onion until translucent, about 5 minutes.
2. Add the wine, lemon juice, tomato sauce, apricots, curry powder, and bay leaf. Simmer, uncovered, for 5 minutes.
3. Remove the bay leaf and discard. Place the mixture in a blender and blend to combine. (Hold down the blender lid with a potholder; the hot mixture will make the lid pop off.)
4. Add the cheese and mayonnaise and blend again. Remove to a large bowl.

5. Fold in the chicken, bell pepper, and grapes. Season with black pepper to taste.

6. Refrigerate, covered, for at least 4 hours or up to 1 day in advance. Serve with a cucumber garnish.

YIELD : 4–6 servings

chicken paillards in crème fraîche

■ ■ ■

This recipe is melt-in-your-mouth delicious.

- 2 whole chicken breasts (about 1½ pounds)
- 2 tablespoons unsalted butter
- Salt and freshly ground black pepper
- 2 tablespoons finely minced shallot
- ½ cup chicken stock or low-sodium chicken broth
- ½ cup dry white wine
- ½ cup crème fraîche
- 1 tablespoon tarragon mustard (Cajun, honey, or coarse-grained)
- 3 tablespoons finely minced fresh parsley (optional, for color)

1. Trim away the center cartilage of the chicken breasts and discard any fat. Remove the fillets on the bottom of each breast and reserve for another use. Using a rolling pin, pound the chicken between sheets of wax paper to just less than ½ inch thick.

2. Melt the butter in a large skillet over medium heat. Pat the chicken paillards dry. Place them in the skillet and cook for about 2 minutes, or until lightly colored. Turn.

3. Season lightly with salt and pepper and stir the shallots into the butter around the paillards. Cook 2 minutes longer.

4. Transfer the paillards to a plate. Raise the heat to high. Pour the stock and wine into the skillet and bring to a boil, stirring to scrape any browned bits from the bottom of the pan. Cook hard until reduced by half, about 2 minutes. Add the crème fraîche and mustard.

5. Return the paillards to the skillet, lower the heat, and simmer, basting the paillards with the sauce until they are heated through and fully cooked (1–2 minutes). Transfer to plates.

6. Adjust the seasoning. Strain the sauce over the paillards, sprinkle with parsley, and serve immediately.

YIELD: 4 servings

Judy Schad, Capriole Farm
Greenville, Indiana

The hills and valleys of southern Indiana, an area known as Kentuckiana (the Ohio River and Louisville are just down the road), are home to the Schad family and Capriole Farm. The 300 dairy goats they milk today are related to the ones Judy bought in 1978 as a 4-H project for her kids. Cheese making begins and ends right here, on the farm.

Judy got started in cheese making when she took a cheese-making class. "I saw cheese making as an extension of the kitchen," Judy says, "and then I started playing around with molds and fungi and also breeding my goats to select for certain qualities." She believes that the distinction of the cheeses she makes is due to the high-quality milk she gets from "the girls." The farmstead-scale production allows for many happy accidents and experiments, but the milk is a constant: "French farmers believe that your particular environment is expressed in what you produce. Our goats, their forage, their milk — that's what makes our cheeses unique."

Capriole's fresh chèvre is hand-ladled to stay light, almost fluffy. The farm's surface-ripened cheeses, such as Wabash Cannonball, and the semi-hard aged cheeses, including Old Kentucky Tomme and Mont St. Francis, are shipped to some of the finest restaurants across the United States for customers to enjoy on cheese boards and dessert trays. "I'm pleased with the profile of the cheeses we do," says Judy. "I've chosen the ones I love." (One of Judy's favorite recipes for cooking with goat cheese is featured on page 223.)

Distinctive milk from her prized herd of goats gives Judy Schad's cheeses their unique flavor and texture

turkey cheese casserole

■ ■ ■

Here's a great way to use Thanksgiving leftovers.

- 4 cups cooked, cubed turkey (about 1-inch cubes)
- 2 cups shredded Cheddar cheese
- 1½ cups chopped celery
- ¼ cup finely chopped green bell pepper
- 2 tablespoons chopped onion
- 1 cup (8 ounces) sour cream
- ¼ cup all-purpose flour
- 2 tablespoons lemon juice
- ¾ teaspoon salt
- Freshly ground black pepper

1. Preheat the oven to 350°F. Grease a shallow, 2-quart casserole.
2. In a large bowl, toss together the turkey, 1¾ cups of the cheese, and the celery, bell pepper, and onion.
3. In a separate bowl, combine the sour cream and flour. Stir in the lemon juice, salt, and pepper, to taste.
4. Lightly toss the sour cream mixture with the turkey mixture.
5. Pour into the prepared casserole. Garnish with the remaining ¼ cup of cheese and bake for 20 minutes, or until bubbly around the edges.

YIELD: 6 servings

pasta with shrimp and spinach

■ ■ ■

When my friend Denise serves this at a dinner party, I am instantly there! Follow with wine and a great cheese board.

- 8 ounces uncooked penne, mostaccioli, or similarly shaped pasta
- 1 cup (8 ounces) plain, nonfat yogurt
- ½ cup crumbled feta cheese
- 2 cloves garlic, minced
- 1 tablespoon chopped fresh dill (or 1 teaspoon dried)
- ½ teaspoon freshly ground black pepper
- 12 ounces medium frozen shrimp, thawed
- 1 package (10 ounces) frozen chopped spinach, thawed
- Salt

1. Prepare the pasta according to package directions. While the pasta is cooking, blend the yogurt, feta, garlic, dill, and pepper in a large mixing bowl.
2. Two minutes before the pasta is done, add the shrimp and spinach to the pot with the pasta. Continue cooking for the remaining 2 minutes.
3. Drain the pasta, shrimp, and spinach thoroughly. Stir into the yogurt mixture and season with salt to taste. Serve immediately.

YIELD: 4 servings

carol's goat's-milk ricotta scallops

■ ■ ■

This delicious treatment of scallops from Carol Lively is fast, easy, and elegant. It is low in carbohydrates and can easily be modified by using different herbs, lemon juice, and even homemade mozzarella instead of ricotta. See the profile of Carol's home cheese making on page 50.

1 pound bay scallops
Salt and freshly ground black pepper
½ teaspoon dried dill
½ cup goat's-milk ricotta cheese
½ cup sour cream

1. Preheat the broiler.
2. Divide the scallops between two baking dishes so they are in a single layer. Sprinkle both dishes with salt and pepper to taste, then sprinkle with the dill.
3. Spread the ricotta and then the sour cream as evenly as you can over the scallops.
4. Broil for 5–7 minutes, or until white inside. Check the scallops frequently so they do not overcook.
5. Remove from the oven and drain off any excess liquid; serve hot.

YIELD: 2 or 3 servings

desserts

coeur à la crème

■ ■ ■

This is a wonderful dessert cheese that is traditionally drained in heart-shaped molds. Serve with fresh fruit, syrup, or melted chocolate.

1 cup (8 ounces) fromage blanc
1 tablespoon granulated sugar
1 tablespoon heavy cream
2 egg whites, beaten until stiff

1. Combine the cheese, sugar, and cream. Fold in the egg whites.
2. Spoon into individual heart-shaped molds lined with butter muslin. Place the molds on a baking sheet and chill in the refrigerator for 6–10 hours.
3. Gently pull up the butter muslin to remove the hearts from the molds.

Note: The egg yolk in this recipe is not cooked. Please see "Egg Information" on page 228.

YIELD: 4 servings

fromage blanc apple butter cheesecake

■ ■ ■

When the first fall apples ripen, I cook up a big batch of apple butter to be used in this recipe for the rest of the year. (Apple butter is simply applesauce that is cooked and reduced until it is nice and thick.)

1½ cups (12 ounces) fromage blanc, at room temperature (72°F)
1 cup apple butter (if you use genuine, unsweetened cider-mill apple butter, increase the granulated sugar by 3 tablespoons)
4 eggs
½ cup plus 3 tablespoons granulated sugar
3 teaspoons vanilla extract
2 teaspoons cinnamon
1 Graham-Cracker Crust (see recipe at right)
1 cup (8 ounces) sour cream

1. Preheat the oven to 350°F.
2. Place the cheese, apple butter, eggs, ½ cup of the sugar, 2 teaspoons of the vanilla, and 1 teaspoon of the cinnamon in the work bowl of a food processor fitted with a steel blade. Process until smooth, stopping once or twice to scrape down the sides of the bowl.
3. Pour the filling into the prepared piecrust and bake for about 40 minutes.
4. Meanwhile, whisk together the sour cream, the remaining sugar, vanilla, and ½ teaspoon of the remaining cinnamon until smooth. Refrigerate until ready to use.
5. When the edges of the cake are set and lightly browned but the center of the cheesecake remains slightly unset, immediately pour the sour cream mixture around the edges and over the top of the cake.
6. Bake 7–10 minutes longer, or until the sour cream bubbles around the edges.
7. Sprinkle the top lightly with the remaining ½ teaspoon of cinnamon and cool to room temperature (72°F) on a rack. Refrigerate overnight before cutting.

YIELD: 8 servings

GRAHAM-CRACKER CRUST

½ cup graham-cracker crumbs (about 8 crackers)
2 tablespoons sugar
2 tablespoons unsalted butter, melted

1. In a bowl, combine the crumbs and sugar, then add the butter. Mix well.
2. Spread the crumb mixture in the bottom of an 8-inch springform pan and pat firmly and evenly. Refrigerate while you prepare the filling.

YIELD: Pastry for one 8-inch pie

apricot crisp with crème fraîche

■ ■ ■

Your guests will savor this light, flavorful dessert. The crème fraîche is a nice complement to the sweetness of the apricot crisp.

½ cup (1 stick) unsalted butter, cut into small pieces
4 cups pitted apricot halves
Juice of 1 medium lemon
2–8 tablespoons granulated sugar
1 cup sifted all-purpose flour
1 cup firmly packed light brown sugar
1 teaspoon ground cinnamon
½ teaspoon salt
1–1½ cups (8–12 ounces) crème fraîche, at room temperature (72°F)

1. Preheat the oven to 375°F.
2. With a little of the butter, lightly grease a 9-inch pie pan or a shallow, round baking dish.
3. Toss the apricots in the lemon juice and sprinkle with the granulated sugar to taste. Pile into the baking dish.
4. Combine the remaining butter and the flour, brown sugar, cinnamon, and salt in a bowl. Rub together with your fingertips until the mixture is crumbly. Sprinkle on top of the fruit.
5. Bake for 35–45 minutes, until the fruit is bubbly around the edges and the top has browned. Let cool briefly. Top each serving with crème fraîche and serve warm.

YIELD: 4–6 servings

tiramisù

■ ■ ■

A traditional Italian dessert, tiramisù *means "pick me up."*

20 ladyfingers
3 eggs, separated
3 tablespoons granulated sugar
1½ cups (12 ounces) mascarpone
1 tablespoon Triple Sec or cognac
1 cup strong coffee
3 ounces semisweet chocolate, grated
1 ounce almonds, chopped and toasted

1. Preheat the oven to 325°F.
2. Cut the ladyfingers in half and spread on a baking sheet. Brown in the oven for 5 minutes per side. Cool.
3. With an electric mixer, beat together the egg yolks and sugar at high speed until thick. Add the mascarpone and Triple Sec and beat by hand until smooth.
4. Beat the egg whites until stiff and fold into the mascarpone mixture.
5. Dip the ladyfinger bottoms into the coffee, cut-side down, so that they soak up some of the liquid but do not become mushy. Do not soak for too long.
6. Place the coffee-soaked ladyfingers, cut-side up, in a 2-quart bowl. Cover with half the mascarpone mixture.
7. Sprinkle half the chocolate and half the almonds over the mascarpone.
8. Dip the top halves of the remaining ladyfingers into the coffee with the cut-side down. Let them soak up some of the liquid, but they should remain firm.

9. Place the coffee-soaked ladyfingers, cut-side up, on top of the mascarpone-covered ladyfingers. Cover them with the remaining mascarpone mixture, chocolate, and almonds.

10. Cover the bowl and refrigerate for at least 6 hours, or overnight, before serving.

Note: The egg yolk in this recipe is not cooked. Please see "Egg Information" on page 228.

YIELD: 10–12 servings

cream cheese chocolate fudge

■ ■ ■

Did you ever see chocolate smiles? Well, you will with this recipe.

⅓ cup cream cheese
2 cups sifted confectioners' sugar
2 squares (1 ounce each) unsweetened chocolate, melted
½ cup chopped pecans
¼ teaspoon vanilla extract
Pinch of salt

1. Cream the cheese in a bowl until soft and smooth. Slowly blend in the sugar.

2. Add the chocolate and mix well.

3. Add the pecans, vanilla, and salt and mix until well blended. Press into a well-greased shallow pan.

4. Place in the refrigerator until firm, about 15 minutes. Cut into squares.

YIELD: 12–16 servings (if you're lucky!)

ronnie's mascarpone fudge

■ ■ ■

Mascarpone, homemade or store-bought, adds to the creaminess of this fudge. Ronnie Glantz developed the recipe for the Vermont Butter & Cheese Company in Websterville.

1½ pounds unsweetened baking chocolate or semisweet chocolate chips
1 cup (8 ounces) mascarpone
¼ cup (2 ounces) peanut butter
¼ cup raisins (optional)
¼ cup walnuts (optional)

1. Butter an 8-inch square glass pan. Melt the chocolate in a heavy saucepan or a double boiler over medium heat. Remove from the heat.

2. Add the mascarpone and blend thoroughly.

3. Swirl in the peanut butter and the raisins and walnuts, if desired.

4. Spread in the prepared pan. Refrigerate overnight, then cut into small serving pieces.

YIELD: About 36 pieces

mascarpone tart topped with fresh fruit

■ ■ ■

Cheese maker and author Paula Lambert developed this recipe, which is reminiscent of the pastries sold in an elegant shop she loves to frequent in Perugia. It is a perfect summer dessert, but you can vary the fruit and serve it year-round. See the profile of Paula and her business, The Mozzarella Company, on page 119.

Sweet Pastry Crust (see recipe at right)
2 cups (1 pound) cold mascarpone (home-made or store-bought)
¼ cup sugar
3 tablespoons Grand Marnier or other fruit-based liqueur
1 pint (2 cups) fresh blueberries
1 pint (2 cups) fresh strawberries
¼ cup apple jelly

1. Butter and flour a 10- to 12-inch tart pan with a removable bottom.
2. Place the pastry crust on a lightly floured piece of wax paper on a work surface. Roll out the dough to a round 1–2 inches larger than the tart pan. Pick up the dough and wax paper and invert it into the tart pan. Peel off the paper. Carefully fit the dough into the pan, patching it, if needed. Trim the edges by rolling a rolling pin across the top of the pan. Prick the bottom of the shell with a fork and refrigerate for 30 minutes. Meanwhile, preheat the oven to 375°F.

3. Bake the tart shell for 20–25 minutes, or until light golden brown. Cool on a rack.
4. In a small bowl, combine the mascarpone, sugar, and 2 tablespoons of the Grand Marnier. Spread the mixture on the cooled crust with a rubber spatula. Refrigerate.
5. Wash the berries, removing the stems and hulls. If the strawberries are large, slice or quarter them. Arrange the berries over the filling in an attractive pattern.
6. In a small saucepan, simmer the jelly and remaining Grand Marnier over low heat, stirring, until it thickens and large bubbles form. Remove from the heat; paint over the fruit with a pastry brush.
7. Remove the sides of the tart pan and slide the tart onto a serving plate. Refrigerate for at least 30 minutes (up to 4 hours). Cut into wedges to serve.

YIELD: 8 servings

SWEET PASTRY CRUST

7 tablespoons unsalted butter
⅔ cup sugar
½ teaspoon grated lemon zest
3 egg yolks
1½ cups unbleached all-purpose flour
Pinch of salt

1. Place the butter, sugar, and lemon zest in the work bowl of a food processor fitted with a steel blade. Pulse until the ingredients are well mixed.

2. Add the egg yolks and pulse to mix well.

3. Add the flour and salt and pulse briefly until blended. The dough will be crumbly. Be careful not to overwork it.

4. Remove the dough from the work bowl, press it into a disk, and wrap in plastic wrap. Refrigerate for at least 30 minutes.

YIELD: Pastry for 1 tart

frosted sour cream spice cake

■ ■ ■

This recipe is an old New England favorite.

  2 cups sifted all-purpose flour
1½ cups packed brown sugar
  2 teaspoons ground cinnamon
1¼ teaspoons baking soda
  1 teaspoon baking powder
  ¾ teaspoon ground cloves
  ½ teaspoon ground nutmeg
  ½ teaspoon salt
  1 cup (8 ounces) sour cream
  2 tablespoons butter, softened
  ¼ cup shortening
  ½ cup water
  2 eggs
  1 cup chopped raisins
  ½ cup chopped walnuts
  Sour Cream Frosting (see recipe at right)

1. Preheat the oven to 350°F. Grease one 13- by 9-inch rectangular pan or two 8-inch round pans and lightly coat with flour.

2. In a medium-sized bowl, combine the flour, sugar, cinnamon, baking soda, baking powder, cloves, nutmeg, and salt.

3. In a large bowl, combine the sour cream, butter, shortening, water, and eggs and beat until smooth.

4. Fold the flour mixture into the sour cream mixture. Stir in the raisins and walnuts. Pour into the pan(s).

5. Bake the rectangular cake for 40–45 minutes, the round cakes for 30–35 minutes, or until a tester inserted into the center comes out clean.

6. Let cool for 10 minutes, then turn out onto racks. Cool completely and frost with the Sour Cream Frosting.

SOUR CREAM FROSTING

  3 cups confectioners' sugar
5⅓ tablespoons butter, softened
  ½ cup sour cream
  2 teaspoons vanilla extract

1. In a medium-sized bowl, combine the sugar and butter until blended.

2. Add the sour cream and vanilla. Beat until smooth and spreadable.

YIELD: Frosting for one 13- by 9-inch cake or filling and frosting for one 8- or 9-inch two-layer cake

cream cheese frosting

■ ■ ■

Try this frosting on a moist, double-chocolate cake. Delicious!

- 1 cup (8 ounces) cream cheese, softened
- 4 tablespoons butter, softened
- 2 ounces unsweetened baking chocolate, melted and cooled (optional)
- 2 teaspoons milk
- 1 teaspoon vanilla extract
- 4 cups confectioners' sugar

1. In a medium-sized bowl, beat the cream cheese, butter, chocolate (if desired), milk, and vanilla until smooth.
2. Gradually beat in the sugar until smooth and spreadable.

YIELD: 2½ cups

yogurt pops

■ ■ ■

A healthy alternative to sugary Popsicles, these cool snacks are fun breakfast treats too.

- 1 cup (8 ounces) plain low-fat yogurt
- ¾ cup frozen fruit juice concentrate (any type)
- ¾ cup low-fat or skim milk

1. Combine all ingredients and pour into six small paper cups.
2. Insert a wooden stick in the center of each.
3. Freeze until firm, 2–3 hours.
4. To serve, peel off the paper cups and discard.

YIELD: 6 servings

fruit raita

■ ■ ■

A traditional Indian dish, raita is a nice cool accompaniment to a spicy dish.

- 3 tablespoons raisins or currants
- 1½ cups (12 ounces) yogurt
- 1 cup (8 ounces) sour cream
- ⅓ cup honey
- 3 tablespoons slivered almonds
- ¼ teaspoon ground cardamom
- ⅛ teaspoon ground cinnamon
- ⅛ teaspoon ground coriander
- ½ pound red or green seedless grapes, halved
- 1 apple, chopped
- 1 banana, sliced

1. Put the raisins in a small bowl and cover with boiling water. Let soak for 15 minutes, then drain.
2. In a serving bowl, combine the yogurt, sour cream, honey, almonds, cardamom, cinnamon, and coriander. Stir in the raisins.
3. Gently mix in the grapes, apple, and banana and chill. Sprinkle with additional cardamom before serving.

YIELD: 6 servings

Mariano Gonzalez, Fiscalini Farms
Modesto, California

The Fiscalini family came to California from Switzerland in 1890, bringing the traditions of many generations of dairy farmers. The family turned to Mariano Gonzalez and his team of cheese makers to transform their nascent cheese-making operation into one of growing sophistication.

Mariano's path to California was not a straight one. Raised in Paraguay, he learned cheese making as a boy on his family's farm. He started with queso blanco, coagulating the milk by acidification. Then in 1987 he went to Shelburne Farm in Vermont, where he learned more about cheese making, took courses at the University of Vermont, and made a plan to return to Paraguay to develop a cheese factory with his father and uncle.

Sadly, his father and uncle both died suddenly. Mariano decided to persevere with his plan anyway. In 1997 he returned to Paraguay, where he hoped to help local farmers market their milk. After four years of frustration at the political and economic conditions in the country, he decided to return to the United States. Cheese-maker friends put him in touch with the Fiscalini family, whose cheese-making operation was just getting started. Mariano started working on the recipe and aging process for San Joaquin Gold, a fontina-style cheese; two types of Cheddar; and Parmesan. Their first aged cheeses were sold in the fall of 2001.

Mariano loves his work. "If I don't make cheese, I'm not happy," he says. "I wanted to make a small-scale farmstead cheese, and when I first heard about the size of this farm I was worried. But once I saw how well the cows are managed, how comfortable and clean they are, I fell in love." His advice to beginning cheese makers is this: "Don't get discouraged. To make a living product like cheese is tricky. It takes a while to get the bacteria in the cheese to be happy." He and his wife have two daughters who love their father's cheese. "I hope they will follow my path and become cheese makers," Mariano says with a smile.

> *When the owners of this vast dairy farm wanted to produce farmstead cheeses, they turned to a talented Paraguayan cheese maker*

irish cream frozen yogurt

■ ■ ■

This frozen yogurt is delicious to enjoy on the veranda on a hot summer's evening.

2 tablespoons plus ⅓ cup water
1 teaspoon unflavored gelatin
¾ cup low-fat milk
¼ cup light corn syrup
¼ cup sugar
3 ounces semisweet chocolate, coarsely chopped
1 cup (8 ounces) low-fat yogurt, stirred
3 tablespoons Irish cream liqueur
⅓ cup nonfat dry milk
1 egg white

1. In a small saucepan, combine the 2 tablespoons of water and the gelatin. Let stand for 1 minute. Stir over low heat until gelatin dissolves. Set aside.
2. In medium-sized saucepan, combine the milk, corn syrup, sugar, and chocolate. Cook, whisking constantly, over low heat until the mixture is smooth.
3. Stir in the dissolved gelatin mixture. Let cool.
4. Add the yogurt and liqueur.
5. Beat the remaining ⅓ cup of water, dry milk, and egg white until stiff but not dry. Fold into the yogurt mixture.
6. Freeze in an ice-cream maker, or, if one is not available, whisk frequently while it freezes.
Note: The egg in this recipe is not cooked. Please see "Egg Information" on page 228.

YIELD: 6–8 servings

frozen yogurt cheese dessert

■ ■ ■

Topped with chocolate sauce and garnished with a fresh sprig of mint, this is a delightful summer treat.

2 cups (16 ounces) yogurt cheese (see recipe on page 77)
½ cup sugar
1 tablespoon vanilla extract
4 egg whites
1 cup strawberries, thinly sliced

1. In a large bowl, combine the cheese, sugar, and vanilla.
2. In a separate bowl, beat the egg whites until stiff. Fold into the cheese mixture.
3. Fold in the strawberries.
4. For best results, let the mixture stand overnight in the refrigerator.
5. Freeze according to the ice-cream maker's instructions or whisk several times as it hardens in the freezer.
Note: The egg in this recipe is not cooked. Please see "Egg Information" on page 228.

YIELD: 6 servings

beverages

kefir fruit drinks

■ ■ ■

Delicious and easy to make, these drinks are especially bubbly and effervescent when using kefir made from live grains.

BASIC BLEND

- 1 cup (8 ounces) fruit juice
- 1 cup (8 ounces) kefir
- 4–6 ice cubes
- 1 teaspoon honey or maple syrup (optional)

Combine all ingredients in a blender and process until smooth. Serve immediately.

YIELD: 2 or 3 servings

BERRY DELICIOUS

- 1 cup fresh or frozen berries
- 1 cup (8 ounces) kefir
- 4–6 ice cubes
- 1 tablespoon frozen orange juice concentrate

Combine all ingredients in a blender and process until smooth. Serve immediately.

YIELD: 2 or 3 servings

CHOCOLATE-BANANA BLAST

- 1 cup (8 ounces) kefir
- 4–6 ice cubes
- 1 banana, frozen
- 2 teaspoons chocolate syrup
- 2 teaspoons peanut butter

Combine all ingredients in a blender and process until smooth. Serve immediately.

YIELD: 2 or 3 servings

TROPICAL SPLENDOR

- 1 cup (8 ounces) kefir
- ½ cup crushed pineapple with juice
- 4–6 ice cubes
- 1 banana, frozen
- 1 kiwi (peeled)

Combine all ingredients in a blender and process until smooth. Serve immediately.

YIELD: 2 or 3 servings

APPENDIXES

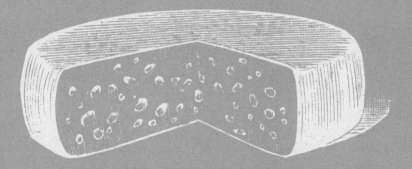

GLOSSARY OF TERMS

Acid curd. The custardlike state that milk acquires when a high level of acidity is created.

Acidity. The amount of sourness in milk. Acidity is produced by the activity of starter culture bacteria, and it precipitates the milk protein into a solid curd.

Aging. A step in cheese making in which the cheese is stored at a particular temperature and relative humidity for a specified amount of time so it can develop its distinct flavor.

Albuminous protein. Protein in milk that cannot be precipitated out by the addition of rennet. Albuminous protein remains in the whey and is precipitated by high temperatures to make ricotta.

Annatto. A natural vegetable extract used to color cheese. *See also* cheese color.

Ash. A charcoal or vegetable derivative used to neutralize the surface of cheese and create a friendly environment for mold growth.

Bacteria. Microscopic unicellular organisms found almost everywhere. Lactic acid–producing bacteria are helpful and necessary for making quality hard cheeses.

Bacteria-ripened cheese. A cheese upon whose surface bacterial growth is encouraged to develop in order to produce a distinct flavor. Brick and Limburger are examples of bacteria-ripened cheeses.

Bandaging. The wrapping and larding of cheese to keep its shape, preserve its coat, and prevent the loss of excess moisture through evaporation.

Blue mold. *See Penicillium roqueforti.*

Brevibacterium linens. A red bacterium that is encouraged to grow on the surfaces of cheeses, such as brick and Limburger, to produce a sharp flavor.

Butterfat. The fat portion (cream) in milk. Butterfat can vary from 2½ to 5½ percent of the total weight of milk.

Butter muslin. A very finely woven cotton cloth used to drain soft cheeses.

Calcium chloride. A white, lumpy solid that is derived from calcium carbonate and used as a drying agent to produce a firmer curd.

Casein. The principal protein in milk that, with the addition of rennet, coagulates and forms the foundation for cheese.

Cheese board. A board made of ash, fir, maple, or birch with no knots and measuring 6 inches square and 1 inch thick, often used to help drain soft cheeses, such as Camembert. Larger cheese boards are often used to hold cheeses during the aging process.

Cheesecloth. A finely woven cotton cloth used to drain curds, line cheese molds, and perform a host of other cheese-making functions.

Cheese color. Annatto, a natural coloring added to milk prior to renneting to impart various shades of yellow to cheese. Obtained from the seeds of the fruit of the annatto tree, *Bixa orellana,* which is native to many tropical countries and cultivated in the West Indies, Brazil, and India.

Cheese mat. A wooden reed or food-grade plastic mat often used to help drain soft cheeses, such as Coulommiers and Camembert.

Cheese salt. A coarse, noniodized flake salt.

Cheese starter culture. A bacterial culture added to milk as the first step in making many cheeses. The bacteria produce an acid during their life cycle in the milk. There are two categories of starter culture: mesophilic and thermophilic.

Cheese trier. A stainless-steel iron used to take samples as a cheese ages to determine whether it is properly matured and ready for eating.

Cheese wax. A pliable wax with a low melting point that produces an airtight seal that will not crack. Most hard cheeses are waxed.

Cheese wrap. A permeable cellophane for wrapping cheese.

Clean break. The condition of the curd when it is ready for cutting. A finger or thermometer inserted into the curd at a 45-degree angle will separate the curd firmly and cleanly if the curd has reached that stage.

Coagulation. The point at which milk congeals into a thickened mass.

Cooking. A step in cheese making during which the cut curd is warmed to expel more whey.

Coulommiers mold. A stainless-steel mold consisting of two hoops, one resting inside the other. The mold is used to make Coulommiers cheese. (A one-piece Camembert mold may also be used.)

Curd. The solid, custardlike state of milk achieved by the addition of rennet. The curd contains most of the milk protein and fat.

Curd knife. A knife with a blade long enough to reach the bottom of the pot without immersing the handle and with a flat end rather than a pointed one.

Cutting the curd. A step in cheese making in which the curd is cut into equal-sized pieces.

Dairy thermometer. A thermometer that ranges from 0°F to 220°F and can be used to measure the temperature of milk during cheese making.

Direct heating. Heating milk for cheese making on the stovetop.

Direct-set starter. Prepackaged starter cultures that are added directly to milk, eliminating the lengthy process of making the prepared starter (mother culture), and used to turn milk protein into a solid white gel for the purpose of cheese making.

Draining. A step in cheese making in which the whey is separated from the curds by ladling the curds and whey into a colander lined with cheesecloth.

Drip tray. A tray that is placed under a mold while a cheese is pressed. The drip tray allows the whey to drain into a sink or other container.

Drying. The air-drying of cheese to form a protective rind in anticipation of the aging process.

Dry milk powder. Dehydrated milk solids that may be reconstituted in water.

Flora Danica starter. A fresh goat-cheese starter that may be used as either a direct-set or a reculturable starter.

Follower. A flat stainless-steel, food-grade plastic, or wooden disk used inside a mold to apply even pressure to the curd.

Geotrichum candidum. A white mold that is encouraged to grow on the surface of a number of soft mold-ripened cheeses, such as Camembert and Brie, producing a delicious, mottled white skin.

Hard cheese. A cheese that is firm or hard in texture because a high percentage of moisture is removed during the cheese-making process. Hard cheeses are pressed and aged for varying lengths of time for full flavor development.

Homogenization. A mechanical process that breaks up fat globules in milk so that they will be evenly dispersed and the cream will no longer rise to the top.

Indirect heating. Placing a pot of milk for cheese making into a bowl or sink full of hot water.

Junket rennet. A weak form of rennet.

Lactic acid. The acid created in milk during cheese making. Cheese starter culture bacteria consume the milk sugar (lactose) and produce lactic acid as a by-product.

Lactose. The sugar naturally present in milk. Lactose can constitute up to 5 percent of the total weight of milk.

Lipase powder. An enzyme added to milk to create a stronger-flavored cheese.

Mesophilic cheese starter culture. A blend of lactic acid–producing bacteria that is used to make cheeses when the cooking temperature is 102°F or lower.

Milkstone. A milk residue that is deposited on cheese-making utensils over time.

Milling. A step in cheese making during which the curd is broken into smaller pieces before being placed into a cheese press.

Molding. A step in cheese making during which the curd is placed into a cheese mold. The cheese mold helps produce the final shape of the cheese and aids in drainage.

Mold-ripened cheese. A cheese upon whose surface (and/or interior) a mold is encouraged to grow. Two types of mold are most commonly used in cheese making: blue mold (for blue cheeses) and white mold (for Camembert and related cheeses). *See also Penicillium roqueforti and Penicillium camemberti.*

Mother culture. *See* prepared starter culture.

Noncorrosive. A material that will not break down or erode in the presence of acid.

Nonfat (skim) milk. Milk that has most of the cream removed and a butterfat content of 1 to 2 percent.

Oiling. The application of vegetable oil to provide a protective layer that keeps the cheese from drying out.

Pasteurization. The heating of milk to 145°F for 30 minutes in order to destroy pathogenic organisms that may be harmful to people.

Penicillium camemberti (P. album). A white mold that is encouraged to grow on the surface of a number of soft mold-ripened cheeses, such as Camembert and Brie, producing a delicious, mottled white skin.

Penicillium candidum. A white mold that is encouraged to grow on the surface of a number of soft mold-ripened cheeses, such as Brie and Camembert, producing a delicious, mottled white skin.

Penicillium roqueforti. A blue mold that is encouraged to grow on the surface and in the interior of a variety of blue cheeses, including Stilton and Gorgonzola.

Prepared starter culture. A mother culture containing live bacteria that may be propagated and used to turn milk protein into a solid white gel for the purpose of cheese making.

Pressing. A step in cheese making during which the curds are placed into a cheesecloth-lined mold and pressed to remove more whey.

Proper break. A term used during the making of Swiss cheese. To make certain the curds are properly cooked, a handful is wadded into a ball. If the ball of curds can be easily broken back into the individual curd particles, it is called a *proper break.*

Raw milk. Milk that is taken fresh from an animal and has not been pasteurized.

Reculturable starter. A culture that can be made into a mother culture and repropagated for many generations of bacteria.

Red bacteria. *See Brevibacterium linens.*

Re-dressing. The changing of cheesecloth on a cheese that is being drained or pressed. This is required to keep the cheesecloth from sticking to the cheese.

Rennet. A milk-coagulating enzyme that is available in three forms. Animal-derived rennet comes from the fourth stomach of a milk-fed calf. It contains the enzyme rennin, which has the ability to coagulate milk. Vegetable-derived rennet is a microbial rennet that contains no animal products. Chymostar Classic is a factory-made rennet containing no animal products.

Renneting. A step in the cheese-making process in which rennet is added to milk to bring about coagulation.

Ripening. A step in cheese making in which milk is allowed to undergo an increase in acidity as a result of the activity of cheese starter culture bacteria.

Salting. A step in cheese making in which cheese salt is added to the curds before molding or to the surface of the finished cheese.

Saturated brine solution. A saltwater solution in which cheese is soaked. Water is saturated when it will no longer dissolve any additional salt.

Soft cheese. A cheese that is not pressed, has a high moisture content, and is either not aged at all or aged for a comparatively short period.

Thermophilic cheese starter culture. A bacterial starter culture that is used to make cheeses that have a high cooking temperature. Recipes for Italian and Swiss cheeses call for thermophilic culture.

Top-stirring. Stirring the top ¼ inch of non-homogenized milk to keep the cream from rising immediately after rennet has been added to milk.

Ultra-Heat-Treated (UHT) milk. "Long-life" milk that is flash-heated for a few seconds at a temperature between 275 and 300°F to give it a shelf life of several months.

Ultrapasteurization. The high-heat treatment of milk to guarantee a long shelf life.

Waxing. The application of cheese wax to keep cheese from drying out and to retard the growth of mold.

Whey. The liquid portion of milk that develops after the milk protein has coagulated. Whey contains water, milk sugar, albuminous proteins, and minerals.

White mold. *See Penicillium candidum, Penicillium camemberti,* and *Geotrichum candidum.*

TROUBLESHOOTING GUIDE

Problem	Possible Causes	Possible Solutions
The cheese tastes very bitter	Poor hygiene was used in handling the milk and/or cheese-making utensils.	Keep the milk in a cold, sanitary environment until ready for cheese making. Keep all utensils absolutely clean and free from milkstone. (Milkstone is a milk residue that is deposited over time on the surface of utensils. It can be removed by using a dairy-acid type of cleanser.) Sterilize all utensils. If using raw milk, pasteurize it prior to cheese making (see page 14).
	Excessive rennet was used.	Reduce the amount of rennet.
	Excessive acidity developed during the cheese-making process.	Take steps to reduce acidity (see pages 20, 23, 42, and 62).
	Too little salt was added to the curd after milling.	Increase the amount of salt added to the curds.
The cheese tastes quite sour and acidic	The cheese contains too much moisture.	Take steps to reduce the moisture content during cheese making (see pages 49 and 51).
	Excessive acidity developed during the cheese-making process.	Take steps to reduce acid production (see pages 20, 23, 42, and 62).
The cheese has little or no flavor	The cheese was not aged long enough.	Age cheese for at least the minimum period stated in recipe.
	Insufficient acidity was produced during cheese making.	Take steps to increase acidity during cheese making (see pages 20, 23, 42, and 62).
After adding rennet, the milk almost instantly coagulates into a curd of tiny grains while the rennet is still being stirred into the milk	There is excessive acidity in the milk. The milk should not start to coagulate until about 5 minutes after adding the rennet.	Take steps to reduce acidity (see pages 20, 23, 42, and 62).

Problem	Possible Causes	Possible Solutions
The milk does not coagulate into a solid curd	Too little rennet was used.	Increase the amount of rennet.
	Poor-quality rennet was used.	Use a high-quality rennet that has been stored in the appropriate manner.
	Rennet activity was destroyed by mixing it with very warm water for diluting.	Dilute rennet in cool water.
	Rennet was mixed in the same container as the cheese color.	Do not contaminate rennet with cheese coloring.
	The dairy thermometer is inaccurate and the setting temperature was too low.	Check the accuracy of your dairy thermometer by holding it in boiling water and making sure it reads 212°F.
	The milk contains colostrum.	Do not use milk that contains colostrum.
The finished cheese is excessively dry	An insufficient amount of rennet was added.	Add more rennet.
	The curd was cut into particles that were too small.	Cut the curd into larger pieces.
	The curds were cooked to an excessive temperature.	Lower the cooking temperature.
	The curds were overly agitated.	Treat the curds gently.
Mold growth occurs on the surface of air-drying or waxed cheese	There were unclean aging conditions and/or too high a humidity in the aging room.	Clean all cheese-aging shelves thoroughly. Lower the humidity of the cheese storage room.
The cheese is quite difficult to remove from the mold after pressing	Coliform bacteria and/or wild yeast contaminated the milk and the curd. They have produced gas that has swelled the cheese during pressing. This production of gas makes it difficult to remove the cheese from the mold after pressing.	Pay strict attention to cleanliness. Clean all utensils scrupulously. Sterilize all utensils in boiling water or in a sterilizing solution. Keep the milk clean and cold prior to cheese making. If using raw milk, pasteurize it.

(continued on next page)

Problem	Possible Causes	Possible Solutions
The cheese, when cut open, is filled with tiny holes, giving it the appearance of a sponge	Coliform bacteria and/or wild yeast contaminated it. Such a contamination will be noted during the cooking process. The curds will have an unusual odor very similar to that of bread dough.	Pay strict attention to cleanliness.
The cheesecloth is difficult to remove from the cheese after pressing. Pieces of the cheese rip off when the cheesecloth is removed.	Coliform bacteria and/or wild yeast contaminated it.	Pay strict attention to cleanliness.
	The cheese was not re-dressed in a fresh cheesecloth when needed. This is particularly true for cheeses made with thermophilic starter cultures.	Re-dress the cheese promptly as noted in the recipe.
The cheese becomes oily when air-drying	The cheese is being air-dried at too high a temperature.	Remove the cheese to a cooler room. The temperature should not exceed 65°F.
	The curd was stirred too vigorously.	Handle the curd more gently.
	The curd was heated to too high a temperature.	Lower the cooking temperature.
Moisture spots are observed on the surface of the aging cheese beneath the wax. The wet spots begin to rot and ruin the cheese	The cheese was not turned often enough.	Turn the cheese at least daily when it first starts to age.
	The cheese contains excessive moisture.	Take steps to reduce the moisture content of the cheese (see pages 49 and 51).
There is insufficient acidity during cheese making	The starter culture is not working.	Antibiotics are present in the milk. Do not use milk from animals receiving antibiotics or any other medication.
		The starter is contaminated. Use a new starter.
		There is cleaning agent residue, particularly chlorine, on the utensils. Rinse all utensils thoroughly.

Problem	Possible Causes	Possible Solutions
There is excessive acidity during cheese making	The milk was improperly stored prior to cheese making or pasteurization.	Immediately after milking, cool the milk to below 35°F. Store milk at that temperature or lower until ready for cheese making.
	Too much starter was added.	Reduce the amount of starter.
	The ripening period was too long.	Reduce the ripening time and add the rennet sooner.
	There is excessive moisture in the cheese.	Take steps to reduce moisture in the cheese (see pages 49 and 51).
There is excessive moisture in the cheese	Acid development was inadequate during cheese making.	Increase acidity during cheese making (see pages 20, 23, 42, and 62).
	The milk had too high a fat content.	Butterfat content of milk should not be much higher than 4.5 percent. If fat content is higher than that and excessive moisture is a problem, remove some cream prior to cheese making.
	The curds were heated too rapidly. Too fast an increase in cooking temperature produces a membrane around the curd particles that prevents moisture from escaping.	Do not heat the curd faster than two degrees every 5 minutes.
	Too much whey was retained in the curd.	Cut the curd into smaller pieces.
	The curd was heated to too low a temperature during cooking.	Heat the curd to a somewhat higher temperature.

RESOURCES

RESOURCES FOR CHEESE-MAKING SUPPLIES

The following companies carry a complete line of cheese-making supplies.

Glengarry Cheesemaking & Dairy Supply
888-816-0903
www.glengarrycheesemaking.on.ca

New England Cheesemaking Supply Company
413-628-3808
www.cheesemaking.com

The following sources carry rennet and some cheese-making kits and supplies.

Beer & Wine Hobby
781-933-8818
www.beer-wine.com

Caprine Supply
800-646-7796
www.caprinesupply.com

Hoegger Supply Company
800-221-4628
http://hoeggergoatsupply.com

The Home Wine, Beer, and Cheesemaking Shop
818-884-8586
www.homebeerwinecheese.com

Lehman's
888-438-5346
www.lehmans.com

Moorlands Cheesemakers
44-1749-850-108
www.cheesemaking.co.uk

COMMERCIAL SUPPLIES AND EQUIPMENT

Alliance Pastorale
33-5-49-83-30-30
www.alliancepastorale.fr

CHEESE-MAKING MEDIA

Cheesemaking 101, with Ricki Carroll (video)
New England Cheesemaking Supply Company
413-628-3808
www.cheesemaking.com
Farmhouse Cheddar, Fromage, Blanc, Crème Fraîche, Queso Blanco, Ricotta, Mozzarella, Mascarpone.

GROUPS OF INTEREST

Slow Food
718-260-8000
www.slowfood.com
From their Web site: "If we wish to enjoy the pleasure that this world can give us, we have to give of our all to strike the right balance of respect and exchange with nature and the environment. This is why we like to define ourselves as "eco-gastronomes." The fact is that our pleasure cannot be disconnected from the pleasure of others, but it is likewise connected to the equilibrium we manage to preserve (and in many cases, revive) with the environment we live in. Slow Food USA's mission is to rediscover pleasure and quality in everyday life precisely by slowing down and learning to appreciate the convivial traditions of the table."

The American Cheese Society
502-574-9950
www.cheesesociety.org
An educational resource organization for American cheese makers and people who love cheese. Shares knowledge and experience on cheese making as a hobby or as a commercial enterprise, with special attention given to specialty and farmhouse cheeses made from all types of milk, including cow's, goat's, and sheep's milk. If you are thinking about becoming a commercial cheese maker, this is the organization to join. There are contacts galore and a great conference in August each year. You will find information on current cheese events, workshops, and artisanal cheese makers on their Web site.

The Dairy Practices Council
732-203-1947
www.dairypc.org
A nonprofit organization pertaining to milk quality, sanitation, and regulatory uniformity. Provides guidelines from the farm to the consumer. Free informational brochure and publications list.

State Regulatory Agencies
To find information on state agencies that regulate dairy farms and cheese plants and the requirements for a farmstead cheese dairy, go to www.cfsan.fda.gov/list.html then choose a topic with "milk" in it. Then go to Milk Safety References, then Interstate Milk Shippers List, then State Grade A Milk Sanitation Personnel. You can ask for information by state.

WEB SITES WITH MARKETING INFORMATION

Agricultural Marketing Service
www.ams.usda.gov

Growing for Market
www.ibiblio.org/farmingconnection/ growmark/home.htm

COMMERCIAL CHEESE-MAKER PROFILES

Capriole Farm
Greenville, Indiana
812-923-9408
www.capriolegoatcheese.com

Cato Corner Farm, LLC.
Colchester, Connecticut
860-537-3884
www.catocornerfarm.com

Cypress Grove Chèvre
Arcata, California
707-825-1100
www.cypressgrovechevre.com

Hancock Shaker Village
Pittsfield, Massachusetts
800-817-1137
www.hancockshakervillage.org

Hawthorne Valley Farm
Ghent, New York
518-672-7500
www.hawthornevalleyfarm.com

Fiscalini Cheese Company
Modesto, California
800-610-3276
www.fiscalinicheese.com

The Mozzarella Company
Dallas, Texas
800-798-2954
www.mozzco.com

Orb Weaver Farm
New Haven, Vermont
802-877-3755

Sweet Home Farm
Elberta, Alabama
251-986-5663
*www.southerncheese.com/Pages/
sweethome.html*

Vermont Shepherd, LLC
Putney, Vermont
802-387-4473
www.vermontshepherd.com

Uplands Cheese Company
Dodgeville, Wisconsin
888-935-5558
www.uplandscheese.com

Westfield Farm
Hubbardston, Massachusetts
877-777-3900
www.chevre.com

NEWSLETTERS, PERIODICALS, AND OTHER EDUCATIONAL MATERIAL

CASEUS
(back issues)
413-628-3808
www.cheesemaking.com
A 100-page, full-color cheese-making magazine for artisanal and small-scale commercial cheese makers. Cheese makers tell their stories, recipes, trouble-shooting ideas. If you're making cheese, this is certainly a must-have publication!

Cheesemakers' Journal
(back issues)
413-628-3808
www.cheesemaking.com
355 pages of cheese information; includes dozens of recipes and stories about cheese-making adventures of home and artisanal cheese makers.

Creamline
Vicki Dunaway, Editor
540-789-7877
www.smalldairy.com
The most comprehensive quarterly newsletter for small-scale cheese makers. This is written in a friendly and completely understandable way. I love it! Let Vicki know Ricki sent you.

The Home Dairy News
Vicki Dunaway, Editor
540-789-7877
www.smalldairy.com
This is it folks — the new monthly newsletter for home cheese making! Don't think twice, just get it — you'll love it. And tell Vicki that Ricki sent you.

Books

Dunaway, Vicki. *The Small Dairy Resource Book.* Beltsville, MD: Sustainable Agriculture Network, 2000. Bibliography of books, periodicals, videos, and other materials of interest to small-scale dairies. The major topics of this book are making cheese, butter, ice cream, and other dairy foods; dairy processing; business and marketing; food safety; dairy animals; and feeds and grazing. The appendix lists suppliers, consultants, dairy processing courses, related organizations, interesting Web sites, and more.

Fletcher, Janet. *The Cheese Course.* San Francisco: Chronicle Books, 2000. A tantalizing array of top-quality cheeses now available, with suggestions for presentation and more than 40 delectable recipes for sweet and savory pairings.

Irvine, Sian, photographer. *Mozzarella.* Boston: Periplus Editions, 1999. Inventive recipes with buffalo mozzarella from leading chefs.

Jenkins, Steve. *Cheese Primer.* New York: Workman, 1996. A passionate guide to the world's cheeses by America's most opinionated authority. Brimming with knowledge, enthusiasm, and decided opinions, it is everything you need to know to judge, savor, choose, store, and serve the terrific variety of cheeses now available.

Kosikowski, Frank, and Vikram Mistry. *Cheese and Fermented Milk Foods.* Westport, CT: F. V. Kosikowski, 1997. Written in simple language that describes the origins and principles, procedures and analysis for producing cheese both on the farm and in the factory. For both technicians and industry, this book is the most comprehensive book available on cheese making.

Lambert, Paula. *The Cheese Lover's Cookbook and Guide.* New York: Simon and Schuster, 2000. More than 150 recipes, with instruction on how to buy, store, and serve all your favorite cheeses.

Le Jaouen, Jean-Claude. *The Fabrication of Farmstead Goat Cheese.* Ashfield, MA: Cheesemakers' Journal, 1990. The most comprehensive book on goat cheese making in the world. If you want to learn about it, sell it, make it, or just plain love it, this is for you.

The Mont-Laurier Benedictine Nuns. *Goat Cheese Small Scale Production.* Ashfield, MA: Cheesemakers' Journal, 1983. This is a comprehensive treatment of all aspects of goat cheese making.

Scott, R. *Cheesemaking Practice.* Gaithersburg, MD: Aspen Publications, 1998. Contains clear and concise cheese-making recipes for on the farm with chemistry, microbiology, and more. An in-depth explanation of the processes involved, this is the science if you want to get serious.

Toth, Mary Jane. *Goats Produce Too!: The Udder Real Thing, Vol. 2.* Coleman, MI: Mary Jane Toth, 1989. Sixth Edition, July 1998. The basics of getting started with easy goat's-milk cheese making and more at home.

Werlin, Laura. *The New American Cheese.* New York: Stewart, Tabori, and Chang, 2000. Profiles of more than 50 of America's great cheese makers and 80 recipes for cooking with cheese. Provides an in-depth look at the art and craft of cheese making in the United States. Also contains a listing of American artisanal cheese makers and retailers where you can purchase the finest cheeses in the United States.

INDEX

Note: References to charts are in **bold;** those for illustrations are in *italics.*